The Heir

# Religion and Transformation in Contemporary European Society

*Edited by*

Kurt Appel,
Christian Danz,
Jakob Helmut Deibl,
Rüdiger Lohlker,
Richard Potz,
Sieglinde Rosenberger

*Advisory Board*

Schirin Amir-Moazami, Eileen Barker, Martin Baumann, Lori Beaman, Angelika Berlejung, Azelarabe Lahkim Bennani, Alfred Bodenheimer, Lieven Boeve, Paolo Luigi Branca, Patrice Brodeur, Nina Caputo, Mauro Ceruti, Jörg Dierken, Luca Diotallevi, Adriano Fabris, Jean-Marc Ferry, Charlotte Fonrobert, François Foret, Guiseppe Fornari, Alfred Friedl, Ingeborg Gabriel, Volker Gerhardt, Chiara Giaccardi, Necmettin Gökkir, Jeffrey Haynes, Susannah Heschel, Klaus Hock, Ernst van den Hemel, Hans Joas, Ulvi Karagedik, Assaad Elias Kattan, Julia Kristeva, Cristina Lafont, Karsten Lehmann, Lucian Leustean, Adrian Loretan, Andrew Louth, Vasilios N. Makrides, Pavel Mikluscak, John Milbank, Sigrid Müller, Sighard Neckel, Klaus Nellen, Peter Nynäs, René Pahud de Mortanges, Detlef Pollack, Sabrina Ramet, Niamh Reilly, Marco Rizzi, Mathias Rohe, Olivier Roy, Thomas Schmidt, Ludger Schwienhorst-Schönberger, Adam Seligman, Pierangelo Sequeri, Riem Spielhaus, Levent Teczcan, Christoph Theobald SJ, Jan-Heiner Tück, Bülent Ucar, Haci Halil Uslucan, Giuseppe Visonà, Herman Westerink, Paul M. Zulehner

VOLUME 30

Leonardo Paris

# The Heir

*A Christology*

Translated from Italian by

Michael Tait and Maria-Caterina Sighel

BRILL | SCHÖNINGH

Cover illustration: Self Portrait by Egon Schiele, 1914

Bibliographic information published by the Deutsche Nationalbibliothek.
The Deutsche Nationalbibliothek lists this publication in the Deutsche Nationalbibliografie; detailed bibliographic data available online: http://dnb.d-nb.de

All rights reserved. No part of this publication may be reproduced, translated, stored in a retrieval system, or transmitted in any form or by any means, electronic, mechanical, photocopying, recording or otherwise, without prior written permission from the publisher.

Title of the original Italian edition: Leonardo Paris, *L'erede: Una cristologia* © 2021 by Editrice Queriniana, Brescia

© 2024 by Brill Schöningh, Wollmarktstraße 115, 33098 Paderborn, Germany, an imprint of the Brill-Group (Koninklijke Brill NV, Leiden, The Netherlands; Brill USA Inc., Boston MA, USA; Brill Asia Pte Ltd, Singapore; Brill Deutschland GmbH, Paderborn, Germany; Brill Österreich GmbH, Vienna, Austria) Koninklijke Brill NV incorporates the imprints Brill, Brill Nijhoff, Brill Schöningh, Brill Fink, Brill mentis, Brill Wageningen Academic, Vandenhoeck & Ruprecht, Böhlau and V&R unipress.

www.brill.com

Cover design: Evelyn Ziegler, Munich
Production: Brill Deutschland GmbH, Paderborn

ISSN 2198-5235
ISBN 978-3-506-79453-6 (hardback)
ISBN 978-3-657-79453-9 (e-book)

# Contents

**Foreword: Christology for a Time of Ecclesial Crisis** .................. IX

    **Introduction** ............................................... 1
    1  Narrative and Freedom ...................................... 1
    2  Between Death and Inheritance .............................. 2
    3  The Stages of the Route .................................... 3
        Note to the Reader ....................................... 5

**1**   **Searching for Jesus** ........................................... 7
    1  Some Choices .............................................. 7
        1.1  Christology From Above – Christology From Below ....... 7
        1.2  Descending Soteriology – Ascending Soteriology ......... 9
        1.3  Gratia sanans – Gratia elevans ......................... 11
    2  Which Jesus? .............................................. 13
        2.1  The Real Jesus ........................................ 13
        2.2  The Historical Jesus .................................. 15
        2.3  The Narrated Jesus .................................... 16
        2.4  The Dogmatic Jesus .................................... 22
    3  Story of a Murder ......................................... 23
        Bibliographical Guidelines ................................ 24

**2**   **Motives for Murder** ........................................... 29
    1  A Difficult Man ............................................ 29
    2  Convicted and Killed ....................................... 31
        2.1  The Law .............................................. 33
        2.2  The Temple ........................................... 34
        2.3  The Messiah .......................................... 35
        2.4  The Triumphal Entry .................................. 35
        Bibliographical Guidelines ................................ 37

**3**   **The Story of a Free Man** ...................................... 39
    1  Freedom Today ............................................. 39
        1.1  The Challenge of Psychology: Conditioned Freedom ...... 39
        1.2  The Challenge of Sociology: Drunk Freedom ............ 41
        1.3  The Challenge of Science: The Dark Background ........ 42
    2  The Freedom of Bonds ...................................... 44
        2.1  Constitutive Relationship ............................. 44

|   |   |   |   |
|---|---|---|---|
|   | 2.2 | Is God the first? | 46 |
|   | 2.3 | Creative Recovery | 47 |
|   | 2.4 | A Life of Bonds | 49 |
|   |   | Bibliographical Guidelines | 54 |

## 4 Towards Death (1). The Father ........................... 59
1 Israel: The Priest Messiah ............................. 59
2 The Least and Forgiveness ............................ 62
3 What Remains of the Law? ........................... 65
4 Complex Inheritances ................................. 68
    4.1 John the Baptist Revisited ......................... 69
    4.2 The Son of Joseph ................................. 70
    4.3 Heir of Sinners ..................................... 72
5 Contested Paternity .................................. 73
    Bibliographical Guidelines ............................ 76

## 5 Towards Death (2). The Children ......................... 79
1 Israel: The Prophet Messiah .......................... 79
2 The Near *Abba* ......................................... 81
    2.1 An Awkward Nearness ............................. 81
    2.2 Excessive Love ..................................... 82
    2.3 The Sons of *Abba* ................................. 83
3 The New Temple ...................................... 85
4 The Son of Mary ...................................... 89
5 Contested Sonship .................................... 94
    Bibliographical Guidelines ............................ 96

## 6 Towards Death (3). The Brothers ......................... 99
1 Israel: The King Messiah .............................. 100
2 A Changing World .................................... 103
    2.1 The Thaumaturge ................................. 103
    2.2 The Kingdom is Here .............................. 105
3 Complex Inheritances Again .......................... 107
    3.1 The Heir of the Poor ............................... 107
    3.2 The Heir of His Disciples .......................... 107
4 Contested Fraternity .................................. 110
    Bibliographical Guidelines ............................ 113

| | | | |
|---|---|---|---|
| 7 | **Towards Death (4). Chance** | | 117 |
| | 1 A Faceless Enemy | | 117 |
| | | 1.1 A Contemporary Demand for Salvation | 117 |
| | | 1.2 Unexpected Aid | 118 |
| | 2 What is Chance? | | 120 |
| | | 2.1 A Theological Voice | 121 |
| | | 2.2 The Word to Literature | 122 |
| | | 2.3 An Attempt to Circumscribe the Chance | 124 |
| | 3 The Chances of a Lifetime | | 125 |
| | 4 Dead by Chance? | | 127 |
| | 5 Heir to Chance? | | 129 |
| | Bibliographical Guidelines | | 131 |
| 8 | **The Heir** | | 133 |
| | 1 At the Test of the Contestations | | 133 |
| | 2 Inheriting | | 135 |
| | | 2.1 Grammar | 135 |
| | | 2.2 Characters | 137 |
| | 3 Inheriting in the Age of the Son | | 138 |
| | | 3.1 Three Contributions | 140 |
| | | 3.2 Fathers and Sons | 143 |
| | 4 Patrimony | | 145 |
| | 5 The Name of the Heir in the New Testament | | 149 |
| | 6 The Testator | | 152 |
| | | 6.1 Handing Over | 152 |
| | | 6.2 Absences | 155 |
| | | 6.3 Mockery | 156 |
| | | 6.4 *Excursus*: Everyday Inheritances | 158 |
| | 7 The Heir | | 159 |
| | | 7.1 The Name of the Father | 159 |
| | | 7.2 The Name of the Brothers and Sisters | 161 |
| | | 7.3 The Manifested Heir | 163 |
| | | 7.4 What We Have Seen | 169 |
| | 8 An Absolute Claim | | 170 |
| | 9 Checkmate | | 172 |
| | Bibliographical Guidelines | | 173 |

## 9 The Heir's Father … 177
- 1 No! … 177
- 2 Yes! … 179
- 3 I Am … 180
  - 3.1 For the Love of My Name … 181
  - 3.2 Resurrection, Mystery of Relationship … 182
  - 3.3 The Unprecedented Word of Correspondence … 183
  - 3.4 Resurrection, Suspended Mystery … 184
- 4 Rethinking God … 185
  - 4.1 Paternity Rethought, or Mutual Identities … 186
  - 4.2 Sonship Rethought, or Shared Power … 192
  - 4.3 Fraternity Rethought, or Freedom in Relation … 198
- Bibliographical Guidelines … 202

## 10 The Space of the Heirs … 205
- 1 The Son and the Sons … 205
  - 1.1 The Space of the Spirit … 205
  - 1.2 The Space of Co-Heirs … 208
  - 1.3 Mediation Beyond Mediation … 211
- 2 Challenges Token Up … 215
  - 2.1 Theological Challenges … 215
  - 2.2 Contemporary Challenges … 216
- Bibliographical Guidelines … 217

**Bibliography** … 221

**Videography** … 241

**Index** … 243

# Foreword: Christology for a Time of Ecclesial Crisis

*Massimo Faggioli*

Some books find the reader in a particular personal situation and say something that resonate powerfully, even more than what can be legitimately expected of a theology book. In the transition during the last couple of years for myself – a male member of our ecclesial, social, and political community – from the status of spouse and father of young children to the status of son who must also take care of aging parents, I found a guiding light in this book on Christology written through the lens of "the heir". For this reason, I am especially grateful to Leonardo Paris for asking me to reflect on his book and in this testing time.

But the book by Leonardo Paris is important for reasons that go well beyond the personal situation of the reader and give *The Heir* the ability to speak in a powerful way. First of all, the lens of "the heir" is a much-needed complement, at this particular stage in the history of Christology, to the concepts of Jesus Christ in an evolution that marks the emergence of a new understanding of Christianity. It is also a corrective to the trajectories of the images of God – from the Eternal Father, to Christ the Lord, to the kenotic Son, to the Brother, to the Friend at my side. God loves and wants to be loved in a relationship that is one of friendship, not of servitude. Jesus refers to his disciples as "friends" in *Jn* 15:15: "I do not call you servants any longer, because the servant does not know what the master is doing, but I have called you friends, because I have made known to you everything that I have heard from my Father". At the beginning of the constitution on revelation of the Second Vatican Council, we read: "God, who is invisible (see *Col* 1;15, *1Tim* 1:17), in his great love speaks to humankind as friends (see *Ex* 33:11; *Jn* 15:14–15) and enters into their life (see *Bar* 3,38), so as to invite and receive them into relationship" (Vatican II, *Dei Verbum*, 2). The biblical and gospel narratives are indeed full of stories of friendship that we would do well to reconsider so as to give adequate measure to our concept of friendship in this age of social media and the virtualization of sociability that brings with it an illusory idea of freedom, equality, and fraternity of relationships.

Yet Paris' book chooses another, and less explored way in the pendulum between high and low Christologies, through the concept of "the heir", drawing first of all on the parable of the wicked tenants (*Mk* 12:7) and the Letter to the Hebrews (*Heb* 1:1–2). The way in which Paris develops a Christology of the heir casts a light on at least four emergent and urgent issues that, to the eyes of this ecclesiologist, are crucial both in the church and in our societies. This book highlights these four issues in an indirect but unescapable way.

The first issue is the tragedy of *abuse in the church* – sexual abuse and the abuse of authority and power. *The Heir* provides us indirectly with an important way of deploying Christology in order to face the most acute crisis in the Church (not only the Catholic Church) since the sixteenth century. It corrects the temptation to count only on legal and administrative measures in addressing a crisis that is not just of discipline, but also theological and spiritual. Paris writes: "He [Jesus] showed that there is no place so dark, so wounded, that cannot be experienced as children and siblings. In order to do this, he had to put his own spin on it; he had to expose himself since reality did not speak words of sonship and brotherhood at all. It was not an observation but a stance on reality. The free action and word of Jesus imposed itself on events, changing their perspective. The more events plummeted, the stronger the need became to *give* and *say* to events a meaning they did not immediately have and did not say".[1] The apparent meaninglessness of abuse in the church can lead to a new sense of ecclesial community, but this new sense remains elusive without a Christology that avoids the temptation to identify the victims of abuse with Jesus Christ as victim. This is crucial at a time when the narratives about the Church run the risk of being crushed within a sort of absolutizing device, where the exclusive focus on the visible victims obscures the oppressed – and with it obscures the struggle and desire for the liberation of all.[2]

The temptation to remain within the woundedness of the victim is one of the shortcuts to which *The Heir* alerts us, together with the temptation of a theology of childhood that pushes children back into an original state of nature.[3] As Paris writes: "With respect to the *Age of the son-child*, one should recognise the distinctiveness of childhood without turning it into a fetish. Both from an educational and a religious point of view, there can be risks. The absolute passivity of children, besides being false, cannot be mythologised as an ideal condition before God. The Father does not desire infant and sleeper children".[4] The contribution of a Christology of the heir helps us deal with a massive socio-cultural turn about the treatment of childhood by institutions (ecclesial

---

1 PARIS, *The Heir*, 170.
2 An example of the pervasiveness, even in contemporary literature, of the discourse of opposition between victim and oppressor as *theological* discourse (in which victims are transcendently good and oppressors personally evil) in the best-selling novel by S. ROONEY, *Beautiful World, Where Are You?* Farrar, Straus and Giroux, New York 2021, 106–108.
3 Still relevant K. RAHNER, *Ideas for a Theology of Childhood*, in *Theological Investigations*, Volume 8: *Further Theology of the Spiritual Life*, 2, Darton, Longman & Todd/Herder and Herder, London/New York 1971, 33–50; J.G. MCEVOY, *Theology of Childhood: An Essential Element of Christian Anthropology*, in *Irish Theological Quarterly*, 84 (2) 2019, 117–136.
4 PARIS, *The Heir*, 195.

and not only):[5] "Our contemporaries, or rather all of us, have not fallen into a moral abyss; we are simply facing crises and challenges typical of the Age of the Son, typical of children becoming adults. What I have wanted to show is how Jesus himself faced this decisive passage".[6]

*The Heir* helps us put the children at the center, in a moment where inheritance of the Christian tradition seems to many of our contemporaries the inheritance of a broken system, with far more debts than assets: "The choice of the category of inheritance was intended to focus on this real sharing of power that puts the children at the centre. If to speak of inheritance is to speak of a power handed over, the cross and the resurrection redefine these concepts because they speak of a gift without return, and, thus, redefine forever both power and inheritance".[7]

The second major contribution of *The Heir* is the theological and ecclesial discourse on *Christianity and power* – not only power in the church. The lens of inheritance helps us give the purely political logics of power (democracy in the Church, separation of powers, checks and balances, etc.) the role they deserve without exposing the Christian tradition to the shortcomings and contradictions inherent in every political philosophy, including the ones inspiring the constitutional liberal order.[8]

This has immediate consequences for the conversation on synodality in the Church, and this contribution is ever so important because we find ourselves in a moment of retrieving an ancient synodal tradition, but also in a phase of building a new phase of that tradition.[9] As Paris highlights directly: "It will not be possible to find a decent way of living together politically without recognising the shared nature of power and finding concrete ways of exercising it. This is particularly evident within the church. It is no longer possible to quote Paul – "There is no longer Jew or Greek; there is no longer slave or free; there is no longer male and female; for all of you are one in Christ Jesus" (*Gal* 3:28) – and appeal to synodality without recognising that this means finding concrete

---

5   See H. ZOLLNER, *Wandel durch Bruch? Mentalitätengeschichtliche Betrachtungen zum Missbrauch in der katholischen Kirche*, in *Katholische Dunkelräume. Die Kirche und der sexuelle Missbrauch*, ed. Birgit Aschmann, Brill, Schöningh 2022, 43–64.
6   PARIS, *The Heir*, 194.
7   PARIS, *The Heir*, 193.
8   For a multi-disciplinary perspective on power in the Church in our times, see H. HASLINGER, *Macht in der Kirche. Wo wir sie finden – Wer sie ausübt – Wie wir sie überwinden*, Herder, Freiburg 2022).
9   See R. LUCIANI – S. NOCETI – C. SCHICKENDANTZ (edd.), *Sinodalità e riforma: una sfida ecclesiale*, Queriniana, Brescia 2022; A. SPADARO – C.M. GALLI, *La riforma e le riforme nella chiesa*, Queriniana, Brescia 2016.

historical forms so that each one is recognised as having the power that the Father has willed to be entrusted to him. In fact, to speak of synodality, even when it is the pope who does so, cannot be the granting of absolute power. This is not a humanistic principle but a theological one. The differences between clergy and laity, men and women, young and old, even between Christians and non-Christians, are always subject to the fact that we are all children of a Father who wanted to share his power with each one".[10]

Paris leads us into a Christological perspective on power that has a lot to say not just to the contemporary intra-ecclesial conversations, but to all those who witness the reconfiguration and dislocation of power also in our political communities: "The Father shares his power. With everyone. And he configures all power as shared. Whoever wants to exercise power – and everyone exercises power because God gives power to everyone – is brought to the edge of this recognition. Its origin is shared because each, as a son, has received his power from others. [...] Whoever exercises power, therefore, does so before God, before the origin of all power. Whoever does not know, or does not want, to experience power as shared, will find himself exercising it against its origin".[11] This Christology of power has the potential of clearing our eyes from views of synodality that betray a naïve romance with worldly dynamics, and at the same time from the spiritualization of power in the Church that are often justifications of the *status quo*.

The third issue on which *The Heir* casts an important light is the impact of *"identity politics" in the church and in theology*. The lens of inheritance focuses on relationality, and this is a much-needed contribution to the theological conversations on identity – sexual identity and gender, equality, subjectivity. A first important concept is the multiplicity and interconnectedness of relationships: "Perhaps the most scandalous trait lies in the fact that God does not rely only on relationship but on relationships. That is, he entrusts himself to relationships that are not his alone. In the events of the passion, the Father's name was linked not only to the relationship that Jesus had with him but also to the different relationships that involved the Son".[12] This relational Christology (and relationship not just with the Father) liberates us from the temptation of conceiving identity (both individual and collective) as independent, absolute,

---

10   PARIS, *The Heir*, 198.
11   PARIS, *The Heir*, 197.
12   PARIS, *The Heir*, 187.

and antagonistic: "These relationships are not concessions but the confirmation that God's identity is *reciprocal* and generates reciprocal identities".[13]

The contemporary theological discourse on identity is at the same time a step forward toward the recognition of the inviolable dignity of the human person, but also suffers from the loss of connections that goes together with, and is a product of, unparalleled technological opportunities for connections. This focus on the relationship between the Father and the Heir, but in the context of a wider relationality of the Heir, provide us with a warning: "If we are not capable of living as brothers, it would have been better if none of this had happened. It would have been better to have been and be children of a servant, or rather children of no one, with nothing to share and nothing to risk. What men and women decide to do is uncertain; what is certain is what God has decided to do and be".[14]

Paris restores a theological discourse on freedom that is free from the traps of a solipsistic anthropology: "He lives the relationship with the Father, and in this he takes up and redefines all fraternal relationships. More radically, it is freedom itself that is being redesigned. It does not begin where others' ends. Rather it begins where others' begins".[15] This helps us liberate from the risks of the theologization of the paradigm of neoliberal individualism functional to the global market which, where the self, "baptized" in a prosperity-gospel Christianity, becomes a one-on-one delivery of salvation distorted as a self-help personal growth.[16]

At the same time, *The Heir* helps us avoid a recrudescence of theological metaphysics that sees necessarily everything in a hierarchical order that must be replicated in an immutable hierarchical religious and ecclesial system: "In inheriting the Kingdom, we inherit a space characterised by blessing, autonomy in relationships, generativity. Christian metaphysics draws this space open because this is the place where sons and brothers can give themselves, the place of the possible realisation of paternal desire".[17]

The fourth issue on which *The Heir* casts a light at a crucial time is on the *theology of Christian tradition*. The collapse of the sense of the tradition in Christianity is deeper than an interruption in the social and institutional mechanisms of transmission and re-elaboration of what has been received,

---

13   PARIS, *The Heir*, 187.
14   PARIS, *The Heir*, 199.
15   PARIS, *The Heir*, 200.
16   *Contra*, see R. WILLIAMS, *The Tragic Imagination*, Oxford University Press, Oxford 2016.
17   PARIS, *The Heir*, 208.

but has to do with an understanding of the self that is not relational or only conditionally relational. As Paris writes: "For Jesus, an immediate relationship with self, which would be independent of the Father and the brothers, would not be the realisation of a dream but the plunging into a nightmare. The hope of being able to generate oneself in the immediacy of self is a wicked hope. It cannot even be called a mirage because a mirage represents something good, albeit illusory. Here, however, we are faced with something worse: it is the very object of hope that is wrong. In the immediacy of self, one is not free, one is alone. One does not really love by aiming at immediacy with the other but devours him or herself".[18]

There is no tradition without community and, in a deeper sense, without fraternity which has to point to the end of tradition: "The eschatological horizon of Christian fraternity is not represented by a mass of individuals who love only the Son but by a choral ensemble of real relationships in which the identity and freedom of each are brought into play in singular relationships".[19]

This relational dimension of the self that emerges from a Christology of the Heir is also very important in our conversations about intercultural dialogue in a globalized Church.[20] This book arrives, with its Christological proposal, as a reminder to behave as adults in handling the tradition in this epoch-making time of transition towards a multi-cultural Christianity: "This adult responsibility implies that the inheritance received is in turn passed on. The forms and forces of this process are entrusted to us, to our freedom. What we have before us is an open space, as much for our own sonship as for the possibility of the children of tomorrow. A theology of inheritance is a theology of transmission, *a theology of tradition*. Something that has been life for us must become life for others. And the 'traditional' forms that guarantee the transmission of the force that makes children must be preserved. Only the adolescent thinks he can invent the future from today – and he is excusable because after all, he only arrived yesterday. The adult feels the weight of having received forms that have enabled him to live as a son and the responsibility to transmit this in a vital way".[21]

This book has something very important to tell. On the one hand we must accept the fact that some parts of the doctrinal and magisterial tradition of the Church have already been liquidated, not just updated or developed. On

---

18  PARIS, *The Heir*, 211.
19  PARIS, *The Heir*, 213.
20  See J.G. MCEVOY, *Cultural Plurality and Inculturation: Foundations for Intercultural Dialogue*, in *Irish theological quarterly* 87 (4) 2022, 259–279.
21  PARIS, *The Heir*, 214.

the other, any realistic and sustainable path towards doctrinal development must reject the prospects of a dissolution of the tradition because it is also an inheritance.[22]

---

22   See A.M. CARPENTER, *Nothing Gained Is Eternal. A Theology of Tradition*, Fortress Press, Minneapolis 2022.

> In a hole in the ground there lived a hobbit. Not a nasty, dirty, wet hole, filled with the ends of worms and an oozy smell, nor yet a dry, bare, sandy hole with nothing in it to sit down on or to eat: it was a hobbit-hole, and that means comfort.[1]

This book could have started like that:

> In a monastery on a mountain lived fifteen nuns. It was not a gloomy monastery, full of draughts and murmurs, nor was it a lonely monastery with no one to visit. Instead, it was a cheerful, youthful monastery, full of singing, prayers and laughter: and so it was a great place to be.

The idea to start writing this book came about last summer when I happened to be giving a Christology course to the fifteen nuns of this hypothetical *incipit*. I had never met them before and it was a fascinating adventure.

At first glance, there seemed to be no particular difficulty: it was a matter of *talking about Jesus and then setting the exams*.

In fact, it soon became clear to me that this course would be neither simple nor harmless. It is not easy to talk about Jesus with nuns, just as it is not easy to talk about flour with bakers, or wood with carpenters. You cannot be superficial – because they notice – and you have to be very careful about the positions you take – because they will certainly have their own ideas on the subject. With nuns, one should also highlight the spiritual impact of theology. For the story of Jesus is not just about facts of the past, or the history of the church, but speaks of the possibility of being in the world before God, with God, of knowing him and loving him – yesterday as well as today. With this awareness also grows the care one must have as one touches delicate places in the way people have shaped their lives – even more delicate if this form is the ancient and radical form of monasticism.

At this point, you can see that it was a dangerous course. Dangerous for me. When you find yourself talking about something so crucial and intimate, you can certainly be *misunderstood*. This can happen, but it is not serious. You

---

1 J.R.R. TOLKIEN, *The Hobbit or There and Back Again*, HarperCollins Publishers, New York 1995, 10.

happen to be more or less clear, more or less happy in your exposition. You happen not to be understood. It is much more serious if you are understood but not *acknowledged*, that is, if your listener tells you: 'This is not the Jesus I believe in'. For a theology to be *ecclesial*, it is necessary for the theologian to recognise those to whom he speaks and for the listeners, in turn, to recognise the theologian. A mutual recognition to walk together in the knowledge of God.

All in all, I think this is what happened. That is precisely why I wanted to write this book, so that what was useful to me and to them may also be useful to others. A possible way to approach the story of Jesus, among many others that have been written. In short, *a Christology*.

# Introduction

## 1      Narrative and Freedom

In planning this Christology, I wanted to make a definite start from the story of Jesus and present it as a story of freedom.

Why should one start from a *story* in order to do theology? I shall try to answer in the words of Marc Bloch:

> Christianity is a religion of historians. Other religious systems have been able to found their beliefs and their rites on a mythology nearly outside human time. For sacred books, the Christians have books of history, and their liturgies commemorate, together with episodes from the terrestrial life of a God, the annals of the church and the lives of the saints. Christianity is historical in another and, perhaps, even deeper sense. The destiny of humankind, placed between the Fall and the Judgment, appears to its eyes as a long adventure, of which each life, each individual pilgrimage, is in its turn a reflection. [...] Doubtless, a religious experience apart from history is conceivable. For the pure Deist, it is enough to have the inner light to believe in God. But not to believe in the God of the Christians.[1]

In Christianity, there are, of course, dogmas, liturgies, precepts, theologies, but all of these desire and claim to be based on a history, the history of Jesus. This is a problem because that history is past, like any history. When it is not past, the story is not history; it is not told but lived. If it is retold, it can give rise to other lives and other stories, yet that history as such is no longer there. This gives the Christian experience an inevitably fragile and narrative character.[2] In this book, therefore, I shall attempt to respect this character.

In speaking of the story of Jesus, I would also like to present it as a story of *freedom*. Not only because this is a theme close to my heart – as it is to many – and not only because it seems to be one of the central turning points in the Christian story since Modernity. What interests me most is the intertwining of storytelling and freedom. To speak of freedom, in fact, one must narrate. Theorems work badly, as do treatises. Much better are films or novels. Freedom is always an act, something dynamic that can be grasped only in the unfolding of a story that is being narrated. Likewise, a good narrative always

---

1   M. BLOCH, *The Historian's Craft*, Manchester University Press, Manchester – New York, 1992, 4. 26.
2   *Cf.* P. RICŒUR – E. JÜNGEL, *Metapher. Zur Hermeneutik religiöser Sprache*, Chr. Kaiser Verlag, München 1974.

has something to do with freedom. Characters are faced with crossroads and choices: they resist or back down, they flourish or fall.

This interweaving also applies to the story of Jesus. I am not interested in simply saying who he is, but rather in understanding how he played out his freedom, how he lived. How he acted, how he confronted his own desire and the desires of those he met, how he faced the choices and crossroads that life put in front of him, how he wove his relationships. In short, how he experienced his own freedom.

## 2   Between Death and Inheritance

With this in mind, I chose two particular perspectives – again, among many possible ones. On the one hand, I focused on the reasons for Jesus' death; on the other, I used a theological key, namely, the concept of inheritance.

First of all, the *reasons for his death*. Regardless of one's judgement on it, there is no doubt that Jesus died because someone wanted him dead. And why? This question highlights well the *narrative* utility of this perspective. Asking why he died, investigating the reasons for it, forces two stages to be held together as parts of a single story: life and death. What Jesus did and said during his life must contain the answer that leads to his death, and, at the same time, his death becomes the test of that same life. Even more interesting is the possibility of reading Jesus' life in the light of other lives. The reasons for his death are largely reasons *not his own*, that is, the reasons of other people. Good or bad, close or distant, these are concrete relationships, so concrete that they will eventually turn against him and kill him. By investigating the reasons for his death, therefore, it is possible to hold the life and death of Jesus together with the lives of others in a coherent and plural narrative.

Secondly, as is evident from the title of this book, the theological key I have chosen to adopt is that of *inheritance*. Like any key, it does not claim to be exhaustive – no key opens all doors –, yet it seems to me that it can offer a number of advantages: 1) that of being intriguing and not obvious; 2) that of boasting solid theological and biblical foundations; and, finally, 3) that of being in dialogue with a series of cultural turning points that have charged the concept with new values which were foreign to the sensibilities of those who used it in the past.

That this key can be intriguing and in dialogue with important cultural issues is what I hope to show in the course of the text. Before I begin, however, I would like to give two examples of how the theme of inheritance is present in the New Testament. The first is in Jesus' own words. Among the very few parables retained as probably authentic in the historical-critical analysis conducted by John P. Meier is that of the wicked tenants[3] (*cf.* below, ch. 8, § 5). In this parable, Jesus describes himself as the heir: "This is the heir; come, let us kill him, and the inheritance will be ours!" (*Mk* 12:7). The second reference is broader and concerns the most radical interpretation of Jesus and his death that there is in the entire New Testament,[4] namely, the *Letter to the Hebrews*:

> Long ago God spoke to our ancestors in many and various ways by the prophets, but in these last days he has spoken to us by a Son, whom he appointed heir of all things, through whom he also created the worlds (*Heb* 1:1–2).

In this letter, Jesus is referred to not only as 'son' but as 'heir', forcing us to look at Jesus' relationship with the Father and his brothers in a more complex way.

## 3   The Stages of the Route

So here is how this book is structured.

In the first chapters, the aim will be to prepare the ground so that the account of this story of freedom does not appear naïve with respect to the different perspectives it intends to weave together. In Chapter 1, therefore, I shall try to show the different approaches that can be taken to the figure of Jesus and some classic choices that are imposed on those who wish to speak of him *theologically*. In Chapter 2, I shall deal with the event of his death from a *historical* point of view in order to clear the field of implausible interpretations and offer a solid anchorage for the considerations that follow. Chapter 3 is an attempt to broaden the perspective on the subject of freedom. The word *freedom* – the concept and the feelings it evokes – is so rich and so vague that, on its own, it offers no real contribution to the reading of the figure of Jesus. That is why I shall clarify how I use the term 'freedom' and what challenges this concept encounters in the contemporary cultural landscape. In this way, I would like to show the possibility of bringing into dialogue two distant horizons of life and freedom such as that of an obscure eschatological prophet of the first century and that of men and women of our world – secularised, scientific and psychological.

---

3  *Cf. Mt* 21:33–46; *Mk* 12:1–12; *Lk* 20:9–19; J.P. MEIER, *A Marginal Jew. Rethinking the Historical Jesus. 5. Probing the Authenticity of the Parables*, Doubleday, New York 2017, 240–253.
4  *Cf.* S. MCKNIGHT, *Jesus and His Death. Historiography, the Historical Jesus, and Atonement Theory*, Baylor University Press, Waco (TX) 2005, 363–366.

At this point, in order to interpret Jesus' death from a theological point of view, I shall propose three reasons plus one. These three reasons are linked to three strong cores of what was Jesus' message and work: they are the idea that God is *Father* (ch. 4), that we are his *children* (ch. 5), and that we are, therefore, *brothers and sisters* of one another (ch. 6). Each of these themes has deep roots in the history of Israel, and yet Jesus takes them up and, in his words and concrete behaviour, radicalises them in such a way that they become something difficult to accept, something disputable and contested. Indeed, the reason why this story ends in death lies precisely in the fact that, in the end, Jesus was considered *too much* by a substantial part of his world. This is what actually killed him. Understanding the reasons for this opposition is not only useful to explain a fact of the past, but, above all, to realise how much, to the extent that it remains faithful to Jesus, Christianity always brings with it something difficult, something indigestible.

The last of the reasons for Jesus' death concerns *chance* (ch. 7) and is a pause and digression. It aims to ask an uncomfortable, yet, in my opinion, question that is necessary today: did Jesus' story end 'badly' *by chance*? Trying to answer this will have the advantage of reminding us how, to be meaningful, this story must confront the questions that every age feels are relevant and urgent.

Finally, the three concluding chapters will address the last days of Jesus' life from the perspective of *inheritance*. Chapter 8 – in many ways the heart of this book – will clarify in what sense I use the concept of inheritance and how this can interpret the passion and death of the Son. To achieve this, I have focused on the continuity and discontinuity between the public life and the passion. These two stages of Jesus' life are not separable as if each could be told in isolation; they are part of a single story. At the same time, there is a real difference between these two stages: *they do not simply say the same thing*, because the passion is the occasion when Jesus responds with his own death to the contestations that have been made to his life. Chapter 9 intends to focus on the true protagonist of the whole affair, who – perhaps unexpectedly – is not Jesus but the one of whom Jesus speaks and to whom he refers his every action, namely the Father. One does not make a good Christology by speaking only of the Son. Rather, the discourse on the Son must bring out a more radical presence, that of God himself, and the way he intends life and configures it. This is why Chapter 10, the last chapter, will attempt to show how the account of the Son's and the Father's story has the capacity to redesign the concrete space in which each of us can live our own life and freedom. It is basically an attempt to speak of the Holy Spirit.

The hope of this book is that the more we understand the dynamics and challenges faced by Jesus – the Son and heir – the more we shall be able to accept the invitation to be, in our turn, children and heirs. I think it will often emerge how much of a challenge this has been for me. Somehow it will be inevitable – and intended – that this will also be challenging for the reader.

**Note to the Reader**

In order to make the reading smooth, I have kept the notes in the text to a minimum. Instead, I have included a box at the end of each chapter to offer bibliographical orientation and indicate possible paths for further study. I hope it will be useful to those who want to understand the roots of the discourse I develop and try to proceed in this direction.

This book was conceived as the second volume of an ideal trilogy. The first volume is L. PARIS, *Teologia e neuroscienze. Una sfida possibile*, Queriniana, Brescia 2017, whose chapters 7 and 8 anticipate some of the ideas expressed here. Similarly, chapters 9 and 10 of the present volume anticipate ideas that I would like to develop in a forthcoming book.

I would particularly like to point out some previous publications that have been taken up and modified here. I thank the editors for allowing me to reuse what has already been partially published elsewhere.

For ch. 3: L. PARIS, *Tra vocazione e scelte, il senso della libertà*, in A. STECCANELLA (ed.), *Scelte di vita e vocazione. Tracce di cammino con i giovani*, Messaggero – Facoltà teologica del Triveneto, Padova 2019, 151–184; ID., *La libertà di Gesù*, in *Presbyteri* 2 (2019) 97–108.

For ch. 8: ID., *Ereditare. La passione del Figlio*, in S. ZENI – C. CURZEL (edd.), *La speranza della croce. Stile del cristiano*, EDB, Bologna 2017, 73–94.

CHAPTER 1

# Searching for Jesus

## 1  Some Choices

Out of respect for the efforts that have been made in the history of theology to speak about Jesus adequately, it is important to lay one's cards on the table right from the start and try to position oneself within the different underlying options of perspective. For Jesus can be spoken of in many ways and by respecting different issues. The perfect method does not exist; the very presence of the four Gospels constitutes the perennial testimony to this impossibility. Everyone will have no choice but to choose a way, a specific way. In the awareness, however, that there are certain basic choices – systemic choices – that fix and orient the path, often even beyond the explicit intentions of the writer. The quality of a theology, in fact, lies as much in the scholar's ability to intuit the appropriate model and tools to build his proposal, as in knowing how to equip it with the necessary correctives and antidotes so that the model and tools do not take over, leading the proposal to become a victim of itself. Indeed, while life is sometimes capable of unpredictable deviations and inconsistencies, ideas possess an inertia that can bring them to their own breaking point. Hence the usefulness of clarifying one's position at the outset with regard to these basic choices, declaring what one is intending to attempt and, at the same time, making explicit the risks one is aware of running.

The theological-systemic polarities examined here are very traditional, and very debatable. They nevertheless retain a certain usefulness, mainly because they allow one to place oneself within an ancient and complex history, recognising one's debts and inheritance. These are *polarities*,[1] inasmuch as the choice, however clear-cut it may be, can never deny the validity of the opposite choice, and, above all, it cannot – or at least should not – exempt itself from taking into account the motives of its antagonists.

### 1.1  *Christology From Above – Christology From Below*

The first polarity, that between Christology from above and Christology from below, derives from the very heart of Christianity, at the point where it clashes with the necessities of language. In fact, wanting to affirm, at the same time,

---

[1] Cf. R. GUARDINI, *Der Gegensatz. Versuche zu einer Philosophie des Lebendigkonkreten* (1925), Matthias Gruenewald Verlag, Mainz 1985.

that Jesus was true God and true man, one is faced with an impossibility: that of saying both things simultaneously. Those who have tried, imagining that they could speak of "theandria" (divine-human),[2] have been faced with the risk of making Jesus a kind of chimera, an in-between being who, in the end, risked not being credible as either God or man. This impossibility is in some way similar to the optical illusions found in psychology tests. We can see one image or the other but not both at the same time, while recognising that the image is the same and that both figures are present. At the same time, there is a difficulty with our language – it is not the same thing to say that the figure in question is 'the face of an old woman hidden in a landscape' or, instead, 'a landscape hiding the face of an old woman' – and something deeper: the difficulty of our thinking to hold together the complex aspects of reality at the same time as we strive to express that reality in simple, clear words. In the case of Jesus, the two positions are clear-cut: we are told either of the Son of God who became man or of a man whom we have recognised as the Son of God. The result will be essentially the same, yet the spiritual and expressive modes of those who choose one option or the other are very different.

If one opts for the first option, which starts from God – from above – the task will be to show how *God's extraordinariness is manifested in the ordinariness of the human.* It will, therefore, be all that is exceptional in Jesus – the birth, the miracles, the prior knowledge of his destiny and his interlocutors – that will attract interest and be emphasised. If, on the other hand, one goes for the second option – from below – the task will be to show how *in the ordinariness of the human the divine is manifested.* Almost the same, but with very relevant narrative consequences for this story. Indeed, the emphases will now fall, rather, on everything that brings Jesus closer to the concreteness of ordinary human gestures – closeness to people, relationships, faith and prayer – all things that were overshadowed in the previous approach. Both approaches are legitimate today as long as one recognises that they are not easily harmonised. For either Jesus literally knew beforehand what was going to happen to him, or he did not; either Jesus needed – as each of us does – to cultivate his relationship with the Father in prayer and silence, or he did not need to since he possessed a clear vision of God and of himself. In the midst of the temple doctors, Jesus had gone either to question and listen to them or else to teach what he already had clear, giving them a foretaste of what he would say later. The basic points of dogma can be saved in either case, but the resulting accounts will inevitably be different.

---

2   Cf. A. GRILLMEIER, *Christ in Christian Tradition. Vol. II. From the Council of Chalcedon (451) to Gregory the Great (590–604). Part Three*, Oxford University Press, Oxford 2013, 333–336.

Following in this the preference of the New Testament as a whole, the great Fathers of the Church certainly side with the first option. They do so because they want to exploit its great advantage and thus avoid the risk attaching to the second. For, by starting from the divinity, one is able to secure the heart of Christology, i.e. the divinity of Jesus, and avoid the fact that, in the end, he turns out to be simply a good person. Today's cultural sensibility, even within the church, tends, instead, to favour the second option. The immediate reason for this preference lies in the attempt to avoid the typical risks of a Christology from above, i.e. to present a Jesus so extraordinary that he is in fact inimitable, unattainable. For those who would like to live like him, pray like him, love like him, the image of the divine Word incarnate is not a possible model. There is, however, a deeper theological motivation: the path that starts out from the human is certainly more difficult – insofar as it risks losing the very heart of the Christian message. However, if it succeeds in the enterprise, it is also much richer. If, in fact, one can show in the human the manifestation of the divine, one will not only have gained the affirmation of dogma but also the concreteness of its manifestation, the roads that allow one to access it. Precisely for this reason, the history of Christology in the Christian West of the second millennium can be read as a long and uncertain journey to celebrate – in different ways – this human way. A parade example would be the genius of Saint Francis of Assisi who was to make the imitation of the poor Christ one of the pivots of his proposal for renewal to the point of bearing in his own flesh the signs of Jesus' passion, or, more simply, of wishing to offer the senses of Christianity a plastic image of the Incarnation, made up of a couple, a child, some straw and some animals. Any living nativity scene carries within it something vaguely ridiculous, yet Francis wanted us to confront precisely this everydayness, to find in it the keys to access the mystery of Christ. Therefore, for the Western tradition to which I belong and for contemporary sensibility, the choice of a Christology "from below" has something obligatory and pushes in the direction of a Christology that knows how to respect the human fully. However, one must always keep in mind its risk, namely, that, after much work, one ends up with a description of a good person who says nothing about God.

## 1.2  *Descending Soteriology – Ascending Soteriology*

With the second polarity, that between descending soteriology and ascending soteriology, one must move much more carefully. In fact, it is assumed that the story of Jesus is a story of salvation, a soteriology.[3] Similarly, it is accepted

---

3   *Cf.* B. SESBOÜÉ, *Jésus-Christ l'unique médiateur. Essai sur la rédemption et la salut. 2. Les récits du salut: Proposition de sotériologie narrative*, Descleé, Paris 1991, 15–30.

by all Christian denominations that it is God who saves, not man who saves himself.[4] This is why the discarded preference of patristic images of salvation has moved in favour of a descending soteriology: as illumination, revelation, deification, justification. And as liberation. The idea is that someone is in darkness, ignorance, distance from God and sin, and God saves them by sending Jesus. In another way, one can imagine a chained man having his chains broken and being set free. Now, in this last example, one can already see the jarring features that introduced into the history of Christology the suspicion that the first option, the descending one, was not enough. One can indeed imagine a stone being illuminated by a strong light, without itself having to do anything. Similarly, one can imagine people being illuminated by a strong light, without their having to do anything themselves. For light, there is no distinction between stones and people. Not so for freedom. You cannot give freedom to people without their being involved in the undertaking. You can break their chains, but to make their free people is another thing altogether. At this point, the path of theology becomes arduous, moving between two precipices: on the one hand, the danger of presenting passive people, *uninvolved* in their own salvation, and, on the other hand, the danger of presenting people so active that they can be said to *save themselves*.

This difficulty must be well understood in order to be able to appreciate the effort of those who, from Saint Anselm onwards, have tried to make the salvation of human beings a path that truly involves them. We can clearly see the limits of this effort today. In fact, the involvement was mainly through the body, through pain, through suffering.[5] The humanity involved was primarily the humanity of Jesus, and his contribution was to suffer in order to "satisfy" God's justice. The negative aspects of this approach need not be addressed. Rather, the risk of failing to see the intention of this operation – namely the involvement of the human – must be avoided. This is also why recent theology has tried to rescue this intention by reinterpreting the classical categories of atonement and vicarious substitution with other categories – gift, representation, love – that could achieve the same goal while avoiding the sad flourish of sacrificial dolorism.

It seems to me that the underlying desire here is certainly to be maintained: a way must be found to involve man in his own salvation. But what way? The history of Western soteriology puts us on notice: finding this way without

---

4  Cf. A. MAFFEIS, *Dossier sulla giustificazione. La dichiarazione congiunta cattolico-luterana, commento e dibattito teologico*, Queriniana, Brescia 2000, 30–31.
5  Cf. B. SESBOÜÉ, *Jésus-Christ l'unique médiateur. Essai sur la rédemption et la salut. 1. Problématique et relecture doctrinale*, Desclée, Paris 1988, 33–86.

falling into self-salvation or sliding into the exaltation of suffering is not easy. However, this seems the most appropriate way to respect the tradition that has preceded us and, at the same time, coincide with a contemporary sensibility that is too aware of the necessity of relationship and personal involvement to be able to find credible a proposal of salvation that does not see both partners – saviour and saved – as active subjects in this process.

### 1.3   *Gratia sanans – Gratia elevans*

Lastly, a third polarity, that between healing grace and elevating grace – this time with more nuanced contours. What does it mean to be saved, to be freed? This question does not concern *who brings about* salvation, as in the previous case, but the *effects* it produces. In another way, one could ask what concept of freedom we are referring to.

There is a salvation that can be indicated by the image of a drowning man who is helped to rise to the surface and breathe. He is saved *from the* sea. This is freedom *from*, linked to *healing grace*: the idea is that where there is an evil, something that enchains or drowns, God's grace snatches from death, removes the evil. Jesus clearly shows that he holds this kind of grace in high regard: he approaches, heals and rehabilitates the sick, the possessed, sinners – without caring too much about defining the nature or cause of the evil or responsibility for it.

There is, however, another kind of grace, which underlies a different kind of freedom. To show its significance in our present context, I would like to give a concrete example. The mother of a sixteen-year-old boy asks me for help because she is worried about her son. I try to understand what it is all about and the picture that emerges leaves me perplexed: the boy drinks moderately (considering the standards of his and my land, i.e. Trentino-Alto Adige!), he has friends, a girlfriend, quite good grades, an easy dialogue with his parents, he is helpful and, in the summer, he works in a hotel. What is the problem, then? The mother's answer is very striking: 'I have the feeling that if I come back in 20 years I shall find him exactly where he is now'. The boy, in short, does not know how to desire. He is not drowning; rather, he is floating on the surface of the water, carried along by the current. He does not know how to fly. The answer to this call for help is much more complicated than if there had been a problem with alcoholism or poor school performance. When someone is underwater, it is not difficult to work out which path to take: the shortest path between one's problem and the surface. But which path should one take once one is floating? An infinite sky of possibilities opens up, provided one manages to leave the surface of the water. It is here that so-called *elevating grace* becomes significant. The concept is meant to express that the grace of Jesus' salvation does not simply remove obstacles but teaches one to take flight, with all the personal creativity that is required to design one's own path.

In today's cultural context, there is a definite need to make the elevating dimension of grace credible. There is an acute need here. If the destination of flight is not clear, even the effort of rising from the water can be meaningless. An expanse of bodies floating on the surface of the water hoping not to sink cannot be Christian hope. If our soteriology is not able to offer perspectives not only to those who are drowning – who, in principle, grasp any hand – but also to those who are floating, knowing how to instil the playful taste of flight,[6] it risks condemning itself to irrelevance.

In this field, much of patristic and Eastern theology can be good companions. For it is, above all, these Christian traditions that have retained the idea that deliverance from sin is neither the first nor the most important gift that Christ's grace offers. Alongside and beyond this is the promise of the Kingdom, of something great and only partly manifest, that men and women can hope for and to which they can commit their lives. Such a prospect is not without risk: the danger is to forget those who cannot yet delight in the dreams of flight because they are too busy not sinking into the sea. However, one must not simply confuse the opposition of the issues with the opposition of people or the class struggle. Those who fight for their survival or struggle through difficulties often need precisely a perspective that opens up the horizon for them. Elevating grace is not the *extra* that is offered to those who have already passed through the straits of needing to be healed. Likewise, the Kingdom is not offered only to those who have shown themselves capable of being delivered from their sin. Rather, the Kingdom is announced to the poor: in other words, the prospect of flight is announced to those who thought they could only aspire to a precarious buoyancy.

At this point, with regard to traditional pairs of options, it should be clear both what we are looking for and what the risks of the venture are.

We are looking for a *Christology from below* that does not remain below – reducing Jesus to a great person – but rather knows how to show God's presence in the concreteness of human gestures and dynamics.

We are in search of an *ascending soteriology* that does not become a titanic feat of self-salvation but one that can truly involve human beings in the adventure of their own salvation.

We are looking for an *elevating salvation* that, by involving the person in what is best and worst, opens up the possibility of living, simply living.

---

6   *Cf.* J. MOLTMANN, *Theology of Play*, Harper & Row, New York 1972.

If the risks are not avoided, Jesus will become a superman who saves himself and learns to fly by himself. A good example for some great men, but also a sad condemnation for the majority of us.

## 2  Which Jesus?

If up to now we have shown the choices that are imposed on those who wish to engage in a Christology, it is now a matter of understanding which cultural and theological issues are to be taken into account when writing about him. One might ask: which Jesus are we talking about? And in what way do we want to do it?

The two thousand years of the history of Christianity and the complexity of the cultural and scientific world in which we live do not permit a naïve approach to the figure of Jesus or, rather, to the different figures we have of him. In fact, we possess such a keen perception of what has been worked out in the field of the history of theology, history in general, psychology, exegesis and philology that we must at least try to respect the efforts of these disciplines that, in different ways, have something to say about the possibility of talking about Jesus. Without taking all this into account – at once a debt to be honoured and a possibility to be exploited – one easily runs the risk of writing about Jesus without actually considering these contributions. Indeed, it is not uncommon to find Christologies that seem unaware of what has happened outside dogmatic theology. As if not much has happened since Chalcedon!

In what follows, I try to carve out four possible figures and issues relating to Jesus in order to try to understand how they should be taken into account. Four different Jesuses – *real, historical, narrated* and *dogmatic* – representing as many points of view. None of them exhausts his person and none of them can be easily ascribed to a literary genre or theological approach. Rather, they are theoretical perspectives for which it may be useful to try to have a name.

### 2.1  *The Real Jesus*

First of all, attention should be paid to the fact that, when speaking of someone who has existed, all we can ultimately do is *talk* about him. Our words may be right or wrong because they may or may not capture the general sense of his life, or they may be more or less appropriate on this or that single aspect. However, the reality of his living person is not directly accessible to us. The *real* person eludes us.

This depends on many factors. The first is obviously related to the difficulty of profiling any person who has the general historical characteristics of Jesus, i.e. a man very distant from us: he lived over two thousand years ago, in a marginal region, marginal himself; he was neither a prince nor a great leader; and (like the majority of people of that time) he wrote nothing in his own hand. His only, uncertain, writings were marked in the sand (*Jn* 8:6–8). Time has erased all traces of them. What history leaves us of people like him is very little. Trying to understand what really went through the mind of someone distant from us can be done only in the knowledge of the uncertainty of such an operation.

However, there is one particular factor that makes it difficult even to glimpse his traits: this is the particular 'trade' that Jesus exercised. He was, in fact, a complex personality: healer, wanderer, preacher, teacher. The description that perhaps best encapsulates him is 'eschatological prophet'. This makes it very complex to reconstruct his person. To give an example: it is different from having to work out who Tsar Nicholas II really was or who Rasputin really was. Clearly, the general figure of the last Russian emperor is easier to delineate than that of Jesus. A king or a philosopher tends to have much greater claims on biographical consistency and coherence of thought than a prophet, a mystic or an artist. A figure such as Jesus did not need to be consistent, as Meier often points out: "Our concern about the principle of non-contradiction might have been greeted with a curious smile by the Nazarene and his audience".[7] Jesus did not, in fact, provide easy keys to interpreting his words and actions. Many explanations can be given of Jesus' prohibition of oaths or divorce – both of which are quite certain[8] – and many of these explanations can be convincing and coherent. But the truth is that we are not there to ask him, and he has not clarified the exact reasons.

There is, however, an even more radical reason why the real Jesus remains difficult for those who write about him, and it has to do with the obvious inadequacy of words to express reality. You can ask me who my brother is, and I – choosing among my brothers the one I know best – can talk to you about him for hours, tell you anecdotes, let you read the books he wrote, show you photographs. Yet, I believe that in the end we would both be dissatisfied. The best thing would be to introduce him to you. Yet even that would not be enough. None of us can be completely transparent to others; none of us can simply *tell ourselves completely* to others. The history of theology, particularly concerning the mysticism that refers to Dionysius the Areopagite and Neo-Platonism, has

---

[7] J.P. Meier, *A Marginal Jew. Rethinking the Historical Jesus. 2. Mentor, Message and Miracles*, Doubleday, New York 1994, 452.
[8] *Cf.* Id., *A Marginal Jew. Rethinking the Historical Jesus. 4. Law and Love*, Doubleday, New York 2009, 74–234.

reflected much on the ineffability of God. No one can exhaust God in his own words. His essence always remains beyond the possibility of being *understood and told* as one expresses a theorem or a chemical formula. Come to think of it, however, this does not apply only to God but to each person – perhaps to each reality. Our language fails to convey the individuality of persons and things.

This is not to despair of the enterprise. It is only a matter of finding a way to keep this issue in mind, remembering that our speaking and writing is only a way to put into words something that remains inaccessible like a magmatic bottom. Like lava, it is too hot to be grasped, too alive to be contained. In itself, this issue is banal, but it is not easy to treat. It would be nice to be able to write, leaving the feeling that the bulk is not yet done, even after many volumes. The evangelists themselves have tried to respect this principle by emphasising the mystery of Jesus' person. When you think you have grasped it, you realise that it has already moved on. A good account of a person is always one that makes you want to leave the book to get to know him, to fill the gap that always remains between words and reality.

### 2.2    *The Historical Jesus*

The real Jesus is a kind of 'unspoken' implicit in any Christology. Quite different is the *historical* Jesus, that figure to which we can have access through historical research. An impressive number of studies has been devoted to this. Indeed, it can be said that, from the point of view of historical research, Jesus is perhaps the single most studied person from the world of Antiquity.

This introduces a problem into the work. Compared with the vast amount of research produced over the last two hundred years, the results have very often created a sense of disappointment. On the one hand, it seems that not much can be gleaned from history, except to demolish what we thought we knew about it. This provokes defensive reactions from believers and theologians. On the other hand, the feeling is that the results of this research have a rather modest influence on dogmatic theology. As if, all things considered, one could go on ignoring this research.

Perhaps the reason for these difficulties lies not only in the reluctance of theologians to change their opinions, but also, more subtly, in the particular epistemological status of history itself. For this reason – with a certain arbitrariness – it seems to me better to divide the results of the historical sciences into two different issues. On the one hand, history collects data and does so with the systems proper to the natural sciences: shards, books, documents, carbon dating, and so on. On the other hand, history is not just that. Once the fragments have been collected – as the work of searching for data can return only fragments, traces of reality that have remained while reality, as such, has passed and been lost – it is a matter of reconstructing *a narrative* that allows us to understand what happened. This is not a surreptitious or illicit task, a quirk the historian indulges late in life, but an essential part of his own work. The history of the battle of Cannae, or of the lives of medieval feudal lords, or of Napoleon's exploits, cannot be merely a catalogue of data. These data must be composed to form a narrative that can draw a horizon of meaning. Again in Bloch's words:

> Even apart from any application to conduct, history will rightfully claim its place among those sciences truly worthy of endeavor only in proportion as it promises us, not simply a disjointed and, you might say, a nearly infinite enumeration, but a rational classification and progressive intelligibility.[9]

These two aspects of historical work underlie very different issues, both of which must be kept in mind when trying to talk about Jesus. On the one hand, there are the data, on the other, the narration of these data. I have chosen to call *historical Jesus* the attempt to respect the historical data we know about his person, because it seems to me that research into the historical Jesus has been mainly concerned with this aspect. Perhaps this is where dogmatic theology's certain sense of discouragement and mistrust originates with respect to the results of this method. If only this aspect is emphasised, the risk is to despair of the possibility of reconstructing a story, a history.

Nevertheless, this issue must be respected. Our age has a strong awareness of what can be scientifically proven and what can be only reconstructed. It would be good to take this into account when attempting to propose a Christology. Supporting theological structures should not be based exclusively on data that cannot be ascertained by historical research or on aspects of Jesus' life that are clearly not historical. Of course, it is not a matter of simply expunging them, but of taking them into account. At the same time, this historical-critical approach must in turn be critical, i.e. aware that respect for data is only one aspect of historical reconstruction, and only one of many aspects of a dogmatic construction.[10]

## 2.3   *The Narrated Jesus*

The second aspect of historical reconstruction is, as we have seen, narration. After collecting the data and getting a reasonable idea of their possible course,

---

9    BLOCH, *The Historian's Craft*, 9.
10   *Cf.* J. RATZINGER / BENEDICT XVI, *Jesus of Nazareth. From the Baptism in the Jordan to the Transfiguration*, Bloomsbury, London 2007, XI–XXIV.

the historian must take on the privilege and burden of transforming this into a meaningful narrative. This can be called a *storytelling* problem.[11] It is a different operation from the previous one, requiring different skills. It will indeed have to take into account the data, but also the narrative sensibility specific to each era, because stories are not told in the same way in every era and in every context. The data remain, but the way of shaping them must take into account the interlocutor, otherwise it condemns itself to irrelevance. This issue says that

> if I want my facts and ideas to travel, I need to be prepared to give them an aerodynamic profile. I need to hone this until the facts or ideas can slice through the air of collective sensibilities, until it is the right shape and size to snowball in the Game.[12]

For there to be history, a history that can be of interest to someone, it has to be told, not just piled up. This is how we human beings hand down our past. So what are the specific characteristics that a narrative must possess in order to find acceptance in our time?

The question is insidious for it is evident that our era has a very acute narrative sensibility, much more complex than in other eras. To try to understand this sensibility, one can look at three forms of expression characteristic of the 19th, 20th and this early 21st century of ours, namely the novel, the cinema and television series, respectively.

### 2.3.1 Narrative and Novel

One of the greatest legacies that Modernity has left us is the novel: great texts in which the biographies and vicissitudes of more or less imaginary protagonists unfold with a complexity and depth that only this expressive instrument has been able to recount. It is precisely from Modernity and the novel that we derive a very specific concern – that for the *psychological* aspects of narrative – that was far less evident in other narrative cultures. Today, from the tale of a person, no matter whether princess or peasant, we expect to be able to understand what goes through their mind, heart and belly. Otherwise the tale is not convincing; it misses the mark.

This is a problematic aspect for those who want to narrate Jesus' story as it is not among the narrative interests of the evangelists. One finds here and there hints at an understanding of Jesus' feelings and thoughts – he is moved, weeps,

---

[11] For an informal presentation of the concept and its use, *cf.* A. BARICCO, *The Game. A Digital Turning Point*, McSweeney's, San Francisco 2020, 267–291.
[12] BARICCO, *The Game*, 288.

gets angry, shows himself disinterested or involved – but this almost always happens incidentally. Proof of this is the fact that some of the questions that are most obvious to our contemporaries remain unanswered in the Gospels. Did Jesus know he was God? When did he realise this and how? Was he a friend of his disciples or did he see them rather as students? What did he feel on the cross? These are psychological and existential aspects that are essential for the narrative sensibility of our time but were not so for those who first told us about Jesus.

This is a problem common to many reconstructions and depends on collective sensibilities that are always changing. Fortunately, access to these aspects does not necessarily come from having an explicit account of emotions and thoughts. In fact, it can be reconstructed – at least approximately – from the very dynamics of events and actions. As long as we are talking about people, we can reasonably make a guess at a certain range of emotions and existential attitudes that are possible in the face of events. If there are enough events narrated, it is possible to reconstruct a certain style, a certain posture of that particular person in the face of what happened to him or her. It is precisely this difficult reconstruction that cinema deals with owing to its very form of expression.

### 2.3.2   Narrative and Cinema

Each great cinematic tradition may have its own emphases and characteristics – American cinema is not Japanese, French, Italian or Iranian – and yet the medium is the same, with its opportunities and constraints. In fact, the filmmaker has a couple of hours during which it is not primarily words that describe emotions – as happens in the novel – but moving images that occupy the screen: looks, postures, actions in which a story is expressed, inner worlds and motivations are defined. In a word, a story is brought to life. Therefore, those who make a film must be able to shape an exterior and interior world using the actions of their characters. Similarly, the viewer of a film will have to be able to walk the reverse path, that is, from the actions to the world that the actions reveal. A capacity that, even without being aware of it, each of us today possesses, and with it a specific sensitivity and set of expectations.

An account of Jesus that claims to be heard today will have to engage with this issue. A dogmatics that really wants to tackle the life of Jesus will have to propose interpretative keys that favour – or at least do not hinder – the possibility of understanding his inner world from his gestures. All the more, this challenge will have to be accepted by a Christology from below which intends to give an account of Jesus' humanity. It is not an impossible challenge. It can be faced by trying to put Jesus' *relationships* in particular at the centre. Relationships, in fact, are what allow us to understand the psychology and existential posture of a person, much more than individual statements. Whether their feelings were of love, hate, trust or resentment can be understood from the way they lived their relationships.

There is another point of view that becomes central if one wants to respect the psychological-existential aspects of *storytelling*, and that is the coherence between life and death. When telling a story, and in particular the story of a murder like that of Jesus, it is essential that the connection between the protagonist's actions and his death is made clear. Faced with the question: 'Why did the hunter kill the wolf?' there can be no hesitation: 'Because the wolf has eaten Little Red Riding Hood and her grandmother'. If a child has not grasped this connection, it is clear that it has not understood the story.[13] This is a connection of great importance since not all dogmatic keys succeed in opening up this link in the story of Jesus. One example may apply to all. When an expiatory interpretative key is used for Jesus' death – that is, the idea that Jesus died to pay the price for our sins, or to restore to God the honour that had been violated – his story becomes meaningful. It does not matter if these categories seem inadequate or even wrong to us today. For almost a thousand years, they enabled Christians to understand what they were seeing when they stood before the crucifix, to have a simple and effective reading of it for their lives. In my opinion, the reason why these interpretative keys struggle to be accepted today is, not only the fact that they present an image of a vengeful and resentful God that we no longer feel able to share, but, above all, the fact that they are narratively very weak. They render the psychology of Jesus incomprehensible, presenting the story of a man who engineers his own death knowing that it will redeem humanity. In the words of Ed Sanders:

> It is not historically impossible that Jesus was weird, and I realize that my own interpretation of his views may make twentieth-century people look at him askance. But the view that he plotted his own redemptive death makes him strange in any century and thrusts the entire drama into his peculiar inner psyche. The other things that we know about him make him a *reasonable* first-century visionary. We should be guided by them.[14]

Even more problematically, these categories break the link between Jesus' life and death. From the point of view of the atonement, in fact, if Jesus had done

---

13   The Little Red Riding Hood tale is often used in theology: O.H. PESCH, *Warum hast du so große Ohren? Rotkäppchen – "theologisch" zu Gehör gebracht*, Herder, Freiburg im Br. 1993; S. PAGANINI, *Cappuccetto rosso e la creazione del mondo. How to interpret a text*, EDB, Bologna 2018.
14   E.P. SANDERS, *Jesus and Judaism*, Fortress Press, Philadelphia 1985, 333.

nothing else in his life but die, that would have been fine anyway. In this scenario, the reasons for his death do not lie in his life, but in the divine plan to accept this sacrifice in reparation for humanity's sin. Thus, the narrative falters, and the healings, the preaching, the miracles become incidental, and can only make sense later on, leaving an impression of lack of coherence.

Dogmatic keys that can make the life and death of Jesus accessible to contemporary sensibilities will have to take this into account.

### 2.3.3 Narrative and Television Series

Further attention to the choice of dogmatic keys on the level of *storytelling* may emerge by examining perhaps the most typical contemporary form of storytelling, namely, television series. When setting out to tell a story today, one must bear in mind that our interlocutors have seen *The Game of Thrones*.[15] Compared with both the novel and the film, indeed, this narrative form has peculiarities that introduce new elements, and make it worthy of attention.

To stay with the cited example, it is a story of more than seventy hours, extremely complex, polyphonic, and with a potentially open ending. This is a set of characteristics that brings the narrative closer to specific features of reality; a suitable medium to speak to the complexity of contemporary lives. This means that the average person is now used to narratives on this level, with these characteristics.

Today's sensibility can ill-afford narratives that fall below a high level of *complexity*. This clashes with a certain pious tendency to oversimplify the person and story of Jesus in order to make it more 'comprehensible'. In fact, this simplicity does not make the story more comprehensible, but boring and irrelevant. Reality is not simple, and the tools with which one wants to talk about it – albeit in a fictional form – must take this into account. This also means that our time is perhaps the most *narrative* age in history, in spite of the fact that we no longer gather around the fire to listen together to the tales of a *griot*.

The television series also allows for radically *polyphonic* narratives in which the narrative can move between various points of view. This makes the course of the plot unpredictable, changing, rich. For those who want to talk about Jesus, this constitutes a problem since the Gospels, unlike much of the Old Testament, have, in fact, only one protagonist whom the narratives strive to present as almost the sole agonist of the story. Unless dogmatic-narrative strategies are found to make the narrative more multi-perspectival, the sensation will once again be one of boredom, faced with a tale dully focused on one character. If, literally, the answer is always 'Jesus', it becomes inevitable to lose

---

15    D. BENIOFF – D.B. WEISS, *Game of Thones* (television series), USA 2011–2019.

interest in the questions. From this sensitivity to the polyphonic dynamics of events there then derives a further consequence, of a soteriological nature. In a polyphonic narrative, in fact, it is not possible to simplify the dynamics of salvation to the point of simply presenting one character as the saviour and all the others as the saved. The saviour will always also be a saved person, at least in some respect, and the saved will always be actors in their own affairs and thus, in some way, saviours. If one looks at the evolution that superhero narratives have undergone in the last fifty years, one can clearly see that there is a focus on making them more wounded, more in need of the help of others, in other words, more involved in a complex dynamic action in which the extraordinary role of the superhero is not flattened on one note but acquires polyphonic characteristics. How one can respect this polyphony without making Jesus lose the soteriological centrality that characterises him is one of the most interesting challenges facing contemporary Christology.

Finally, the television series is an *open-ended* narrative structurally. The type of narrative dictates that the tale has no real conclusion. No one has ever understood if and how the mother of the contemporary television series, *Lost*,[16] ended. One might expect this to create unease in the viewer, but it does not. As in life, the focus is not on the ending but on the structure of the journey. As we noted above, this means that ways will have to be found to present a story in which each part of the narrative has the possibility of containing sufficient meaning in itself, regardless of its conclusion. The individual events – the episodes or pericopes – must contain tensions that prompt one to look back and wait for the sequel but, at the same time, also ensure sufficient intrigue to be worthwhile in their own right. The fragment must contain the whole without exhausting it.

The narrated Jesus is perhaps not the most complex issue for the theologian, but it is certainly the one that requires him to engage in greater dialogue with the sensibilities of his own time. Not least because theology does not have the exclusive right to narrate Jesus' life. The act of narrating is so basic to human beings that it can be done in many different ways and for different reasons, and this also applies to the story of Jesus: it can be taken up by the historian and the theologian but also by the novelist (from the Portuguese Saramago to the French Carrère),[17] by the comedian (from the Italian Fantozzi to the English

---

16   J.J. ABRAMS – D. LINDELOF – J. LIEBER, *Lost* (TV series), USA 2004–2010.
17   J. SARAMAGO, *The Gospel According to Jesus Christ*, Harcout Brace & Company, San Diego (CA) 1994; E. CARRÈRE, *The Kingdom*, Penguin Books, London 2018.

Monty Python)[18] and by the politician, without these different narratives being entirely distinguishable.

## 2.4 The Dogmatic Jesus

For those who wish to speak ecclesially about Jesus, the last issue to be considered is the *dogmatic Jesus*. In many respects, it is the most obvious issue with which the theologian is confronted professionally. The story of Jesus must situate itself critically within a tradition of narratives and beyond. It must consider the history of theology, dogma, and the church, but also the many incarnations that this story has encountered in the lives of the saints and in different ecclesial experiences in the course of a history that is now over two thousand years old. The story of Jesus must account for the fact that from this life emerges the face of the Father and the action of the Spirit, that is, that this story is part of the larger field of the Trinitarian life of God.

For this reason, every theological style must take into account that other styles are possible; every form must accept that other forms are possible, where *form* and *style* arise precisely from the intertwining of narrative and dogmatics.[19]

The best way to address this issue critically is to try to clarify in one's own mind what *dogmatic keys* one is using to give shape and style to one's narrative. The image of the key can be of great use as a reminder that its purpose is to open doors and, at the same time, that no key opens all doors. Choosing a key or a type of key will enable one to speak of the Christian mystery by offering a perspective on it, highlighting some features and inevitably leaving others in the shadows. Being aware of this will allow the necessary countermeasures to be put in place so that the inevitable partiality of the choice does not become its own victim. It will also allow one to look with gratitude at the efforts that other theologians and other traditions make, following other paths and making other choices, in order to make the story of Jesus understandable.

For this reason, I would like to try to clarify from the outset what theological choices and dogmatic keys I have adopted here.

---

18   N. PARENTI, *Superfantozzi,* Italy 1986; T. JONES, *Monty Python's Life of Brian,* UK 1979.
19   C. THEOBALD, *Le christianisme comme style. Une manière de faire de la théologie en postmodernité,* Les Éditions du Cerf, Paris 2007, 16–205; ID., *Selon l'Ésprit de sainteté: genèse d'une théologie systématique,* Les Éditions du Cerf, Paris 2015, 181–201; H.U. VON BALTHASAR, *The Glory of the Lord. A Theological Aesthetics. I. Seeing the Form,* Ignatius Press, San Francisco 2009; E. SALMANN, *Presenza di spirito. Cristianesimo come stile di pensiero e di vita,* Cittadella, Assisi 2011, 7–23 and 295–314.

## 3   Story of a Murder

From a narrative point of view, the story of Jesus is the story of a murder. Not a crime novel – as the identity of the murderer is not so clear and perhaps not even that important – but the story of a man who was killed *for what he did and said*. One may object to the word 'murder', arguing that Jesus' death is, rather, an execution, a plot, a sacrifice, a deicide, a betrayal, or much more. This is precisely why I would like to insist on the idea of murder, as it forces one to look at the facts *before* their interpretation. Before deciding who the victim was, who his executioner was, what the motives for or the legitimacy of his execution was, one must pause at the raw datum: a man was killed.

In this apparently reductive perspective, Jesus' death is approached from a narrative rather than a theological point of view. When a murder is narrated, the point lies in understanding *why the protagonist was killed*. A theology that wants to follow this track and rise to the challenge of the narrated event, will have to try to give theological value to this point, without going beyond it before it has even seen it. Not only to his death or only to his life; not only to Christ's natures or to his resurrection, but to the whole event.

To make the centrality of Jesus' death effective, it may be useful to examine it, that is, to recognise it as an event that is not immediately transparent. Why was this man killed? What did he say and do so that the reaction was death? What reasons were there for wanting him dead? They will have to be reasons that are both narratively plausible and theologically convincing. On the basis of these reasons, it will be possible to shed light as much on his public life, which these reasons gave rise to, as on his passion itself. By dying, in fact, Jesus suffered the consequences for what he had done, and, at the same time, in the way he faced death, he had the possibility of reaffirming, disavowing or deepening what he had wanted to uphold with his life.

Looking for these reasons inevitably has a disturbing effect. Finding a reason for Jesus' death may seem equivalent to giving a justification for it. Yet, if we want to understand his life and death, we must resist this problem and face the fact that someone had reasons for killing him. Appealing to madness or sheer evil – which is equivalent to insanity – leads us astray. It is something similar to what happens when we read about some heinous murder or social tragedy. 'They're crazy!' we exclaim. But then we end up not understanding and remain on a very superficial level. If one wants to understand, one has to delve into the motivations behind the drama.

Such a perspective should serve to hold together and give coherence to three different aspects of Jesus' story: his public life, death and resurrection. Certainly, these stages are marked by discontinuity, and yet their continuity must be clear, because it is greater. Life, death and resurrection are, in fact, different aspects of a *single* personal event in which the true face of God was made visible. It would be a mistake to think of the central mysteries of Christianity as linked to one or the other stage of the story: *incarnation* to birth-life, *redemption* to death, *revelation* to resurrection. As if the incarnation of the Son were limited to the birth-life or the revelation of God occurred only with the Risen One. Actually, it is the totality of the events of Christ's life, death and resurrection that speaks of each of these mysteries. Offering theological keys that make these connections narratively effective and allow an overall view of the entire story of Jesus is the task of Christology.

### Bibliographical Guidelines

For a general introduction to **classical Christological and soteriological categories**: B. Sesboüé, *Jésus-Christ l'unique médiateur. Essai sur la rédemption et la salut. 1. Problématique et relecture doctrinale*, Descleé, Paris 1988; *2. Les récits du salut: Proposition de sotériologie narrative*, Descleé, Paris 1991; M. Gronchi, *Trattato di Gesù Cristo figlio di Dio salvatore*, Queriniana, Brescia 2008, 917–953.

The need to **involve human freedom in the relationship with God** is well expressed by Benedict XVI: 'Aristotelian philosophy, as we well know, tells us that between God and man there is only a non-reciprocal relationship. Man refers to God, but God, the Eternal, is in Himself, He does not change: He cannot have this relationship today and another relationship tomorrow. He is within Himself, He does not have ad extra relations. It is a very logical term, but it is also a word that makes us despair: so God himself has no relationship with me. With the Incarnation, with the event of the Theotókos, this radically changed, because God drew us into Himself and God in Himself is the relationship and allows us to participate in His interior relationship' (Benedict XVI, *Meditation during the First General Congregation*. Special Assembly for the Middle East of the Synod of Bishops, 11 October 2010). For a commentary: P. Sequeri, *L'amore della ragione. Variazioni sinfoniche su un tema di Benedetto XVI*, EDB, Bologna 2012. The classical references are: Thomas Aquinas, *Summa theologica*, I, q. 13, a. 7; Id., *Scriptum super Sententiis*, I, d. 30, q. 1, a. 3, ad 3. For the connection between anthropological, Christological and theological: A. Bertuletti, *Dio mistero dell'unico*, Queriniana, Brescia 2014, 261–337 and 536–590.

When attempting an ascending soteriology, it is easy to run into the themes of **sacrifice, atonement, vicarious substitution**, etc., even without meaning to. For these themes and their contemporary revivals see: Sesboüé, *Jésus-Christ l'unique médiateur. Essai sur la rédemption et la salut. 1*, 257–380; F.G. Brambilla, *Redenti nella sua croce. Soddisfazione vicaria o rappresentanza solidale?*, in G. Manca (ed.),

*La redenzione nella morte di Gesù. In dialogo con Franco Giulio Brambilla*, San Paolo, Cinisello Balsamo 2001, 15–83; ID., *La soteriologia in prospettiva drammatica*, in *La Scuola Cattolica* 128 (2000) 209–269; R. MAIOLINI, *Il tema teologico-fondamentale del morire di Gesù come motivo di credibilità. Considerazioni a partire da un confronto con la soteriologia "drammatica" di Raymund Schwager (1935-2004)*, in *Quaderni teologici del seminario di Brescia, Di fronte alla morte*, Morcelliana, Brescia 2009, 49–105; E. SALMANN, *Contro Severino. Incanto e incubo del credere*, Piemme, Casale Monferrato 1999, 247–297; N. HOFFMANN, *Sühne. Zur Theologie der Stellvertretung*, Johannes Verlag, Einsiedeln 1981; K.-H. MENKE, *Stellvertretung. Schlüsselbegriff christlichen Lebens und theologische Grundkategorie*, Johannes Verlag Einsiedeln, Freiburg 1991. For a general overview, cf. C. THEOBALD, *Selon l'Ésprit de sainteté: genèse d'une théologie systématique*, Les Éditions du Cerf, Paris 2015, 289–318.

The danger of an ascending soteriology and a Christology from below leading to perspectives of **self-salvation** must be examined in the light of Pope Francis's focus on neo-Gnosticism and neo-Pelagianism, both of which are seen as the re-presentation of the same ancient Gnostic heresy under the conditions of modern and contemporary subjectivism (*Evangelii gaudium*, nn. 94. 233; *Lumen fidei*, n. 47; *Gaudete et exultate*, nn. 36–62; for a commentary, I. GUANZINI – K. APPEL, *Il neognosticismo*, San Paolo, Cinisello Balsamo 2019). However, it is important to consider whether, alongside the danger of the elitist titanism of those who believe they can know everything or save themselves, there is not another: the quiet resignation of those who believe they can know and do nothing. Similarly, while we should certainly avoid Christianity's allying itself with the delirium of contemporary freedom that believes it can self-reproduce and dispose of the reproduction of others, we should also avoid its allying itself with a generalised distrust of human freedom. Indeed, I wonder whether, behind much contemporary atheism, there is not more mistrust in self than lack of trust in God. People do not believe because they do not believe they have anything to give to God.

For the theme of the reality and its singularity, uniqueness and ability to be expressed or not, the possible paths are many and so diverse that I can only mention some of those that have intrigued me: L. PAREYSON, *Esistenza e persona*, Il Melangolo, Genova 2002, 215–230; M. CACCIARI, *Labirinto filosofico*, Adelphi, Milano 2014, 275–342; E. SALMANN, *Der geteilte Logos. Zum offenen Prozeß von neuzeitlichem Denken und Theologie*, Studia Anselmiana, Roma 1992, 17–80; L. FEUERBACH, *Über Materialismus und Spiritualismus, besonders in Beziehung au die Willensfreiheit*, in ID., *Gesammelte Werke. Teil 11. Kleinere Schriften 4 (1851–1866)*, De Gruyter Akademie Forschung, Berlin 1990, 103–115; F. TOMASONI, *Ludwig Feuerbach. Biografia intellettuale*, Morcelliana, Brescia 2011; K. MARX, *Concerning Feuerbach*, in ID., *Early Writings*, Penguin Books, London – New York 1992, 421–423.; ID., *Critique of Hegel's Dialectic and General Philosophy*, in ID., *Early Writings*, Penguin Books, London – New York 1992, 379–400; V.S. SOLOVIOV, *Philosophical Principles of Integral Knowledge*, Wm.

B. Eerdmans Publishing Company, Grand Rapids (MI) 2008; L. MECACCI, *Cervello e storia. Ricerche sovietiche di neurofisiologia e psicologia*, Editori Riuniti, Roma 1977, 127–140. Next to this, one could place the entire psychological tradition of concentration on single-case, in respect of which I would like to mention only one author – omitting the obvious reference to Sigmund Freud – because of his connections with many of the previous authors: A.R. LURIA, *The Mind of a Mnemonist. A Little Book about a Vast Memory*, Harvard University Press, Cambridge – London 1987; ID., *The Man with a Shattered World*, Harvard University Press, Cambridge 1972.

On the **difference between the real Jesus and the historical Jesus**, cf. J.P. MEIER, *A Marginal Jew. Rethinking the Historical Jesus. 1. The Roots of the Problem and the Person*, Doubleday, New York 1991, 21–40. The author makes three different aspects clear. First, that "the total reality of a person is in principle unknowable – despite the fact that no one would deny that such a total reality did exist. This simply reminds us that all historical knowledge about human persons is limited by the very nature of the case. We may take some comfort from the thought that a good deal of the total reality of a person would be irrelevant and positively boring to historians even if it could be known" (MEIER, *A Marginal Jew.1*, 24). Secondly, while placing the real Jesus beyond our reach, Meier comforts us with the possibility – from the availability of original material – of reconstructing for Jesus "a reasonably complete biographical portrait" (MEIER, *A Marginal Jew.1*, 24). Finally, he performs an analysis of the various terms that are used to unravel this knot: real Jesus, historical Jesus, historiographical Jesus, earthly Jesus, etc. (*cf.* MEIER, *A Marginal Jew.1*, 24). Each author can only come up with his own categories and subdivisions to render the different aspects of the complex operation of recovering the past. These categories are not fixed – and cannot be – as it is very different to trace the historical contours of a person or event from Antiquity, the Middle Ages, Modernity or contemporary times. Indeed, the quantity of available sources, their verifiability, and access to direct witnesses change in such a way that, if one used the criteria of Antiquity for a contemporary figure, one would be overwhelmed with data whereas, if one used the criteria applicable to a contemporary for a man or (worse) a woman from two thousand years ago, one would be condemned to silence.

For the **narrated Jesus**, see A. GESCHÉ, *Dieu pour penser. VI. Le Christ*, Les Éditions du Cerf, Paris 2001, 55–129. One can elaborate on the so-called Fourth Quest in F. TESTAFERRI, *Una "quarta ricerca" del Gesù storico?*, in *Teologia* 38 (2013) 382–400; D.C. ALLISON JR., *The Historical Christ and the Theological Jesus*, Wm. B. Eerdmans Publishing Company, Grand Rapids (MI) 2009; C. THEOBALD, *Le christianisme comme style. Une manière de faire de la théologie en postmodernité*, Les Éditions du Cerf, Paris 2007, 459–482; D. MARGUERAT, *La ricerca del Gesù storico tra storia e teologia*, in Teologia 33 (2008) 37–54. In this Quest, difficult to classify is the Jesus of J. RATZINGER/BENEDICT XVI; *cf.* G. FRANCO (ed.), *Alla ricerca della verità. Discussioni sul Gesù di Nazaret di Joseph Ratzinger – Benedetto XVI*, Lupo Editore, Copertino 2009. For insights on the subject of **Jesus' self-consciousness**: INTERNATIONAL THEOLOGICAL COMMISSION, *The Consciousness of Christ Concerning Himself and His Mission (1985)*; I. SALVADORI, *L'autocoscienza di Gesù. "In tutto simile a noi eccetto il peccato*, Città Nuova, Roma 2011; G. CANOBBIO (ed.), *La fede di Gesù*, EDB, Bologna 2000; K. RAHNER, *Foundations of Chritian Faith. An Introduction to the Idea of Christianity*, Darton Longman & Todd, London 1978, 176–321; G. ESSEN, *Die Freiheit Jesu. Der neuchalkedonische Enhypostasiebegriff im Horizont neuzeitlicher Subjekt- und Personphilosophie*, Pustet, Regensburg 2001.

For the **dogmatic Jesus**, the bibliography could be endless. I indicate only a few classic works for ancient Christology and for a general overview: A. GRILLMEIER, *Christ in Christian Tradition. Vol. I. From the Apostolic Age to Chalcedon (451)*, Mowbray & Co. Limited, London 1965; *Vol. II. From the Council of Chalcedon (451) to Gregory the Great (590–604). Part One. Reception and Contradiction. The Development of the Discussion about Chalcedon from 451 to the Beginning of the Reign of Justinian*, Mowbray & Co. Limited, London 1987; *Part Two. The Church of Constantinople in the Sixth Century*, Mowbray & Co. Limited, London 1989; *Part Three. The Churches of Jerusalem and Antioch from 451 to 600*, Oxford University Press, Oxford 2013; *Part Four. The Church of Alexandria with Nubia and Ethiopia after 451*, Mowbray & Co. Limited, London 1996; B. SESBOÜÉ, *Jésus-Christ dans la tradition de l'Eglise*, Descléè, Paris 1982; B. STUDER, *Trinity and Incarnation. The Faith of the Early Church*, The Liturgical Press, Collegeville (MI) 1993; R. OSCULATI, *La teologia cristiana nel suo sviluppo storico. I. Primo millennio*, San Paolo, Cinisello Balsamo 1996; *II. Secondo millennio*, San Paolo, Cinisello Balsamo 1997; K. RAHNER, *Current Problems in Christology*, in ID., *Theological Investigations. Volume I*, Helicon Press, Baltimore 1961, 149–200; W. PANNENBERG, *Jesus. God and Man*, SCM Press, Canterbury 1968; M.R. PECORARA MAGGI, *Il processo a Calcedonia. Storia e interpretazione*, Glossa, Milano 2006.

Some of the **classical Christological problems** are proposed and re-discussed relentlessly. Suffice it to think of the classical arrangement of Christology in Leontius of Jerusalem (GRILLMEIER, *Christ in Christian Tradition II/2*, 271–312): human nature is enhypostatised in the Lógos (i.e. it exists in the divine hypostasis of the Lógos, without possessing a hypostasis of its own), in order to affirm both the duality of natures and the unity of the hypostasis (that of the Lógos). In the Dutch Christology of the last century (Hulsbosch, Schillebeeckx, Schoonemberg, *cf.* A. COZZI, *Conoscere Gesù Cristo nella fede. Una cristologia*, Cittadella, Assisi 2014, 319–326), the model is completely overturned: it is the divine nature that is enhypostatised in the person of Jesus (i.e. it exists in the human hypostasis of Jesus, without possessing a hypostasis of its own). This second position, although considered inadequate (CONGREGATION FOR THE

Doctrine of the Faith, *Mysterium Filii Dei*, 1972), can indicate a need, the urgency of a sensitivity, that cannot simply be ignored and calls for a return also to the classical models in order to understand how to be appropriate simultaneously to them, to us and to Christ.

CHAPTER 2

# Motives for Murder

## 1 A Difficult Man

The Gospels do not try to mask – indeed, in many cases they tend to accentuate – the misunderstanding that characterised the story and person of Jesus. Both enemies and friends may have followed or persecuted him, but they still struggled to understand who he was and what exactly he wanted. The Gospel passages that most dramatically record this misunderstanding are not those relating to his death, such as the betrayal of Judas (*cf. Mt* 26:14–16) or the discouragement of the disciples at Emmaus (*cf. Lk* 24:13–35), but rather those that show how during his life, with him present, those who loved him could not understand him. The account of Jesus getting lost in Jerusalem (*cf. Lk* 2:41–50) may not be historically reliable but it records a fact that the evangelists want to convey: his family did not understand him, and perhaps thought him mad (*cf. Mk* 3:21). Historically more reliable is the account of John the Baptist's request from prison: "Are you the one who is to come?" (*Mt* 11:3).[1] The one who, to all intents and purposes, had been Jesus' teacher, from whom he had borrowed the practice of baptism and with whom he had shared to a large extent the eschatological perspective, dies without having resolved his reservation about him, or so the Gospels tell us. He is not sure.

If one trace of the real Jesus remains with us, it seems to me it could be this: he was a difficult man. From his parents to Pilate, it seems that everyone had to wade through a plurality of possible interpretations to fathom him. Therefore, the history of Christology will not have to be ashamed of its own posthumous labours.

The difficulty seems to derive directly from his life, the unusual choices he made and, above all, the impossibility of relating him to pre-existing models.

To the onlooker, in fact, he could appear as a kind of prophet, healer, wandering preacher from the peripheral and traditionalist region of Galilee.[2] In itself, none of these most obvious aspects was shocking. Not the fact that he was a layman, not the fact that he was celibate, not the fact that he spoke and taught, not the healings and miracles – which at the time might have been far more acceptable than nowadays – not the fact that he announced the

---

1 MEIER, *A Marginal Jew.* 2, 131–137.
2 MEIER, *A Marginal Jew.* 2, 19–99.

eschatological advent of God. Instead, it is the *set* of characteristics that made and make him an enigma. To take an example, John the Baptist was just as, if not more, original, but he was easy to place in the category of the eschatological prophet. Under this label one could understand his fasting and dress, fiery words and the novelty of baptism. Prophets have always used original signs to express the meaning of their preaching. In the case of the Baptist, this prophetic sign was baptism. If a choice had to be made, Jesus was placed in the same category as the eschatological prophets: "Who do people say that I am? And they answered him, "John the Baptist; and others, Elijah; and still others, one of the prophets" (*Mk* 8:27–28). The immediate association is with the eschatological prophets (*Mt* 16:14 adds Jeremiah) and their last representative, John the Baptist. However, too many elements do not fit in with this or go in the opposite direction, e.g. the banquets or the joyful message. He is, in fact, not an ascetic like John, even though he shares much of his message; he is not an Essene – indeed, the Essenes are not even named in the Gospels and in the sources that generally refer to him – even though he shares some aspects of their eschatology; he is not a political revolutionary, although his own followers will always be perplexed on this point; it is not clear whether his eschatological traits, i.e. the fact that he announces the nearness-presence of God, go as far as apocalyptic, i.e. as far as announcing the end of the world. This point, in particular, will be so ambiguous that several generations will have to pass after his death before the question is settled.

Paradoxically, the social category to which Jesus seems to be closest is that of the Pharisees. The even harsh clashes he seems to have had with them and even the role they may have played in his condemnation should not mislead. The reason for these clashes lies in the fact that Jesus and the Pharisees had many interests in common and, therefore, many possible topics of disagreement. This is the reason why other social groups, such as the Romans or the priests, did not clash with him until the latter part of his life: for much of the time, they simply ignored him, and *vice versa*.

The most interesting aspect highlighted by this difficulty in locating Jesus is not so much his uniqueness but the complexity of his relationships and of the inheritances of which he is the interpreter. He is not simply *different* from those around him; he is *original*. He owes much to them, but reinterprets the debt in his own way. He owes much to the Baptist, he owes much to his family and the Galilean context of his origin, to the Pharisaic passion for absolute observance of the law, to the priestly focus on the temple. In a word, he owes much to Israel and its various traditions. In the end, what will lead to his death will be precisely the fact that he re-proposes this inherited burden in such a way as to be altogether inacceptable to those who, rightly, considered themselves its custodians.

From a historical point of view also, the essential starting point is that this character is killed off at some point. He failed to be accepted, and so triggered his own end. Before attempting a theological reading of the motives that set off this hostility, it is worth dwelling on the historical motives we have, in order to try to eliminate the more far-fetched ones and gather reliable material.

## 2    Convicted and Killed

The story of Jesus' death is not a crime novel because it can be said that there is no mystery to unravel.

> Dogmatic positions have obscured the obviousness of the explanation. [...] Jesus and his followers thought of there being a kingdom in which Jesus was the leader, and he was executed as 'king of the Jews', while his disciples went free. This shows that the Romans regarded him as dangerous at one level but not at another: dangerous as one who excited the hopes and dreams of the Jews, but not as an actual leader of an insurgent group. [...] The real conflict was between Jesus and his contemporaries in Judaism.[3]

Any subsequent explanation and in-depth study must start from this fact and its consequences. One can discuss the concrete reality of the group of Twelve, the number of disciples and the size of the crowds that followed him, yet the limits are set. He was considered dangerous, a subversive, and for this he was condemned to the punishment of political subversives. "Not only for the later faith of the disciples, but also on a historical level, the death-sentence of Jesus on the cross is that of the Messiah".[4] Explanations that would see him as a purely spiritual teacher devoted to loving practices, without any social pretensions, would not offer a clue to the fact of his condemnation. Yet he was not a great revolutionary. His followers were not persecuted to any great extent and, above all, they did not start any revolt. The combined reaction of the jubilant crowds and the core of loyalists was limited to a severed ear. It is precisely this that prompts us to investigate possible religious explanations. The official cause of the subversive messiah does not find sufficient support in the facts to

---

3   SANDERS, *Jesus and Judaism*, 295.
4   G. JOSSA, *La condanna del Messia. Problemi storici della ricerca su Gesù*, Paideia, Brescia 2010, 198.

clarify the matter. There must have been ulterior motives that made people go to the trouble and expense of having Jesus killed.

However, as we probe the motives for Jesus' death, it is good to clear the field of a number of possible answers that would make the story simply implausible. I will eliminate three: the idea that he was killed because he was a *zealot*, the idea that he was killed because he *preached love*, the idea that he got himself killed to *atone for the sin* of the world.

I have already spoken about the last motive. It is not denied that Jesus' death was salvific; it is simply not plausible that this was the existential spring that moved the actors. It may have been a metaphysical motivation but not a psychological one. To go in this direction is to imagine characters who move outside common comprehensibility. This may work for Jesus but not for the other actors. We would end up with Judas fulfilling a religious – almost priestly – duty by handing over the lamb, and with the priests prophetically foreseeing the redemptive value of the murder they are plotting (*Jn* 11:47–53).

The second motive is more dangerously appealing. It must be recognised, however, that to imagine a Jewish world that could have killed a man because he was good or because he preached love – as if he were the only man of the time to do so – is far-fetched. The Gospels themselves testify to us that, by and large, the best of Israel knew well the centrality of love: "You are right, Teacher; you have truly said that he is one, and besides him there is no other; and to love him with all the heart, and with all the understanding, and with all the strength, and to love one's neighbour as oneself, this is much more important than all whole burnt offerings and sacrifices" (*Mk* 12:32–33). The greatest danger of this interpretation, however, lies in the fact that it makes the story extremely flat, a kind of comic strip in which pure goodness is on one side and pure wickedness on the other. Any psychological and human complexity disappears, and the story turns into a Manichaean clash. The very need to pause and meditate on the facts is lost, as everything is reduced to an almost physical confrontation between positive and negative poles. However, this is not what the story is telling us, but something much deeper, more refined and dramatic.

The last possible cause of Jesus' death to be disproved – that Jesus was a zealot – is quickly refuted: at the time of Jesus, zealots did not exist! It is, however, paradoxically, the most plausible cause. Certainly Jesus could not have belonged to a political revolutionary group that came into being only thirty-five years later (in 67–68 A.D.);[5] yet some of the fears that the Nazarene

---

5   *Cf.* JOSSA, *La condanna del Messia*, 115–150; ID., *Gesù e i movimenti di liberazione della Palestina*, Paideia, Brescia 1980.

aroused were similar to those later aroused by the zealots: fears of revolution, of disorder and of social upheaval.

These are implausible motives, therefore. We can set them aside for the moment but not forget them. There will come a time when we shall have to ask ourselves to what extent the suspicion of a social revolution, a conception of love extravagant to the common sensibility, and Jesus' willingness to consider his own death in a representative and not just an individual sense, may not be of help in better understanding the story.

There are, however, other causes for his death that are more historically ascertainable and more psychologically plausible. They can be considered only individually, but must be bear in mind that they are not alternatives. In the most plausible hypothesis we can arrive at, it was a combination of these causes that led to Jesus' condemnation and death.

## 2.1   *The Law*

The hypothesis that Jesus was condemned as a lawbreaker has little historical basis. It seems more like a theological interpretation and a narrative device. Indeed, if one tries to understand *how* and *when* precisely Jesus transgressed the law, the results are very poor. Perhaps he did so only when he ordered a man not to bury his father in order to follow him (*cf. Mt* 8:21) – but even this could be hyperbolic language rather than a description of a fact. For the rest, it does not appear that he transgressed any of the commandments. He did not transgress the Sabbath,[6] for example, but, if anything, he proposed a looser interpretation of it. As for the laws of purity, the truth is that it is not clear what he did. There are certainly instances in which Jesus contrasts his own word with the word of the commandment or introduces new prohibitions – such as the one on divorce and oaths – or, if at all, the 'commandment' of love. However, it does not appear that any of these acts or sayings are capital offences. In many cases, for example on the Sabbath, there could be different interpretations, and Jesus places himself, perhaps on the margins, but within a range of possible interpretative options. Thus, in the case of the antitheses, "But I say to you" (*cf. Mt* 5:21–48; 19:9), these can be interpreted as *restrictive reinterpretations* or *deepenings* of the law that, in principle, were not debatable. It is clear that, in itself, it would be better not to divorce, to swear as little as possible and not to call one's brother crazy. As for the commandment of love, we have already seen how belief in love cannot be presented as a valid reason for condemnation.

However, it would not be fair to dismiss this motivation too quickly. Jesus' way of behaving may have appeared to many as excessively free with regard

---

6   MEIER, *A Marginal Jew.* 4, 235–340.

to the law. Not so much as to provoke condemnation, but enough to explain widespread irritation among various social classes and religious groups within Israel, such as to justify the hostility, or at least the scant support, he encountered at the time of his capture and trial. Perhaps there was no reason to condemn him under the law, yet neither was there any reason to defend or save him. For many, his attitude could have been a threat to traditions considered important to their religious and social identity. Something similar, it seems to me, to the irritation one might have with Socrates: a man considered too *sui generis* to be generally appreciated. With one difference, however: whereas for Socrates the right to life and death was in the hands of his own fellow citizens, not so for Jesus. In his case, what was needed was a motivation that was also valid for an authority – that of Pilate – which, in itself, was indifferent to this kind of ethnic-religious motivation.

## 2.2 The Temple

At different times in Jesus' life, the evangelists record that he did and said something about the destruction of the temple: John places this episode at the beginning of his activity (*Jn* 2:13–25), thus making it a programmatic gesture; the Synoptics place it, instead, at the end (*Mt* 21:12–13; *Mk* 11:15–19; *Lk* 19:45–48), as a concluding one. This second hypothesis seems the most historically plausible. As the case of Jeremiah showed, predicting the destruction of the temple (*Jer* 7) clearly provoked violent reactions (*Jer* 26). What exactly Jesus said, however, and especially what his contemporaries understood, is much less clear. For an initial reconstruction, however, this is sufficient:

> All this suggests to me a modest phrasing of what at its core has high historical probability: Something done and/or said by Jesus prognostic of Temple/sanctuary destruction was at least a partial cause of the Sanhedrin's decision that led to his death.[7]

And again:

> *He was not crucified until after he had had time to make a demonstration against the temple*, which is clearly the last act he *performed* before being executed (except for the Last Supper with his disciples). The rifle might have already been pointed, but it was the demonstration against the temple that caused the trigger to be pulled.[8]

---

[7] R.E. BROWN, *The Death of the Messiah. From Gethsemane to the Grave. A Commentary of the Passion Narratives in the Four Gospels. Vol. I*, Doubleday, New York 1994, 459–460.
[8] SANDERS, *Jesus and Judaism*, 305.

## 2.3 The Messiah

It is very difficult to establish to what extent it was clear what Jesus claimed to be and especially how this claim might have sounded to the ears of his contemporaries. However, Jesus evidently had a very particular conception of his own person.

On the other hand, it can be ruled out that he affirmed something similar to the dogma of Chalcedon about himself: that is, that he was *true God and true man*. Given the time it took Christians to formulate such a definition, it is unrealistic to think either that Jesus expressed himself with such clarity, or that anyone would have understood him, had he done so. If he had, it seems to me that the accusation of blasphemy would have been entirely justified from a Jewish point of view. Subsequent history has shown – as a not entirely predictable fact – that Jewish theology could not accept the dogma of the Trinity without turning into something else.

Any other expression – Messiah, Lord, Son of God, Son of Man, Word of God – could only be ambiguous, something which a Jew could interpret in either an orthodox or blasphemous sense. Many of these possible statements ran more the risk of being exaggerated or ridiculous than of being imputable to blasphemy. The most obvious example is the claim to be the messiah. In itself, this is not blasphemy for those who await the messiah but, rather, a ridiculous claim.[9] However, the hostility towards Jesus may not have needed a formal accusation of blasphemy; rather, it may have fed on a widespread perception of blasphemous egocentrism on his part. There is something similar here to what we have already seen in the case of the law. Not a formalised accusation, but severe irritation that may have been as much the unwillingness to defend someone perceived as megalomaniac as the impetus to demand condemnation.

## 2.4 The Triumphal Entry

If the episode of the triumphal entry into Jerusalem had taken place in the terms in which it is described, both by the Synoptics (*Mt* 21:1–11; *Mk* 11:1–11; *Lk* 19:28–40) and by John (*Jn* 12:12–19), it would have been a sufficient pretext to justify Jesus' condemnation.[10] A man entering an occupied city making royal claims, recognised as the son of David, i.e. a legitimate aspirant to the throne, hailed by a large crowd, would have caused immediate armed intervention and arrest by the Romans– probably not only his own, but also that of a number of his followers. Together with the evangelists' own acknowledgement that the

---

9  *Cf.* JOSSA, *La condanna del Messia*, 196.
10  *Cf.* SANDERS, *Jesus and Judaism*, 306–308.

gesture was not immediately understood ("His disciples did not understand these things at first ...", *Jn* 12:16), this suggests that "from a political point of view Jesus' entry into Jerusalem [was] an insignificant episode: [...] it was over in a few minutes".[11] For as the crowd has gathered, so it disperses. Jesus has the opportunity to preach again without anyone seeming to remember these regal features, either at the time or shortly afterwards when it comes to taking a position against those who want to crucify him.

Again, rather than a specific fact, it is the overall picture that is circumstantial. An alleged eschatological prophet, who often speaks of the Kingdom, with possible or presumed regal-Davidic aspirations, may have created widespread irritation and, above all, offered a good pretext for an admissible denunciation by the Roman authority. It is not by chance that this was to be the official reason for the condemnation of "Jesus of Nazareth, the King of the Jews" (*Jn* 19:19 and, in a different way, *Mt* 27:37; *Mk* 15:26; *Lk* 23:38).

A quick analysis of these causes offers a result that is ambiguous overall. In itself, none of the motives seems to be sufficient to justify condemnation. Yet the condemnation is itself the most certain fact of this story: "To be 'historical' the historical Jesus must have been crucifiable"[12] because he was, in fact, crucified, and it also seems that a certain amount of effort was required to achieve this outcome. This is a much more interesting result than it might seem at first glance, one which opens up a number of paths and considerations.

Firstly, it forces us to go deeper, while also leaving a certain need for interpretation. Anyone who wants to tell this story and give an account of the motivations of the actors on stage will necessarily have to give their own reconstruction of the facts.

Given the uncertainty of the data, however, the safest thing will be to try to offer an open interpretation that respects the *mix* of motives present. Given that this murder apparently involves a combination of responsibilities – one of his own betraying him, someone accusing him and someone else carrying out the sentence, after a double trial – one can legitimately assume that the motives could have been many and varied. Each could have had his own motives for wanting Jesus dead, motives that did not necessarily converge.

It is very important to note, however, that this uncertainty seems to be based essentially on an uncertainty on the part of the evangelists themselves.

---

11  G. Jossa, *Voi chi dite che io sia? Storia di un profeta ebreo di nome Gesù*, Paideia, Torino 2018, 241.
12  J.D.G. Dunn, *Christianity in the Making. I. Jesus remembered*, Wm. B. Eerdmans Publishing Company, Grand Rapids (MI) 2003, 784.

Indeed, from the various narratives, one does not get the impression that the writers *want to hide the true reasons* for Jesus' death in order to insert others, but that they *do not know them at all*. "It seems quite clear that they [the evangelists] did not know why Jesus was executed from the point of view of the Jewish leaders".[13] This is not surprising. Even in many contemporary trials it can happen that the chronicler, even when present at the events, is not clear about the underlying motives, especially when dealing with an event involving many people.

The most interesting aspect, however, is not the fact itself but rather the way in which this gap in knowledge is treated by the evangelists. On the one hand, it is the pretext to bring out the wickedness and lies of the leaders of the Jews; on the other hand, to bend the story in a theological sense, which is the true intent of the Gospels. For them, the story of Jesus is not the result of petty human intrigues but an event of theological revelation.

This risks overshadowing a further historical cause of Jesus' death which I want to mention here only as it will constitute an important aspect of the remainder of my discourse. That is, the possibility that *chance* played a role in this affair. Often, when it is difficult to identify clearly the motive for a murder involving a large number of people, the difficulty lies in the fact that there is no clear motive, since the affair is technically a *mess*. No motive is sufficient, yet events turn ugly, and no one can understand what is going on. Things soon turn tragic for those caught up in the mess: both for the accused, who usually ends up badly, and for the accusers, who may go home with the feeling that things have gone far beyond what they wanted or imagined. This last possibility is of great interest mainly because it is very plausible, yet much overlooked. But, above all, because it is explanatory for contemporary narrative sensitivity. A narrative that fails to integrate this dimension of cynical unpredictability, which is typical of the story, is instinctively false and artificial to our ears.

### Bibliographical Guidelines

For the results of the **historical-critical method** regarding Jesus, I have made extensive use of J.P. MEIER, *A Marginal Jew. Rethinking the Historical Jesus. 1. The Roots of the Problem and the Person*, Doubleday, New York 1991; *2. Mentor, Message and Miracles*, Doubleday, New York 1994; *3. Companions and Competitors*, Doubleday, New York 2001; *4. Law and Love*, Doubleday, New York 2009; *5. Probing the Authenticity of the Parables*, Doubleday, New York 2017.

---

13  SANDERS, *Jesus and Judaism*, 299.

As an **introduction**, see: G. Jossa, *Voi chi dice che io sia? Storia di un profeta ebreo di nome Gesù*, Paideia, Torino 2018; G. Theissen – A. Merz *The Historical Jesus: A Comprehensive Guide*, Fortress Press, Philadelphia 1998; J.D.G. Dunn, *A New Perspective on Jesus. What the Quest for the Historical Jesus Missed*, Backer Academic, Grand Rapids (MI) 2005. A very loose and narrative, but very well documented, introduction is J. Martin, *Jesus. A Pilgrimage*, HarperOne, San Francisco 2014. For specific aspects, one can consult the articles in the monumental T. Holmén – S.E. Porter (edd.), *Handbook for the Study of the Historical Jesus, I–IV*, Brill, Leiden – Boston/MA 2011.

For a **critical approach**: N. Ciola – A. Pitta – G. Pulcinelli (edd.), *Ricerca storica su Gesù. Ricerche e prospettive*, EDB, Bologna 2017; G. Segalla, *Sulle tracce di Gesù. La "Terza ricerca"*, Cittadella, Assisi 2006; C. Keith, *The Narratives of the Gospels and the Historical Jesus. Current Debates, Prior Debates and the Goal of Historical Jesus Research*, in Journal for the Study of the New Testament 38 (2016) 426–455; F.G. Downing, *Feasible Researches in Historical Jesus Tradition. A Critical Response to Chris Keith*, in Journal for the Study of the New Testament 40 (2017) 51–61.

On the **death of Jesus** from a historical-critical point of view: J.D.G. Dunn, *Christianity in the Making, I: Jesus Remembered, 5: The Climax of Jesus' Mission*, Eerdmans, Grand Rapids 2003; G. Jossa, *La condanna del Messia. Problemi storici della ricerca su Gesù*, Paideia, Brescia 2010; G. Barbaglio, *I racconti della Passione. Indagine storica sul processo e la morte di Gesù di Nazaret*, EDB, Bologna 2015; S. McKnight, *Jesus and His Death. Historiography, the Historical Jesus, and Atonement Theory*, Baylor University Press, Waco (TX) 2005; J.B. Green, *The Death of Jesus*, in T. Holmén – S.E. Porter (edd.), *Handbook for the Study of the Historical Jesus, III: The Historical Jesus*, Brill, Leiden – Boston/MA 2011, 2383–2409. For an introduction that interprets Jesus' death within a broader array of earlier and later "traumas": D.M. Carr, *Holy Resilience. The Bible's Traumatic Origins*, Yale University Press, New Haven/CT – London 2014, 141–155. For a solid (and extensive) biblical foundation: R.E. Brown, *The Death of the Messiah. From Gethsemane to the Grave. A Commentary of the Passion Narratives in the Four Gospels. Vol. I–II*, Doubleday, New York 1994.

CHAPTER 3

# The Story of a Free Man

The motivations for Jesus' death that we have analysed so far are, evidently, those of *others*, not his own. At the same time, however, they are caused by Jesus' behaviour and will, in turn, give rise to actions to which he will have to respond, as far as he is able.

What I would like to capture in this story is the unfolding drama of actions and reactions, the interweaving of moves and countermoves. From this dynamic, the freedom of Jesus can become visible as it unfolds. For freedom cannot be seen except in actions, and these need narratives to be understood.

But what is freedom, especially today?

## 1 Freedom Today

Perhaps freedom is always the same, but certainly not its realisation and the challenges it encounters to realise itself in the concreteness of history and biographies. Understanding what the challenges of freedom are today should make it possible to approach the story of Jesus with soteriological perspectives that make it easier to grasp what his story has to offer. If the freedom of today's men and women needs to be liberated, and if Jesus can have something to say to this liberation, then the order of our investigation can only be this: starting from today's questions, we turn to yesterday's stories to understand whether it is still worth telling them again.

Among the many possible angles and nuances that could be adopted to speak about freedom today, I have tried to identify *three challenges* around which to focus attention. They are not exhaustive, but they can constitute perspectives to accompany a Christology that seeks to place itself in the midst of the changes that our age is experiencing.

### 1.1 *The Challenge of Psychology: Conditioned Freedom*
The different approaches that have characterised psychology in the last century certainly cannot be reduced to one. They differ radically in the way they look at the person, at his or her faculties, and in the way they configure educational or therapeutic intervention. However, we must not overlook one specific fact that characterises a world in which psychology is present and intervenes as one of the factors that define the human: human action is analysed by trying

to give reasons for it, that is, by introducing causes, influences, motivations and conditions affecting the action itself. The *ab-solute* place of decision-making is populated with presences of various kinds that give the overall effect of a sort of colonisation at the heart of freedom: presences that are biological, biographical, relational, neuroscientific, ethological, social, etc. The existential environment that each of us inhabits is populated by these presences, and each of us naturally tends to think of our choices as conditioned by a multiplicity of factors. This can lead us to despair of our real freedom, but also, more modestly, leads us to think of freedom as something with very limited room for manoeuvre.

Let us take the case that, while talking to a therapist or even just to a friend, we realise that we have made a certain decision for some unconscious reason. It does not matter whether this unconscious factor was something removed or relational (the recurrence of some childhood dynamic), or biological (some hormonal or metabolic imbalance), or even social (the influence of a cultural prejudice): whatever, it was something that conditioned us without our being aware of it. Our reaction tends to be twofold: on the one hand we are happy to have understood it because it gives us hope that we shall be able to act more consciously and freely later on, but, on the other hand, it also leaves us with a veil of sadness because it opens our eyes to how little we are aware of ourselves, how conditioned we are. It is not a question here of the difficulties that can arise from ignorance, sin or weakness of will. The challenge here is far more radical in that we perceive a threat that comes not from outside but from within our own freedom. It forces us to see that even the choices we consider most essential to defining us – the woman, man or religious order we have chosen, our profession, religious faith itself – actually seem to be the result of a mixture of motivations largely beyond our control and awareness. I find myself not only *doing what I do not want* (*cf. Rom* 7:15–20), but *not even knowing what I want* (*cf. Rom* 8:26–30) – indeed, 'being willed' by forces of which I can only become aware in retrospect.

The possibility of thinking of freedom (and the intellect) as the safe place to control ourselves, to start something new, is drastically reduced.

Faced with such a challenge, Christology, with the weight of its history, runs the risk of floundering. The effort to emphasise the uniqueness of Jesus, his difference from us, his singularity, may prove an obstacle to grasping that Jesus is not only *different from* us but, first and foremost, *similar to* us – *consubstantial*, the Council of Chalcedon would say. Hence, to recognise how even his freedom was a conditioned, contextualised, constrained freedom. But, at the same time, also a *dependent* freedom in the sense that it depended on encounters, relationships and *bonds*. It was nourished by the encounters and contingent challenges it received from the context in which it was realised and from the people it encountered, like the freedom of everyone, at all times. To be able to bring out the concreteness of Jesus' freedom, one must, therefore, strive to grasp the bonds on which it was nourished, the debts it honoured and took up. Otherwise, one will always have the feeling of witnessing a story, perhaps fascinating, but far from being meaningful for the concrete freedom of an ordinary person, which is something we all are.

### 1.2   The Challenge of Sociology: Drunk Freedom

The second challenge comes from the field of sociology. Here, the most interesting fact for our topic seems to me to be the following: the number of fronts on which we are called upon to choose is potentially infinite, as is the amount of options available. Like children in a huge toy shop (or an endless gallery of horrors), we do not escape a sense of drunkenness. It is not materially possible to evaluate the excessive number of options. The disproportion of possibilities makes the choice risky and potentially irrelevant. We intuit that, to be on top of this possible multiplicity, we would need a subject far more powerful than we are, a kind of superman.

One of the possible strategies of defence against this hypermarket of options is to escape, not from choice but from the subject itself. A series of pathologies afflicting contemporary men and women highlight precisely the struggle to live up to the complexity and excess that characterise the process of subjectivisation. Rather than being overwhelmed by the sea of possibilities, they prefer to renounce themselves and thus not have to choose.

The possibility of thinking of freedom as responsible for something that knows, evaluates and controls is also drastically reduced today.

From this point of view, the time in which Jesus lived was less complex. The concrete options of choice available to a 1st century Galilean[1] are not comparable to those of a 21st century European – as I am. However, I do not believe that the difference is so great ultimately. One should neither underestimate the room for manoeuvre granted to the man of the past, nor overestimate the *real* number of options of the man of today. Even a Galilean craftsman had options – to marry or not to marry, to follow in his father's footsteps or not to follow in his father's footsteps, to devote himself to religion with greater or lesser conviction. Otherwise he would not have been free at all. On the contrary, each of us today realises that, even in the sea of *theoretical* possibilities,

---

1   *Cf.* P. GAMBERINI, *Questo Gesù (At 2,32). Pensare la singolarità di Gesù*, EDB, Bologna 2005, 42–44.

in the end, the *real* options are not infinite. There are before each of us a number of viable paths, and it is on these that we stake our lives.

There is, however, a deeper level of the question that brings into play the very way in which we imagine the life of faith, namely, our freedom before God and his freedom. I want to mention here an idea that I know is controversial and yet seems to me to underlie the possibility of talking about the freedom of Jesus as a concrete way to our freedom. The idea is that, even in the case of life before God, we should not imagine *only one* possible way, as if God had placed us in a large supermarket in which only one of the products on display was the right one for us. Or, even worse, as if only one shopping cart with its contents is the right one for us – a much more complicated case because it involves a series of choices that must *all* be right. I don't believe this is the case. Rather, in the large supermarket in which we certainly are, there are *certain* configurations that are good for us, within which we have been given a real choice. This is basically the experience we have when we actually go to the real supermarket: there are a lot of items, and everyone has to be able to get to the checkout with a shopping cart that is reasonably suitable for himself and the people he has to take care of. Clearly, it makes no sense to fill it only with fizzy drinks or exotic sauces, but, at the same time, one can legitimately opt for a menu of fish, meat or the ingredients for lasagne.

The banality of the example should not deceive us with respect to the seriousness of the matter, especially in the case of Jesus. Too often, in fact, his person is portrayed as that of an actor in a drama already written, for better or for worse. Jesus thus becomes the only one who enters the supermarket with the right shopping list, while the rest of us enter it with nothing more than some vague indications. Instead, it is important to tell his story as the story of someone who knew how to choose within real options – albeit in a smaller supermarket than the one we have today.

## 1.3 *The Challenge of Science: The Dark Background*

Finally, there is a challenge that comes from the world of science, particularly from those disciplines that contribute to forming the so-called neurosciences. Again, this is not one specific problem but an overall effect that is created by the enormous amount of data and hypotheses that combine to explain what we tend to feel is the most private and identifying place of whom we are, namely, our brain. Experiencing one's freedom in the face of the pervasiveness of scientific discoveries entails confronting the hypothesis that we are puppets in the hands of forces over which we have no control and which we do not really fully understand.

It is not simply a matter of recognising that *much* of what we do, think or feel is conditioned by factors that we are unaware of and that influence us. This is the challenge of psychology. Instead, it is to confront the assumption that *everything* we do is conditioned by deterministic factors, and that the feeling that we are free agents is ultimately an illusion. Now, psychology by its very nature tends to steer clear of the hypothesis of total determinism, if only for practical reasons: if man cannot control his life at all, there is little point in seeing a psychotherapist. But even the psychology of everyday life – the one that each of us implicitly applies in order to be able to act in the world – naturally keeps away from this hypothesis. Taking it seriously would have catastrophic consequences on every aspect of our being in the world: legal, ethical, emotional, professional and so on.[2]

This hypothesis can be quickly discarded, therefore, especially in the concreteness of everyday life, and yet it touches everyday life itself, leaving a dark horizon, a sort of dull unease that, once it appears, never goes away. We can say that we cannot be people of our time without being confronted with the hypothesis, perhaps immediately dismissed, that our freedom is an illusion and that our life is a jumble of impersonal forces living in our place.

Christianity cannot respond to this challenge with a definitive reassurance or assurance; nor should it. What it can, instead, counter to nothingness is the fragility of a face, of a singular realisation.

Faced with a person who feels overwhelmed by necessity, who sees no meaning and no possibility of fulfilment, no one can give definitive, objective proof of the goodness of the world; the possibility of non-sense remains. It is not even possible to offer one's own person as a model and solution to the problem; no one would stand up to the challenge. What can be done is to show examples of possible realisation – in oneself and in others. Nothing absolute, only fragments, which can, however, arouse the desire that the path of one's own subjectivisation is worthwhile. Perhaps even the face of Christ could be presented with the register of this modest singularity which places him alongside his brothers rather than proposing him as the sole answer to every possible question. He would not be diminished by it: to the extent that the face of Christ is the face of a possible sonship, it is stronger than if it were a universal model, an abstract equation.

---

2  *Cf.* M. De Caro – A. Lavazza – G. Sartori (edd.), *Siamo davvero liberi? Le neuroscienze e il mistero del libero arbitrio*, Codice Edizioni, Torino 2010. For a critical position, *cf.* P. Legrenzi – C. Umiltà, *Neuro-mania. Il cervello non spiega chi siamo*, il Mulino, Bologna 2009.

The radical nature of the challenge of non-sense should not be a problem for Christology: Christ's proclamation of salvation is radical. The condition is that there be a true confrontation with the abyss opened wide by such a prospect. Indeed, the challenge to freedom is such that it cannot simply be resolved but rather experienced as part of the existential horizon we inhabit. As I have tried to show elsewhere,[3] confronting this idea means neither embracing it nor panicking. It does mean, however, putting in place a series of philosophical-theological efforts to defuse this metaphysical hypothesis, but, above all, spiritual tools to live in this new horizon in a Christian manner that is meaningful.

The same applies to a specific aspect of this discussion, namely, the possible presence of chance. It will be a matter of showing how Jesus' activity was exposed as much to the abyss of meaninglessness as to the weight of chance in life, and was able to *carry* and *redeem* these aspects of human existence.

The overall picture that emerges from the interweaving of these three challenges could be summarised somewhat brutally as follows: *our freedom 1) is conditioned, 2) by an unmanageable sea of possibilities, and 3) with the risk that it does not actually manage anything at all.* If Christology wants to proclaim the salvation of the man and woman who also inhabit this cultural context, its task will not be simply to deny these challenges but to pass through them. The story of Jesus should show how it is possible to move between different possibilities, conditioned by one's own unique and singular history, living it as the place of the manifestation and realisation of one's own sonship. It is in this interweaving, and not in some other place, that each one learns to say 'Father' when addressing God.

## 2 The Freedom of Bonds

### 2.1 *Constitutive Relationship*

The possibility of facing the challenges of the current context can only run through a discussion of some of the solutions and perspectives that the same context has generated. In particular, I would like to try to outline some features of an anthropological perspective that seeks to start, not from the isolated subject but from a subject originally in relation. This perspective has a number of complex roots including, by way of example, psychology – in particular the

---

3  Cf. L. PARIS, *Neuroscienze e pastorale. Spunti per un confronto*, in *Rivista del clero italiano* 99 (2018) 429–441.

psychodynamic strand and what has been called the 'relational turn' – but also some currents in phenomenology[4] or neuroscience.[5]

The basic assumption on which many of these perspectives converge concerns the relational nature of the person. By its nature, the process of subjectivisation involves the other. Some aspects of this position are obvious: in order to live we need to relate to food, to eat. If we were to ask ourselves, 'Does food come first or does the body come first?', we would immediately notice that the problem is circular: there is no body without food (we are literally made from what we eat), but there is no food without a body that is hungry (i.e. it is our intention directed at the animal or plant that transforms them into food). The essential point, however, concerns the constitution of the person. Just as the body feeds on food, so personal identity feeds on relationships. Here again, the relationship is circular, and it is not possible to ask whether it is first the subject that seeks relationships or the relationships that provide substance to the subject. Many of the current theoretical positions regarding freedom differ precisely in the balance they create between subject and relation. Some postulate the insubstantiality of the subject at the mercy of relations, while others postulate relations at the mercy of the subject. The essential point remains, however: there is no subject without relation.

The theological interest of this assumption is obvious, and it is fundamental that it is not reduced too quickly into an ethical-moral key, as a call to make relationship – love – the centre of one's personal identity. Before being a moral appeal, this position identifies a trait that is purely anthropological, ontological, and constitutes a formidable theological challenge.

Thinking of freedom in a relational key[6] means thinking of freedom not as something to do with individual, unimportant choices but as the ability to define ourselves comprehensively through the choices we make. "Free acts in the proper sense are what we can call self-constitutive acts: these are *sources of personal identity through time*".[7] In this perspective, being free does not mean being able to create something radically new but, rather, having the possibility to choose, within the possible contingent, what we want our face, our future identity to be. This is possible because others offer themselves to us as real possibilities of realisation. I choose what I want to become through concrete gestures, but the object of the choice is not at all *ab-solute*: it is, instead, what

---

4   V. Costa, *Alterità*, il Mulino, Bologna 2011.
5   *Cf.* M. Ammaniti – V. Gallese, *La nascita della intersoggettività. Lo sviluppo del sé tra psicodinamica e neurobiologia*, Raffaello Cortina, Milano 2014; G. Rizzolatti – C. Sinigaglia, *Mirrors in the Brain. How Our Minds Share Actions and Emotions*, Oxford University Press, New York 2008.
6   *Cf.* L. Paris, *Teologia e neuroscienze. Una sfida possibile*, Queriniana, Brescia 2017, 217–314.
7   R. De Monticelli, *La novità di ognuno. Persona e libertà*, Garzanti, Milano 2012, 201.

I actually encounter around me. It is people, with their being at once similar to me (people like me) but also different from me (they are not me), who constitute the hypotheses that allow me to choose. In this perspective, there is no freedom outside the relationship, because outside the relationship there is no subject,[8] there is no possibility of choice between the subject I am and the subject I could be by taking the other as a possible example.[9]

This is the typical dynamic of desire as developed by the Lacanian movement. The subject constitutes itself starting from the other, from what it finds outside itself, establishing with it a relation of desire, that is, a relation that allows it to approach the other without assimilating it to itself but maintaining it in its otherness.

This is not the place to analyse this perspective and its theological relevance in detail. However, I would like to emphasise two aspects that are of great importance for Christology.

## 2.2   *Is God the first?*

The first aspect concerns the tension created between the theological and anthropological dimensions of relationality. Certainly, from a theological point of view, the fundamental constitutive relationship of the human is the relationship with God. This is expressed by the concepts of *creation* (origin is in the relationship with God), *covenant* (life is in the relationship with God), *justification* and *redemption* (possibility is in the relationship with God). However, in a historical-psychological perspective, which analyses the concrete establishment of human relationships, the relationship with God cannot be the first, because the first relationship is with the mother, and then the father, brothers, and friends take over.

This creates an interesting need: that of articulating the relationship between the historical order of relationships, their importance and their ontological scope. On the one hand, it is evident that the first relationship in time is not necessarily also the most important over the course of life; in fact, it is assumed that other, temporally subsequent relationships, such as that of a couple, for example, or that with one's children, must take over from the original ones in terms of importance. However, from the point of view of the formation of subsequent relationships, it is not without significance that some

---

8  "The first-person perspective is relational in that it would be impossible for a being truly alone in the universe to have a first-person perspective": L.R. BAKER, *Persons and Bodies. A Constitution View*, Cambridge University Press, Cambridge – New York 2000, 69–70.

9  *Cf.* A. FERRARA, *The force of the Example. Explorations in the Paradigm of Judgment*, Columbia University Press, New York 2008.

relationships are the first, as well as the fact that these first relationships have taken one certain concrete form rather than another. This is not to fall into any psychological determinism, but neither is it to underestimate – for reasons of ontological pre-eminence – the concrete weight that human relationships, particularly family relationships, can have in shaping the relationship with God.[10]

This applies to each of us, but it must also apply and be made clear in the case of Jesus. Insofar as his was a true – and normal – human subjectivisation, he too had to construct his own identity, starting, *first of all*, from the concrete relationships out of which his life was woven. However, his relationship with the Father, which is the first from a metaphysical point of view, as it is for each of us, was not the first in the concrete shaping of his person from a psychological and evolutionary point of view. To grasp the nexus that links his fundamental relationship with the Father to all the other relationships that formed the fabric of his life is one of the points of interest of a Christology that seeks to be contemporary. That is, it is a matter of constructing a Christology of bonds that does not load all the weight of the person of Jesus on to a single bond, but that knows how to grasp its constitutive and dynamic complexity.

## 2.3  *Creative Recovery*

A second consideration, with respect to the concept of freedom, concerns the relationship between *beginning* and *choice*. In the Modern perspective, there was a tendency to consider freedom precisely because of its capacity to start something new, new causal chains compared with the determined chains of the natural world.[11] In this perspective, the value of freedom does not lie in the possibility of choosing, since it is impossible to choose if there is nothing to choose from, regardless of any presupposition. Instead, it lies in the possibility of creating something out of nothing, in an obvious and problematic analogy with the creative freedom of God. In a relational perspective, on the other hand, freedom does not create anything, but applies the possibility of choosing between different options that are contingent, given. It is the concreteness of the existing real that provides the material to which human desire applies

---

10    *Cf.* G. Rossi – M. Aletti (edd.), *Psicologia della religione e teoria dell'attaccamento*, Aracne, Roma 2009, esp. the articles by R. Cassibba, P. Granqvist and M. Aletti.

11    For Descartes, "the spontaneity of the spiritual substance is thus the first guarantee of the freedom of the will. The irreducibility of spirit and will to material elements – this is the ultimate meaning of ontological dualism between soul and body – guarantees their complete independence from any causal determination of corporeal substance": M. Mori, *Gli spiriti e le macchine. Il determinismo moderno*, in M. De Caro – M. Mori – E. Spinelli (edd.), *Libero arbitrio. Storia di una controversia filosofica*, Carocci, Roma 2014, 267.

itself in order to reject or accept it through a choice. The metaphysical and theological significance of this shift in focus should not be underestimated, particularly with regard to Jesus.

If freedom is to be able to make one's life something that speaks of oneself, then what is needed is a real space in which to say one's name, beyond necessity and beyond contingency. It will be precisely in such a space that the bonds, the relationships that constitute this real space and provide the construction material for each one's biography, will emerge. For no one invents his or her life from scratch. Everyone builds their own personality, their own work, their own style, from the contributions that many others provide them with. If there were not these bonds that nourish us and offer us words, thoughts, money, possibilities, roads, houses, we could not even begin. At the same time, these bonds appear to us as the ballast that does not allow us to fly.

At this point, it seems to me that the most correct perspective is to see freedom as the *creative recovery* of what we have received. We all receive from others almost everything we have, and, at the same time, if we are able, we leave our own distinctive mark on this material. We do not invent the music and most of the time not even the score, and yet the interpretation is ours and says who we are, for better or worse. Jesus also did this. He certainly said something new, yet he did not start from scratch, but rather from words, thoughts and gestures encountered in his own living relationships.

In order to understand the concreteness of Jesus' freedom, so as to be able to make him a model for our own concrete freedom, it may be useful to start from the perspective of a creative recovery that integrates freedom *from* and freedom *for*.[12] Indeed, Jesus cannot be described merely as the one who was free lord of himself: his biography is too radically marked by the bonds that bound and constrained him. Jesus was not simply free in relation to the Father, nor did he want to be; instead, he was bound by a constitutive relationship with the God whom he called Father, and in relation to whom he felt he was called and bound to a mission that did not simply come from himself but preceded him. Not even in relation to us, to those he called brothers and sisters, was Jesus free: he was bound by bonds of friendship, bonds of people, but, above all, the same mission that bound him to the Father also bound him to us. In this sense, Jesus was not and is not free from us, but bound himself to our fate

---

12   Cf. I. BERLIN, *Two Concepts of Liberty*, in ID., *Liberty*, Oxford University Press, Oxford 1995, 166–217. The author outlines these two concepts of freedom – negative and positive – and undoubtedly favours the former to the detriment of the latter. The choice in favour of negative versus positive freedom is a clear indication of the author's suspicion of the ideologies and visions – more political and military than religious – that have plagued the 20th century.

and exposed himself to our love and stupidity in a completely irreversible way. If freedom is simply doing as we please, Jesus was not and will never be free.

However, the opposite does not work either: seeing Jesus as the one who is totally absorbed in his own mission,[13] totally entrusted to the relationships that constitute him, totally free of himself *for others*, risks turning him into an ideologue, dehumanising him and not doing justice either to him or to the Father. Jesus is not just the obedient one; he is not just the crucified one; he is not just at the mercy of others. For he is Son and Saviour, but he is also Lord. In the way the Gospels tell us, he is never presented as being overwhelmed by divine or human events that he does not dominate but, rather, as one who chooses his own path and makes the mission entrusted to him his own. In this sense, Jesus is a man who constructs his own biography in dialogue with those who precede him and with the bonds that constitute him, but taking up each of these bonds in a creative way. The handing over of Jesus is not a kidnapping. He is called by someone and captured by someone else and, at the same time, it is he who responds, who positions himself in the dramatic scene. In the events he lives, he brings out his own character, his own name. It seems to me that, from this perspective, it is easier to glimpse an aspect that both Scripture and Tradition risk underestimating. Jesus is not only the Son, the Lord, the Christ: he is also Jesus. An individual person, a way of looking or walking, a style in approaching people. I am not speaking here of that Christ-like form of love, dedication, and passion for the Kingdom that was Jesus' and must become every Christian's. I am talking about those singular aspects that were uniquely his, that only those he met could recognise – and therefore remain largely closed to us – and yet cannot be overlooked. Jesus was not humanity, he was a man: only by seeing this can one grasp the free and individual way in which he made his life what it was.

These singular traits of freedom emerge – in Jesus as in any of us – from the personal way in which we creatively take up the relationships and inheritances that constitute us and imprint our features on them. We have real and weighty relationships, but, within these bonds, we are actors in our turn.

## 2.4  *A Life of Bonds*

So then, one can look at the life of Jesus as a creative recovery of a series of previous bonds. Jesus receives something and takes it up, rethinks it, reinterprets it, making it something that makes him and his message unique. His uniqueness does not lie in his independence but in his bonds.

---

13   *Cf.* H.U. VON BALTHASAR, *Theo-drama. Theological dramatic Theory. III. Dramatis Personae: Person in Christ*, Ignatius Press, San Francisco 1992, 149–259.

### 2.4.1 Israel

First there is the link with Israel's heritage. The choice of the early church to consider the Old Testament canonical established forever that one cannot think of Jesus outside his Jewish context: human, religious, cultural. The God of Jesus is the same God of Abraham, Moses and Jeremiah, but he is also a creative recovery of him.

The person and freedom of Jesus emerge most clearly where we see that his message is not a total novelty but, rather, is radically grounded in a previous revelation. One thus grasps a religious dynamic that is also ours, albeit with due distinctions, namely, being part of a tradition, but also being its unique interpreter. A task that risks failure as much for those who break the bonds that bind them to tradition – and this is the case with heresy – as for those who hide behind tradition and use it as an alibi for not putting themselves at stake, for not delivering their own living, specific contribution.

### 2.4.2 A Family

A second set of bonds are what we might call the family bonds of which we know something, namely, his family and his home environment – Galilee, Nazareth, Mary and Joseph – but also some other bonds – Zechariah, Elizabeth and John. These are his starting points, his limitations and his opportunities. Even if historical-critical research were to cast doubt on this or that aspect of Jesus' family,[14] it cannot be denied that, he came from somewhere and that this origin influenced him. It should be noted that Jesus did not come "from starry skies descending" (as in the famous Christmas carol of St. Alphonsus Liguori), but was "born of a woman, born under the law" (*Gal* 4:4). It is not just a devotional exercise to ask what aspects of Jesus' preaching and life were influenced by his family background. When Jesus announces, "Blessed are those who hunger and thirst for righteousness" (*Mt* 5:6), and, at the same time, admonishes, "Unless your righteousness exceeds that of the scribes and Pharisees, you will never enter the kingdom of heaven" (*Mt* 5:20), he is implicitly also telling the story of his father, Joseph, who was "a righteous man" (*Mt* 1:19), one whose righteousness exceeded that of the scribes and Pharisees. It is not so strange to think that the idea that you do not stone adulteresses – if anything you send them home "quietly" (*Mt* 1,19) – is something he may have learned in the family. When we look at the way in which the adolescent Jesus leaves his family to stay in the temple to do what he felt it was his duty to do (*Lk* 2:41–52), we are basically seeing a repetition of the attitude of the woman who, alone, "set out and went with haste to a Judean town in the hill country" (*Lk* 1:39) to find her

---

14   *Cf.* Meier, *A Marginal Jew.* 1, 205–371.

cousin. Apparently, in this family, when one perceives that something needs to be done, one does not give too much consideration to cost and opportunity. One just does it. In the same key, moreover, is the manner in which Mary interacts with Jesus at the wedding feast of Cana: there is something to be done, and any delay is to be ruled out, especially in small things, such as caring for a pregnant woman and paying attention to wine at feasts.

### 2.4.3 John the Baptist

A third bond, with which we return to more historically reliable ground, is that of Jesus with his teacher.[15] Jesus did not simply invent fundamental aspects of his own message and work but inherited them from the one of whom he would say: "Among those born of women no one has arisen greater than John the Baptist" (*Mt* 11:11). Baptism, the idea of the Kingdom and its eschatological imminence, the openness of salvation even beyond the descendants of Abraham (*cf. Mt* 3:1–12), but also a common destiny of increasing hostility and death are aspects that bind him to his mentor. It is precisely in the case of the Baptist that one can see the singular freedom of Jesus in action: he takes the idea of the Kingdom from John and, at the same time, transforms it: he is not an axe placed at the base of a trunk but a woman who searches in the house for a lost coin, anxiously and thoughtfully. For Jesus, the Kingdom is more mercy than imminent wrath. "And blessed is anyone who takes no offence at me!" (*Mt* 11:6), which is like saying: blessed is he who sees his own idea heavily distorted and is able to recognise, in this distortion, something better than what he himself had thought. The Baptist is challenged to recognise in Jesus his own heir, even if not in the form he himself would, perhaps, have wished. That is why it is also true that "the least in the kingdom of heaven is greater than he" (*Mt* 11:11), since the kingdom of which Jesus speaks is both similar to and different from that which the Baptist announced.

This way of understanding freedom as a creative recovery may cause annoyance: it seems to reduce the absolute originality of Jesus, his exceptional nature. However, this is an error of perspective that derives precisely from a mistaken conception of freedom. Jesus is not all the greater when he is detached from and set against those who lived with him. Quite the contrary: his greatness, witnessed by his entire life and death, was precisely that of thinking of himself, not in opposition to others but, rather, in sharing with them, to the point of being in solidarity even with sinners (*cf. 2 Cor* 5:21). It is for this reason that highlighting his relationships as meaningful and real does not have the effect of diminishing him, but, on the contrary, of bringing out his saving power.

---

15   *Cf.* MEIER, *A Marginal Jew.* 2, 19–176.

### 2.4.4  So Many People

This applies in a very special way to the fourth category of relationships I would like to point out, namely, all those bonds – disciples, women, friends, the poor, sinners, encounters – that touched, wounded, accompanied, provoked and shaped him. Jesus did not become what he became in an empty space but by inhabiting a space of relationships. He said what he said because someone listened to him, and he did what he did because others were with him. Others were actors *with him*, to the point that, in his house, "he did not do many deeds of power there because of their unbelief" (*Mt* 13:58). There is one relationship in particular where this stands out, namely, the one with the Syro-Phoenician woman (*Mk* 7:24–30 and *Mt* 15:21–28), which is, perhaps, the most surprising interaction in the entire New Testament. A pagan woman asks Jesus for help for her possessed daughter. Here, an amazing and very harsh dialogue takes place:

> He said to her, "Let the children be fed first, for it is not fair to take the children's food and throw it to the dogs." But she answered him, "Sir, even the dogs under the table eat the children's crumbs." Then he said to her, "For saying that, you may go – the demon has left your daughter" (Mk 7:27–29).

We realise that it is not a question of whether it was Jesus who converted her or she who converted Jesus; this is a mistaken perspective that assumes that one of the two possesses the truth and simply communicates it to the other. Instead, what happens between these two extraordinary individuals is that only *together* do they succeed in thinking of a God who is not the Father of Jesus alone, or of Israel alone, but of everyone, even of a pagan and possessed child. A God who gives even to dogs the bread of his children, because, from his hands, comes the bread of all.[16]

If Jesus' mutual involvement with his interlocutors is not understood, one category of people in particular will suffer, namely, the poor; precisely those humble ones who, as Mary had already sung, are lifted up by God (*cf. Lk* 1:52). The poor in Jesus' life are not simply those who are benefited by him, in a one-way relationship. Instead, they are, in a much more radical way, those whom Jesus does not want to be without. Jesus' identity is made up of his bond with the poor. If there is a reason why Jesus can be recognised as the Son of God, it is not because he performs miracles or extraordinary deeds – even Beelzebub could perform these. Rather, it is because he binds his life to the least, and, in this, he has the same name as the One who – as he learned from Israel – "watches over

---

[16]   *Cf.* G.C. Pagazzi, *C'è posto per tutti. Legami fraterni, paura, fede*, Vita e pensiero, Milano 2008.

the strangers [and] upholds the orphan and the widow" (*Ps* 146:9). Jesus is perfect because he acts like the Father who "makes his sun rise on the evil and on the good, and sends rain on the righteous and on the unrighteous" (*Mt* 5:45). To give life is proper to God, to bind one's life and name to the small and undeserving is proper to God alone. The devil, the divider, does not do this, which is why it is recognised that Jesus is from God and not the devil.

### 2.4.5 The Father

There is one final relationship – and it is the fundamental one – in which Jesus' freedom emerges most clearly as a personal and creative recovery of the relationships that constitute him, and that is his relationship with the Father. If being free means doing one's own will, then Jesus, who does the Father's will, is a slave. Whereas he is Son precisely insofar as he takes up what is the Father's – that is, care and love for his creatures – and makes it his own, imprinting it with a unique trait, thus defining his own identity.

If, during the public ministry, the actions of the Son and the Father can be confused, so that the blind see thanks to Jesus and his Father together, during the passion, this relationship becomes both more tense and clearer. It is not the Father who lives the passion; it is not the Father who dies for all: it is Jesus. And yet never as during the passion is it shown that Jesus wants to remain faithful to the relationships that constitute him, that with the Father and the one with us. Jesus is free because he chooses to remain son and brother, and he wants to remain so in a fidelity that will lead him to catastrophe. Even faith in the resurrection finds its testing ground here: if freedom consists in being autonomous, then he who is nailed by his fidelity to the Father to consider those who nail him as brothers is simply a loser. If, on the other hand, freedom consists in being able to speak one's own name in fidelity to one's previous relationships, then no one is as free as the Son on the cross. He does not receive the freedom of resurrection as a prisoner whose chains of death are broken; rather, he manifests that he who makes relationships his life is truly free *from* death, free *in* death. In this sense, the cross becomes the centre of the world, the place where freedom shows itself for what it is.

It appears at this point how the story of Jesus should not be read as a script already written by others, even the Father, but as a score performed in a singular and personal way by the one who was Jesus. In this way, he does not seize for himself all the freedom of his children but, rather, opens up the space for other singular freedoms to play out the theme of God's love in their own way.

And now, having gained an idea of the data that history makes available to us and the criteria of freedom that we are looking for, we can move on to the properly theological work, trying to delve into the account of this death. We shall try to understand how what Jesus did and said in his life could have generated such a reaction as to lead him to condemnation, and, above all, how he was able to respond to these accusations, not so much in a defence at his trial, but in the very way in which he faced death.

This is a theological work: the motivations that will emerge will not simply be the explanation of a historical event but will be part of a broader dogmatic understanding of the relationship between human beings and the God of whom Jesus spoke and for whom he lived. In short, these motivations speak to us of the reaction that a human being can always have when faced with the appearance of such a God.

### Bibliographical Guidelines

The theme of **secularisation** in a world characterised by the need for choice is outlined in C. TAYLOR, *A Secular Age*, Harvard University Press, Cambridge (MA) 2007 (for a contextualisation, cf. P. COSTA, *The Post-Secular City. The New Secularization Debate*, Brill Schöning, Paderborn 2022), while, for the theme of choice, the work of reference is H. JOAS, *Faith as an Option: Possible Futures for Christianity*, Stanford University Press, Redwood City (CA) 2014. I have chosen these authors because, unlike others who deal with the sociological analysis of our time, they offer perspectives that are altogether less whingey (U. BECK, *World at Risk*, Polity Press, Cambridge 2009; ID., *I rischi della libertà*, il Mulino, Bologna 2000; R. SENNETT, *The Corrosion of Character: The Personal Consequences of Work in the New Capitalism*, W.W. Norton & Company, New York 1998). These authors focus on a series of risks that affect not this or that aspect of human life on earth but its very survival – such as the atomic bomb or the ecological crisis. These are not risks that can be eliminated. What is needed is a theoretical position – and a spiritual disposition – that know how to integrate them within one's own vision without letting them overwhelm one. With different emphases, we find this in Hans Jonas and Jürgen Moltmann, as well as in Pope Francis' encyclical *Laudato si'* (H. JONAS, *The Imperative of Responsibility: In Search of Ethics for the Technological Age*, University of Chicago Press, Chicago 1984; J. MOLTMANN, *Ethics of Hope*, Fortress Press, Minneapolis 2012).

For in-depth **psychological** analysis, the author I have taken for reference is Jacques Lacan, made accessible and popularised recently in Italy by the work of Massimo Recalcati (M. RECALCATI, *Jacques Lacan, I: Desiderio, godimento e soggettivazione*, Raffaello Cortina, Milano 2012; *II: La clinica psicoanalitica: struttura e soggetto*, Raffaello Cortina, Milano 2016). Recalcati has shown in the past (ID., *L'uomo senza* *inconscio. Figure della nuova clinica psicoanalitica*, Raffaello Cortina, Milano 2010; ID., *Ritratti del desiderio*, Raffaello Cortina, Milano 2012) how a series of typical contemporary pathologies – panic attacks, addictions, eating disorders – attest to the subject's difficulty in becoming a subject of desire. The fatigue of subjectivisation produces pathologies – technically with a psychotic background – in which there is not a subject struggling between his own desires and the demands of reality, but a subject who cannot find his own desire. In a recent text (ID., *Le nuove melanconie. Destini del desiderio nel tempo ipermoderno*, Raffaello Cortina, Milano 2019), this analysis has been revised and extended to a series of individual and social pathologies (perversion, security anxiety, money bulimia). The particular interest of these latter analyses lies in the connection they make with the spectrum of non-meaning I mentioned in the section on science.

For a recent **theological revival of the Lacanian strand**: P. SEQUERI, *L'umano alla prova. Soggetto, identità, limite, Vita e pensiero*, Milano 2002; R. MAIOLINI, *Tra fiducia esistenziale e fede in Dio. L'originaria struttura affettivo-simbolica della coscienza credente*, Glossa, Milano 2005; D. D'ALESSIO, *Nello specchio dell'altro. Riflessioni sulla fede nate dal confronto con Jacques Lacan*, in *La Scuola Cattolica* 131 (2003) 181–267; R. GABOARDI, *"Un Dio a parte. Che altro? Jacques Lacan e la teologia*, Glossa, Milano 2016.

For an introduction to the psychology of **mirror neurons**: M. AMMANITI – V. GALLESE, *La nascita dell'intersoggettività. Lo sviluppo del sé tra psicodinamica e neurobiologia*, Raffaello Cortina, Milano 2014; G. RIZZOLATTI – C. SINIGAGLIA, *Mirrors in the Brain. How Our Minds Share Actions and Emotions*, Oxford University Press, New York 2008; with a critical perspective in G. HICKOK, *The Myth of Mirror Neurons. The Real Neuroscience of Communication and Cognition*, W.W. Norton & Company, New York 2014.

Of particular interest is the theme of the **single-case** that can be found in L.R. BAKER, *Persons and Bodies. A Constitution View*, Cambridge University Press, Cambridge – New York 2000; A. FERRARA, *The force of the Example. Explorations in the Paradigm of Judgment*, Columbia University Press, New York 2008. In theology, it is thematised, with different emphases, in G.C. PAGAZZI, *La singolarità di Gesù come criterio di unità e differenza nella chiesa*, Glossa, Milano 1997; G. DEPEDER, *La singolarità di Gesù Cristo. Indagine nella cristologia italiana contemporanea*, Messaggero, Padova 2013; P. GAMBERINI, *Questo Gesù (At 2,32). Pensare la singolarità di Gesù*, EDB, Bologna 2005.

Special attention is merited by the Balthasarian reading that identifies **identity and mission** in Christ (H.U. VON BALTHASAR, *Theo-drama. Theological dramatic Theory. III. Dramatis Personae: Person in Christ*, Ignatius Press, San Francisco 1992, 149–259; G. MEIATTINI, *Sentire cum Christo. La teologia dell'esperienza cristiana nell'opera di*

*Hans Urs von Balthasar*, Pontificia Università Gregoriana, Roma 1998). From my perspective, this is a move with potentially catastrophic theological and spiritual consequences; indeed, it has the defect of erasing important aspects of what I have called the real Jesus, or, in other words, of proposing a model from which the dimension of *enjoyment* is expunged. Jesus, and consequently anyone who tries to conform to him, becomes one whose subjectivisation is exhausted in the relational dimension of the desire for the paternal mission, with problematic Trinitarian consequences and unmanageable vocational ones.

The bibliography relating to **freedom** is obviously endless. For an introduction, the following are useful: R. Maiolini, Libertà, Cittadella, Assisi 2015; A. Grillo, *Genealogia della libertà. Un itinerario tra filosofia e teologia*, San Paolo, Cinisello Balsamo 2013; C. Ciancio, *Libertà e dono dell'essere*, Marietti, Genova – Milano 2009; R. De Monticelli, *La novità di ognuno. Persona e libertà*, Garzanti, Milano 2012 and the always fascinating I. Berlin, *Liberty*, Oxford University Press, Oxford 1995 (for a discussion of this see A. Honneth, *Three, Not Two, Concepts of Liberty: A Proposal to Enlarge Our Moral Self-Understanding*, in Zuckert R., Kreines J. (edd.), *Hegel on Philosophy in History*, Cambridge University Press, Cambridge 2017, 177–192). For what I have tried to develop here, the main references are: L. Pareyson, *Ontologia della libertà. Il male e la sofferenza*, Einaudi, Torino 1995; A. Honneth, *Freedom's Right. The Social Foundation of Democratic Life*, Polity Press, Cambridge 2014; for the theological framework underlying this idea of freedom, I refer to L. Paris, *Sulla libertà. Prospettive di teologia trinitaria tra neuroscienze e filosofia*, Città Nuova, Roma 2012.

For the **relational turn** in psychology: E.R. Kandel, *Psychiatry, Psicoanalisis, and the New Biology of Mind*, Psychiatric Publishing Inc., Washinton D.C – London 2005; D.J. Siegel, *The Developing Mind. Second Edition*, The Gilford Press, New York 2012; L. Cozolino, *The Neuroscience of Human Relationship. Attachment and the Developing Social Brain*, W.W. Norton & Company, New York – London 2014. For an overview of perspectives and a mine of references, also in dialogue with theology, see F. Ceragioli, *«Il cielo aperto» (Gv 1,51). Analitica del riconoscimento e struttura della fede nell'intreccio di desiderio e dono*, Effatà, Cantalupa 2012, 105–341. The key to the balance between subject and relationship is dealt with Ceragioli, *«Il cielo aperto»*, 99–101, 213 and 476, where the author offers a considerable number of cues and references to address the issue of recognition from a relational perspective, relying in particular on Infant Research. For the alert reader, it is striking that such an examination touches only tangentially on Lacanian currents that have made this theme one of their strong points. The reason emerges in the course of the text and is essentially linked to this balance between subject and relation. In fact, according to Ceragioli, in the Lacanian line of thought, the equilibrium is resolved with a very strong unbalance in the direction of the relation: the subject is empty – this is the conclusion of the Hegel–Kojève–Sartre–Lacan line – and draws its consistency from the other who inhabits it, with his presence, with his language, with his laws. The non-relational remainders are, in fact, linked to the biological dimension. Now, precisely such a balance is what Ceragioli seeks to avoid in order to defend a position that gives the relationship a role counterbalanced by a relatively autonomous consistency of the subject. Possibly a consistency that does not rest directly on biology.

CHAPTER 4

# Towards Death (1). The Father

In this chapter and the next two, we try to understand how Jesus positioned himself with respect to certain crucial theological questions. In particular, it will be matter of understanding both the continuity and the discontinuity of his message and his gestures with respect to what he had received – a creative recovery that was to prove to be anything but harmless but, rather, was to provoke reactions of hostility and, in the end, death. These were not unmotivated or hysterical reactions: the reason why Jesus was contested was not, first and foremost, misunderstanding. It would be too simple if that were the case; after all, it would just be a mistake. Instead, it is precisely because someone *understood* what he was saying and doing that the contestation took place. In short, those who criticised him had their reasons. Entering into this double movement of action and reaction can enable us to come to a better understanding of the extent to which Jesus was scandalous – and still is today.

The first issue to be addressed is the one that in some way confronts every man or woman who seeks to be religious at the beginning, namely, the discovery that he or she is not up to the relationship. Those who seek to be religious usually discover that they are sinners.

## 1 Israel: The Priest Messiah

Jesus does not start from scratch to reflect on and respond to this problem. He draws, first of all, on the extensive reflection he inherits from Israel. Israel, in fact, are the people of the covenant – or rather the people that transgress the covenant again and again. Their entire history can be read as a covenant continually transgressed and continually renewed (*Neh* 9; *Ps* 106; *Hos* 11:1–11). At the heart of this transgression is, of course, the law, i.e. the way God himself gives the people as a guide for the covenant. How does one get out of this game that risks becoming absurd in the long run? Is one really doomed to fall again and again?

There are concrete strategies that can be used to deal with this tangle of problems – for example, the observance of the law or temple sacrifices – but these can only be understood in the light of certain general coordinates that guide all Old Testament reflection.

The first is that God is merciful, or, if you prefer, that God is Father. If God himself did not take the first step, to have a *surplus* of gift – *for-give* – there would be no hope for anyone. God is the one who "passes over the over the transgression of the remnant of your possession" (*Mic* 7:18), the one who – "abounding in steadfast love" (*Ps* 86:5) – "forgives all your iniquity, who heals all your diseases, who redeems your life from the Pit, who crowns you with steadfast love and mercy" (*Ps* 103:3–4). In particular, this is his attitude towards the least and the little ones (*Is* 49:13; *Wis* 6:6), but also towards sinners: "Let the wicked forsake their way, and the unrighteous their thoughts; let them return to the Lord, that he may have mercy on them, and to our God, for he will abundantly pardon" (*Is* 55:7). If this were not so, the creation – of which man and woman immediately showed themselves not to be the height – would not be conceivable, nor would the exodus – a continuous dance of gift, transgression and forgiveness –, but neither would the daily life of each one. That is why one of God's names is "father": "Father of orphans and protector of widows" (*Ps* 68:5). It is not, however, in titles that God demonstrates his fatherhood, but rather in the concreteness of the way he behaves: "As a father has compassion for his children, so the Lord has compassion for those who fear him. For he knows how we were made; he remembers that we are dust" (*Ps* 103:13–14). And again: "I led them with cords of human kindness, with bands of love. I was to them like those who lift infants to their cheeks. I bent down to them and fed them" (*Hos* 11:4). It is his paternal mercy (*Is* 63:15–16) that makes the covenant game possible. If God were simply the one "who judges righteously" (*Jer* 11:20), everything would have ended after the first transgression – a possibility well represented by the Flood (*Gen* 6–9): as if God had had to reflect on the attitude he wanted to adopt and realise that, for the covenant with his people to have a chance, he would have to take it on unilaterally, not subjecting it to the capacity of men and women to be faithful to it, but binding it only to *his own faithfulness*.

Of course, all this does not exempt the people from doing all they can to be faithful to the covenant, trying to live within the law, nor from invoking God's mercy in a formal and ritual structured way with temple sacrifices. This is what the priests are for: they are those who, serving the temple, offer sacrifices so that God does not forget his mercy. Israel is aware that sacrifice is not enough: "The sacrifice acceptable to God is a broken spirit; a broken and contrite heart, O God, you will not despise" (*Ps* 51:17). The prophets, in particular, made Israel aware of this: "For I desire steadfast love and not sacrifice, the knowledge of God, rather than burnt offerings" (*Hos* 6:6). Chapter 1 of Isaiah leaves no doubt about this (*cf. Is* 1:10–20). God shows himself to be satiated and fed up with fat and blood, annoyed with feasts, prayers and "futile" (*Is* 1:13) offerings, and desirous of only one thing: that good and justice be done to the orphan and the widow, that is, to those little ones he cares for. On closer inspection, the awareness of this does not make things any better. As long as it is a matter of organising a well-performed cult, one could even manage that. But this sacrifice of the heart is something else entirely. How does one live up to it? Impossible, unless one starts from the assumption that God's attitude is not that of a judge who comes to check the facts but of a father who cares for his children and seeks to lead them in the ways of life (cf. Ps 16).

Even this is not enough, however. If one wants to live in this covenant, one cannot in the end do without a new priest, one who does not offer calves and rams but who is able to perform a new worship capable of making us all able to stand before God. On that day "he shall cry to me, 'You are my father, my God, and the rock of my salvation!' I will make him the firstborn, the highest of the kings of the earth" (Ps 89:26–27). It is the hope of a *messiah from Aaron* or, even better, from *Melchizedek*,[1] of a saviour who is truly a priest, capable of removing sin and offering God a people worthy of him.[2]

This perspective is loaded with questions: what form could such a messiah take, that of a sufferer or that of a super-priest? What will become of the temple, worship and law at that point? What form will the concrete life of people take, living in his light? But, above all, what should we do now, to live while we wait for him? Should we retreat into small communities of the 'perfect' like the Essenes, or propose new mass rituals – like baptism – that would allow even the most distant to approach and ask for forgiveness once and for all? It will not escape our notice that such different solutions – such as the 'open' one of the Baptist, to which even soldiers and tax collectors approach, and the 'closed' one of the Essenes, to which practically no one approaches – have one thing in common: they are answers to the problem of sin and justice which have, at least, a problematic relationship with the *mainstream* solution represented by the temple.

Jesus inherits these questions and perspectives and, by his action and words, offers his own reading of them.

---

1 Cf. G. IBBA, *Qumran. Correnti del pensiero giudaico (III B.C.–I A.D.)*, Carocci, Roma 2007, 108–109; ID., *La teologia di Qumran*, EDB, Bologna 2002, 44–53.
2 For the theme of the priesthood in the Christology of the *Letter to the Hebrews*, cf. R. PENNA, *I ritratti originali di Gesù il Cristo. Inizi e sviluppi della cristologia neotestamentaria*, II: *Gli sviluppi*, San Paolo, Cinisello Balsamo 1999, 265–324.

## 2 The Least and Forgiveness

The fact that Jesus leans more towards the popular option of the Baptist than the elitist option of the Essenes is evident, first of all, not from his words, but from his lifestyle and his 'friendships'. What he has to bring is intended first and foremost for the poor and the little.[3] In a word, to the least: "… and the poor have good news brought to them. And blessed is anyone who takes no offence [scandal] at me!" (*Mt* 11:5–6; *cf.* also *Lk* 7:11).

After what we have said about Israel's heritage, however, it is not quite clear where the scandal lies. Why should Jesus' preference for and closeness to children, to women, to the poor and the sick have come as a surprise? It could be a practical reason; there is, indeed, a discrepancy between those who are 'blessed' in theory and practice. Even among Christians today, in fact, there is no doubt *in theory* that children, women, the poor and migrants are categories on whom not only does God not look down but who are, indeed, his favourites. Yet, *in practice*, things can be quite difficult: putting these categories at the centre and making them the standard for the blessed person comes up against a whole series of objections and practical resistance. Feminist theology, black theology or the various theologies of liberation bear witness to the fact that time has not made these steps any easier even *within* Christianity and its theology.

Things are more complicated than that, however, particularly if we are looking at Jesus' attitudes from our perspective, two thousand years later. The risk is, indeed, that, even with a certain amount of rhetoric, we have *good reason* today to appreciate women, children and the poor. We appreciate the innocence of children and can read Jesus' calls to "become like children" (*Mt* 18:3) as an invitation to live with simplicity, obedience and purity before God. The feminine world and the qualities that, rightly or wrongly, are associated with it, today enjoy a strong appreciation within much of the intellectual world. This may lead one to read Jesus' attitudes towards them as the wisdom of one who knows how to grasp the treasure of special moral and human qualities, even behind a socially disadvantaged condition. Even more so is this true for the poor in general. It is not uncommon today – let us say starting with St Francis for Christians and J.-J. Rousseau for all – to identify in those who are simple, ignorant and poor characteristics that the educated, the rich and the powerful do not have. Greater willingness to relate and share, greater freshness and

---

3  M. Bordoni, *Gesù di Nazaret Signore e Cristo. Saggio di cristologia sistematica. 2. Gesù fondamento della cristologia*, EDB, Bologna 2017, 167–181.

immediacy towards life, a more genuine spirituality and greater capacity to enjoy the little things that form the fabric of a simple life.

I do not want to go into these assessments. In fact, I fear that there is in this a certain superficial intellectual flaw that betrays a lack of interest in the *real* children, women and poor. I say superficial because, to give just one example, it is all too evident to anyone who deals with childhood in a manner commensurate with the knowledge we have today that there would be very few evolutionary psychologists prepared to subscribe to the peaceful and submissive image of children that is sometimes found in commentaries on the Gospel texts. The problem, however, does not lie here. Even if it were true that these social categories have such positive characteristics, this was not the view held of them at the time Jesus spoke. If it had been – that is, if even the average hearer of Jesus had been willing to recognise the substantial innocence of childhood – the scandal would be inexplicable: if children are pure, there is no scandal whatsoever in affirming that God prefers the pure, even less so from a religion that made purity, however one wants to understand it,[4] one of its strong points.

If there is a scandal, it must lie elsewhere, namely, in the last category, often associated with the previous ones, that of *sinners*. Not of repentant sinners – no scandal there either – but of hardened sinners. Here things get more difficult: how can it be argued that God prefers sinners? And above all, what do these have in common with the other categories? Perhaps women and children are actually sinners too? Something in common with them was actually there, in the eyes of those who listened to Jesus. All these categories are disadvantaged, even in their relationship with God. For different reasons – either ignorance, or pettiness, or social status – they are people who may find it difficult to approach the sacred, to understand and experience the world of religion. They find themselves in the *objective inability*[5] to break out of their condition. This is not a moral evaluation but a disenchanted observation that grasps the person's need. No matter whether the reason is economic, moral or social, the truth is that, unless someone helps them, they will not be able to change their situation.

This is why sinners are the key-category of this group. If one does not grasp this, and makes children, for example, the centre of the discourse, one will find oneself having to praise the purity of women, the poor … and sinners. Strange as it may seem, this would entail no offence and no theological gain (no gospel) with respect to the idea of God. Instead, claiming that God approaches anyone in need – and even those who are bad are in need, perhaps more than

---

4 MEIER, *A Marginal Jew.* 4, 342–352.
5 BORDONI, *Gesù di Nazaret Signore e Cristo.* 2, 167–181.

others, and perhaps less aware than others – is exactly what scandalises. It means taking the idea that God is a merciful father, *and taking it to its extreme consequences*. If God, like a father, is the one who wants the life of his children, then the more someone is in need of life, the more God will become close to him, a neighbour. The parable of the Good Samaritan (*Lk* 10:25–37) is not first and foremost a story about foreigners and heretics being (sometimes) better than we are, but rather represents a God who makes himself a neighbour to those in need. And in doing so he is so strange as to seem foreign!

The consequences of this approach are disruptive, both practically and theoretically. They are the reason why Jesus feels justified in approaching – indeed, going to lunch and dinner with – categories that, to contemporary sensibilities, might correspond to *mafiosi* and paedophiles. "Those who are well have no need of a physician, but those who are sick. Go and learn what this means: 'I desire mercy, not sacrifice'. For I have come to call not the righteous but sinners" (*Mt* 9:12–13).

The very concept of mercy is turned upside down. Forgiveness, in fact, has its own internal logic: one does wrong, realises it, asks for forgiveness, and if the one who has suffered the wrong is merciful, the sinner is forgiven. Forgiveness is granted to the one who asks for it and, perhaps concretely, shows signs of his repentance. This is a dynamic very present in the Old Testament, as it corresponds in practice to the whole history of the relationship between God and his unfaithful people. Or almost the whole, because some passages present a different posture of God: not that of a merciful lord with the unfaithful, unrepentant servant but that of a betrayed lover who has married a prostitute and runs after her while she is still engaged in her former trade (*Hos* 1–3). He assumes the pose of one who is resentful and vindictive, but it is evident that, in reality, he hopes for nothing more than to be able to experience with her the love of when he was young: "Therefore, I will now allure her, and bring her into the wilderness, and speak tenderly to her. [...] There she shall respond as in the days of her youth [...]. On that day, says the Lord, you will call me, 'my husband', and no longer will you call me, 'my Baal'" (*Hos* 2:14–18).

In this view, for Jesus, forgiveness comes before repentance, indeed it is the condition of it. Only if the little one and the sinner – both lost in their condition – receive a *surplus* of gift, through God's unilateral initiative, can they have a chance. That is why Jesus approaches anyone in need; that is why forgiveness is *pre-emptive* – it comes before it is asked for, and even before the awareness of sin (the case of the adulteress in *Jn* 8:1–11 or the paralytic in *Mk* 2:3–12); that is why Jesus' proclamation is good news especially for these categories. For those who have a sufficiently good life, such that they can try to present themselves before God with their works, the initial gift in itself might be enough: they have received a life and used it in a reasonably decent way. But for those whose lives have fallen apart, or never flourished, the gift is not enough, has been wasted or been lost. Precisely for these, the announcement of *for-giveness* is a joy, a sigh of relief: there is more life than I could hope to deserve or ask for. That life I need and do not possess. This is the meaning of the parable of the workers of the last hour (*Mt* 20:1–16). To live a day you need a denarius – the wages for a day's work. Someone has worked hard enough to earn it; he will return to his home at the end of the day and live. But what about those who arrived at the last? They have not earned their day; they are destined to die. Instead, they too are given – or for-given/super-given – what they need. That is why the parable concludes by saying: "So the last will be first, and the first will be last" (*Mt* 20:16).

This is not a paradox but the consequence of God's paternity. If God were only righteous, the first ones, those who can help themselves, would be at an advantage. If, on the other hand, he is a father who wants to gather his children like an eagle keeping watch over her brood (*Deut* 32:11) – Jesus would prefer a similar image for himself: "as a hen gathers her brood under her wings" (*Lk* 13:34) – then "the tax collectors and the prostitutes are going into the kingdom of God ahead of you" (*Mt* 21:31). And it is not because they turn out to be better than the others in the end. They are, in fact, the worst. But precisely because of this, they are also the ones who rejoice in the moratorium of mercy offered by Jesus. A generically good God is not enough for them; they need someone who, like a father, is willing to receive them without too many questions about performance.

As we can see, this is a creative recovery. An idea that was already present is taken seriously and reconfigured by Jesus, bringing it to consequences that may be difficult to integrate into the lives and religiosity of many, and not only in his time.

## 3     What Remains of the Law?

Describing Jesus as a hippie who, in the name of love, blithely ignores the laws and traditions of his people and is, therefore, persecuted is to do a disservice to his character. However, it is an understandable one, especially when referring to the relationship between Jesus and the law. It is indeed a difficult relationship. Difficult in his time, as Jesus had a strange position on this point, and difficult today, as it is not easy to reconstruct it. That is why one may decide to opt for an easy criterion – love, transgression, freedom, mercy – and make it a universal key that overcomes the difficulties.

Reconstructing Jesus' position on the law is difficult for several reasons. The first of these lies in the fact that, not only do we find it difficult to understand what *he thought of* the law, but even more difficult to understand *what the law prescribed* in his time. In other words,

> The more we probe, the more we awake with dismay to the realization that this problem of the relation of the *historical* Jesus to the *historical* Jewish Law may be more intractable on the Law side than on the Jesus side. [...] The quest for the historical Pharisee can at times prove more difficult than the quest for the historical Jesus.[6]

What precisely law and tradition were, and who observed what, is not easy to reconstruct. If we think about it, this is also true today: if someone, two thousand years hence, wanted to reconstruct the 'church's' thinking on premarital relationships at the beginning of the 21st century, they would find themselves in a mess: different positions, practice that often does not correspond to theory, different interpretations of rules that are theoretically very clear.

A second difficulty is that we often end up projecting back interpretative criteria that are misleading. The distinctions between inner law and outer law, between form and substance, between ritualism and faith, ultimately between spirituality and religion – where spirituality is the living heart of the shell represented by religion – are in common use today but would have been incomprehensible to Jesus and his time.

Finally, a third difficulty lies in the fact that, unfortunately Jesus left us no interpretative key for his stance on the law. Not even a broad orientation. Was Jesus a rigorist or a laxist? It is a question that was legitimate and could be answered even in his day: Hillel was more lax and Shammai was stricter, to cite the example of the two most famous Jewish teachers of the first century. For Jesus, this – convenient – distinction does not work. He forbids fasting, he forgives prostitutes and eats with tax collectors, he affirms that "the Sabbath was made for humankind, and not humankind for the Sabbath" (*Mk* 2:27): so he is a laxist. But then he forbids divorce, considers even the mere 'coveting' of one's neighbour's wife as adultery, invites people to pluck out their eyes or cut off their hands rather than sin, and threatens Gehenna to anyone who insults their neighbour, so much so that the disciples exclaim: "Then who can be saved?" (*Mt* 19:25). So he would appear to be a super-rigorist.

---

6  MEIER, *A Marginal Jew. 4*, 21.35.

To begin to find one's way through this quagmire, perhaps it is best to start with an idea: Jesus did not transgress or abolish the law.[7] In Israel, the law is *for all* – that is, regardless of the interpretation that different groups may give to various aspects of the law – a gift from the Lord given to his people so that they may walk in his presence, live out his covenant and be happy. Even its interpretations and specific discussions – the *halakhah* – are the 'path', the reflection on behaviour, necessary to understand how to correspond to this covenant. The law is, therefore, a gift of love, made so that the relationship is true and reciprocal: the law allows salvation not simply to descend from above, but to involve life. With the law, soteriology can be ascending and involving, relational. Jesus does not intend to deny this or even to supersede it. And yet many – yesterday as today – have been convinced or suspicious of this.

This depends, it seems to me, on his particular way of reasoning, which characterises various aspects of his acting and speaking, and which we could call, for the moment, an *eschatological* perspective. I will try to clarify this point by using a paradigmatic example: the discussion on divorce. Jesus forbade divorce, in a context in which both at a proximate (Judaic) and remote (neighbouring cultures, Greeks, Romans) level, *all* foresaw, in one way or another, the possibility of interrupting the conjugal relationship.[8] Why did he do this? It is more difficult than it seems to identify the precise reason, but I would like to dwell on a line of *reasoning* that emerges from the dispute reported in *Mt* 19:1–9. Asked by the Pharisees whether it is permissible to repudiate one's wife – as permitted by the law of Moses – Jesus responds by arguing:

> It was because you were so hard-hearted that Moses allowed you to divorce your wives, but from the beginning it was not so (*Mt* 19:8).
> Have you not read that the one who made them at the beginning 'made them male and female,' and said, 'For this reason a man shall leave his father and mother and be joined to his wife, and the two shall become one flesh'? So they are no longer two, but one flesh. Therefore what God has joined together, let no one separate" (*Mt* 19:4–6).

The way of thinking underlying this response must be grasped. The law – of Moses – must be read in the light of 'as it was in the beginning', that is, how the human being was as soon as he came out of God's hands. The concrete reality – made up of unfaithful wives (or husbands), unbearable in-laws, wickedness,

---

7 "If I were forced to choose *either* the old-time view that Jesus (intentionally or not) abolished the Law *or* Sanders's view that practically nothing in Jesus' teaching opposes or rescinds the Law itself, I would feel much more comfortable accepting Sanders's position" (MEIER, *A Marginal Jew*. 4, 3).
8 For the whole subject, *cf.* MEIER, *A Marginal Jew*. 4, 74–181.

pain and failures – must be read and experienced in the light of the eschatological principle of how God had conceived man and woman at the beginning of time. This is optimistic, to say the least; it is a dream. It is life as God dreamt it. One can say that it is eschatological only if one grasps that, here, the eschatological is not something that is to come, that is future, but that it is present because it is from always, from the beginning. "It was intelligible – to say nothing of being doable – only to those who accepted Jesus as the eschatological prophet who in some sense made present the kingdom of God that was soon to come".[9] A kingdom that was coming because it had always been.

In this way, Jesus appeals to the heart, to God's dream. He recalls that the whole law comes from that dream: God's desire to dwell with man as a father dwells with a son. The court, therefore, becomes that of this paternal dream. At the same time, more merciless and more lenient than any other court. For it is not easy to decide whether one prefers to be judged by a stranger or a loved one. He who loves us may forgive, but he also sees our shame more keenly. A particular effect of the paternal court – that is, the law read through the eyes of paternity – is that, unlike a secular court, it is better for the bad and worse for the good. A generically good person has no problem with the secular court: he has done nothing imputable. He may, however, have problems with a fatherly gaze that sees missed opportunities, pettiness, wasted potential. The opposite is true for someone who has done something really bad: he would be condemned by the secular court, but, in front of his father, he can hope to come out of it somehow safe and sound.

So what happens to the law for Jesus? It remains and it does not remain. For he who lives according to God's eschatological dream *never* transgresses the law. And yet he is not using the law of Moses as a reference, but the dream of 'as it was in the beginning'.

## 4  Complex Inheritances

Where did Jesus get this way of interpreting the law? Can we find figures who embodied for him this way of living and judging? I would like to propose two, with a different degree of historical reliability: his teacher, John the Baptist, and his father, Joseph. To these I would add a third 'figure', perhaps the most difficult to accept, that of sinners.

---

9  MEIER, *A Marginal Jew. 4*, 127.

## 4.1   John the Baptist Revisited

The figure of John is, indeed, the first to be dealt with if one wants to speak of Jesus in terms of inheritance. Clearly, Jesus had, for some time, a *teacher*, from whom he then partly distanced himself, but from whom he also inherited much. And this incredible man, who happened to be the teacher of the Master, of the one who would later be considered the Redeemer by one of the most influential religions in history, is a strange prophet with his own message and his own vision of Israel and its future. John's story would be worth telling – as indeed Flavius Josephus thought[10] – even if his most famous disciple had never existed. He lives and works in the desert areas around the Jordan, the same areas where, Elijah and Elisha, the prophets he is inspired by, had worked. His message is clear and consists of a few recognisable elements: 1) God's judgement is imminent; 2) for this it is necessary to change one's life as soon as possible, with the simple and definitive rite of baptism; 3) the judgement will be brought by a mysterious strong figure, whom Christians identified with the disciple, Jesus, but who could also have been Elijah himself; 4) all this is set against the background of the imminence of the Kingdom.

Such a figure does not present his contemporaries with great difficulties of interpretation because he is placed in the wake of other characters, ascetic and eschatological-apocalyptic prophets, who announce the imminent radicalism of God's presence. It can certainly be disturbing; one must not forget that the main legacy that Jesus inherits from John is the fate of persecution and death. In fact, the Baptist's message too is presented as a critique and alternative to several of the basic institutions of the Judaism of his time. He does not lash out against the sensibilities associated with the temple and the law but implicitly stretches their limits. The simplicity of baptism in the Jordan is an obvious alternative to temple worship for obtaining God's forgiveness for sins. It has the advantage of being much simpler and more immediate, even for social classes that might have had problems approaching the temple in Jerusalem. Even with respect to the law, John goes, as it were, to the essentials. A message of justice that is simple and practicable and does not involve the minutiae of the Sabbath, purity or tithes. It can apply to the soldiers: Do not "rob anyone by violence or by false accusation, and be content with your wages"; to the tax collectors: "Collect no more than the amount prescribed for you" (*Lk* 3:13); and to everyone: "Whoever has two coats must share with anyone who has none; and whoever has food must do likewise" (*Lk* 3:11). Blood and lineage do not count for much in this concrete change of life since "God is able from these stones to raise up children to Abraham" (*Lk* 3:8). This is disturbing news for those who

---

10   *Cf.* MEIER, *A Marginal Jew.* 4, 56–62.

think they can get preferential treatment because they are descended from Abraham, and yet it does not sound like heresy. It radicalises ideas that had already been heard in the prophets (*2 Kings* 5; *Is* 25:6–7; 56:7). And, indeed, contemporaries recognised John as a prophet (*Mt* 14:5). For those who do not convert, "even now the axe is lying at the root of the trees; every tree therefore that does not bear good fruit is cut down and thrown into the fire" (*Lk* 3:9). John is, therefore, interpreted as the last *opportunity* offered to all to convert, before – with the coming of the "more powerful" (*Mk* 1:7; *Lk* 3:16) – judgement descends upon the people.

Jesus' gesture of creatively recovering someone else's legacy is evident here. He retains practically everything of John's message while imposing a change of perspective as radical as his faithfulness. The imminence of judgement remains, baptism remains, and the presence of the Kingdom becomes even more pressing, as John himself expected. "By comparing himself with John, he [Jesus] places himself more or less in the category of an eschatological prophet who does not derive his authority from institutional channels like the law or the temple".[11] Yet the general tone changes. The conviction of the imminence – indeed, the presence – of the Kingdom is not interpreted by Jesus in the tones of judgement and condemnation but of mercy. We could say that what changes is the very face of the judge: not a strong, implacable one, holding the tools to separate the good from the bad and throwing the latter into the fire, but a strong father who offers everyone the forgiveness that will allow them to change their lives. This change of emphasis in the direction of forgiveness is not indifferent to the law. In John's perspective, the ways through which God demands man's observance of the law may actually change, but the substance remains unchanged: if one does not live by the law, one is doomed. With Jesus, on the other hand, it is the very prospect of the law that is threatened, insofar as it is subjected to the merciful and paternal face of God, the judge and father. Jesus, we might say, is very much – too much according to some – unbalanced in the direction of mercy. For him, the law cannot be understood outside God's paternal attitude. This is not a matter of heresy: Israel is well aware that the law comes *after* God's love: it is out of love that God gave the law in that it is his gift and not a cunning invention of man to get closer to him. And yet this imbalance remains, with consequences that are difficult to manage.

## 4.2   *The Son of Joseph*

The second character I would like to propose as the 'father' of Jesus' attitude towards justice and law is none other than Joseph, the one whom everyone considered to be his father.

---

11    MEIER, *A Marginal Jew. 4*, 166.

We do not know much about him, and what we are told has little chance of being historical. Yet some facts are interesting. He is a law-abiding man, not a revolutionary or a protester. Suffice it to say that, in the canonical Gospels, he does not utter a single word: he just acts, and does so according to the law. Almost always. In fact, he is presented as one who obeys Roman laws – going to be counted with his family in his country of origin (*Lk* 2:1–2) – and Jewish laws – taking his first-born son to the temple "according to the law of Moses" (*Lk* 2:22). We can imagine that, if he really did move with his family to Egypt, there too he observed the laws of the place, as he had always done. *Almost always*. For the fundamental gesture of his life, that little big gesture without which the story of Jesus would have ended before it began, that gesture for which he is remembered as a "righteous man", could be seen as a transgression, or at least a heavy evasion, of the law.

> When his mother Mary had been engaged to Joseph, but before they lived together, she was found to be pregnant from the Holy Spirit. Her husband Joseph, being a righteous man and unwilling to expose her to public disgrace, planned to divorce her quietly (*Mt* 1:18–19).

This man is righteous at the very moment he evades the law: "If a man commits adultery with the wife of his neighbour, both the adulterer and the adulteress shall be put to death" (*Lev* 20:10). He is a man who respects the law and yet fulfils it under the guidance of another voice, one more ancient and more original, that of God or rather of the angels (*Mt* 1:20; 2:13). The law for him is reinterpreted on the basis of a dream in which the angels speak. Not a promise here of a future or eschatological fulfilment – there is nothing in Joseph that allows us to see him as an eschatological prophet – but an original promise that links his fatherhood to the loving fatherhood of God.

In this unusual attitude towards the difficult relationship between law, justice and the image of God, we see the possibility that Joseph was the father of Jesus, not in the transmission of genes but in the transmission of desire, of a look at reality. His son collected this inheritance from him and made it his own. One can observe this fatherhood many years later in the case of an adulteress (*Jn* 8:1–11).

> In dismissing those who would put this woman to death, Jesus is undoubtedly doing the will of the Father, but, at the same time, he is putting into practice something he learnt at home, listening to the story of how he himself risked not coming into the world if Joseph had not found within himself the strength to welcome his betrothed, pregnant with a child that was not his, and had surrendered Mary's life to the implacability of an inhuman law.[12]

---

12   L. VANTINI, *Il sé esposto. Teologia e neuroscienze in chiave fenomenologica*, Cittadella, Assisi 2017, 275.

There is certainly the problem that the historicity of the accounts of Joseph is "hopeless".[13] In this particular case, however, this is not only not a problem but could even be an advantage. Instead of being an accurate inheritance, linked to the genius of one man, the figure of Joseph presented by Matthew becomes the symbol of a people, an environment, a context. In the religious *revival* of first-century Galilee, with people going back to giving their children the names of the great figures of their religious past (Joseph, Mary-Myriam, Jesus-Joshua, James-Jacob, Simon-Simeon, Judas),[14] a question arises: does returning to tradition mean returning to stoning young girls – since this is no longer practised?[15] In that case, one can say that it is an environment – if not a historical figure – that conveys to Jesus a different way of returning to tradition, to the true sense of the law.

I like to think, therefore, that, behind the exclamation of those who consider him "Joseph's son" (*Lk* 4:22; *Jn* 6:42), there is not only an attempt to lead him back to the simplicity of his origins but also the recognition that, in his way of acting and speaking, one finds the clear trait of the righteousness of an obscure Galilean "of the house of David" (*Lk* 1:27), of whom no word was worth remembering because his word was engraved on the bones and gestures of the one he raised as his own son.

## 4.3 *Heir of Sinners*

There is a final category of people of whom Jesus is, in an entirely original way, heir, namely, sinners. He certainly does not inherit their way of acting, yet he can be said to make himself the channel of their condition and their secret hope.

"John the baptizer appeared in the wilderness, proclaiming a baptism of repentance for the forgiveness of sins. [...] In those days Jesus came from Nazareth of Galilee and was baptized by John in the Jordan" (*Mk* 1:4.9). By standing in line with sinners, Jesus places himself on their side, he becomes heir to their demands. It is not only "for our sake God made the one who knew no sin to be sin, so that in him we might become the righteousness of God" (*2 Cor* 5:21), but, more correctly, it is he himself who makes himself sympathetic to sin, who treats *himself* as a sinner.

This use of the word 'heir' to indicate Jesus' relationship with sinners is not forced. Anyone who has received a complex inheritance, involving debts as well as credits, knows this well. One does not inherit only the good things, but

---

13    U. Luz, *Matthew 1–7. A commentary*, Fortress Press, Minneapolis 2007, 93.
14    Meier, *A Marginal Jew. 1*, 205–208.
15    Luz, *Matthew 1–7*, 94.

also the bad. Wounded pieces of history that are left to us by those who came before us and that we can decide whether and to what extent to accept or reject. If we decide to make them our own, or if we cannot escape them, there is the possibility of being crushed by them, but also the possibility of healing them. Inheriting a shabby company can mean the ruin of the heir, as well as the possibility that that company will rise again and that the dark period will be remembered as a small episode in the history of a big name.

Jesus decides not to shirk this inheritance. He does not present himself as the one who stands before sinners to remind them of their debts but as the one who stands on their side to transform their wounded history into a great story of salvation.

Obviously, this cannot be done without paying a price.

## 5      Contested Paternity

The idea of a God so unbalanced on the paternal-merciful side – today we would say on the maternal side – can be contested. And with good reason. As long as we are talking about an eschatological appeal, evoking another, future world, while the present world continues with its rules and punishments, it can be accepted. But if it is a matter of enforcing this God and this justice in the real world, things are different.

Firstly, because it is false. God is not like that. One cannot count the examples in which the God of the Old Testament clearly expresses the fact that he has given a law to be followed, and that, for those who do not follow it, there are grave consequences, not a final pardon. The splendid Chapter 28 of *Deuteronomy* is an example that suffices for all: "If you will only obey the Lord your God by diligently observing all his commandments that I am commanding you today" (*Deut* 28:1), there will be *blessing*: for you, for your children, crops, livestock, houses and cities; "blessed shall be your basket and your kneading bowl" (*Deut* 28:5). "But if you will not obey the voice of the Lord your God by diligently observing all his commandments and decrees, which I am commanding you today" (*Deut* 28:15), then it shall be a *curse*: for you, for your children, your crops, your cattle, your houses, and your cities; "cursed shall be your basket and your kneading bowl" (*Deut* 28:17). However, this is not just an Old Testament image of God. In *Matthew's Gospel*, Jesus himself is familiar with the "weeping and gnashing of teeth": for those who have no faith (*Mt* 8:12); for the wicked represented by the tares thrown into the fiery furnace (*Mt* 13:42); but also for those who come to the banquet without their fine clothes (*Mt* 22:13);

and for those who do not know how to keep watch while waiting for the master to return (*Mt* 24:51). It is the good Father who proclaims by the mouth of Jesus: "You that are accursed, depart from me into the eternal fire prepared for the devil and his angels" (*Mt* 25:41) to those who did not recognise him in the poor. One who "reaps where he has not sown and gathers where he has not scattered" (*cf. Mt* 25:24–26). To convince people that he is, instead, a Father who forgives before repentance is to deceive.

But let us assume that this is true. Such justice is not good for man. It creates irresponsible people who believe they can do anything, trusting in the final blow. Like Guido da Montefeltro in Dante's *Comedy*, who is snatched from the hands of Saint Francis and taken to hell because "assolver non si può chi non si pente, / né pentere e volere insieme puossi / per la contraddizion che nol consente [one cannot absolve one who does not repent, / nor can one repent and will together, / for the contradiction that does not allow it]" (*Inferno*, XXVII, 118–120). Pope Boniface VIII's promise of absolution turns out to be false. Even if it does not produce false people, this image of God tends to create immature men and women, and, what is more serious: no covenant can really be established with such people. With this mercy, any reciprocity is passed over, as, in practice, God does everything, without man being asked for anything. Any ascending involvement in the dynamics of salvation is overwhelmed by the pure descending movement of God's love. At this point, our justice is better. It is clearer, offering each person the direction for his or her behaviour and life, so that this life may be pleasing to God. Without rules, there is no game, not even the serious game of life with God.

There is, however, a more radical reason why all this is problematic. In fact, it is such an unbalanced position towards sinners that it tends in the end to consider everyone a sinner. Paul is so aware of this change of perspective that he goes so far as to say: "For God has imprisoned all in disobedience so that he may be merciful to all!" (*Rom* 11:32). He who seemed to treat everyone with respect actually considers all women prostitutes and all men corrupt-corrupters.

Finally, one could, more gently, raise a practical question: can one really raise children or educate people with this image of God? All this forgiveness makes any social rule unmanageable, and it is especially those with responsibilities to others who realise this. Clearly, civil law becomes impossible, but also the management of a family: the praise of prostitutes may be appreciated by adults – aware that their own history is also wounded (*cf. Jn* 8:9) – but it is not welcome to parents. This *pre-emptive* forgiveness also makes order unmanageable in religion, yesterday as today. To give a current example: how could access to Eucharistic communion be regulated with these criteria? Instead of confession being the condition for communion, it would be *vice versa*: communion as a condition for confession. In essence, to the extent that Jesus' call is not a *boutade* but is envisaged as a social project, there are good reasons to reject it, for the sake of the men and women of our time, for the sake of our own sons and daughters.

These are human objections which lead us to think that our righteousness is better than the righteousness of Jesus, at least for us. But there are also objections on God's side. Such a paternal God is in danger of not making a good impression. He seems not to know justice, and especially seems not to know and respect his own holiness. He gets so close to sin, which at this point 'encompasses' everyone, that he himself is drawn into sin. Too close and mixed in with human misery, without a criterion that would allow him, at least, to know what is near and pleasing to him and what is distant and unwelcome. Both humanity and God are in danger of being overwhelmed by a condition that can be expressed, provocatively, by Groucho Marx's joke: "I would never want to belong to a club that accepts among its members a guy like me". However, this is not a joke but a reaction that we can often find in those who belong to Jesus' 'club', i.e. the apostles, and in those who aspire to join it. Are we really a mass of sinners headed by a God who cannot distinguish between those who respect him with their lives and those who do not? Both those who cherish the name of God and those who cherish the dignity of human beings have good reason to protest at this and raise objections.

There is, however, one final objection, the most cynical. We could express it like this: 'Let us assume that you are right. If God is truly a forgiving Father, we shall kill you and God will forgive us. That way, if you are wrong, we shall have wiped a blasphemer from our midst; if you are right, however, we shall be forgiven. You will agree with us that we have no alternative'. Again, this is not a tease; it literally happened: Jesus was killed and sinners were forgiven. In this regard, it is worth noting some aspects of a parable that will come in handy later – that of the murderous vine-dressers – whose paradoxical features are often overlooked (*cf.* below, ch. 7, § 5). Some tenants do not want to give their master what is due to him and, therefore, beat and kill those sent by him to collect his share. The first element of strangeness lies in the mind of the master who then sends his son, thinking: "They will respect my son!" (*Mt* 21:37). The second element, which slips the tale into the absurd, is the logic of the tenants: "This is the heir; come, let us kill him and get his inheritance!" (*Mt* 21,38). They think that they will inherit the vineyard that belonged to the son they themselves murdered! It will be useful to pause over this absurdity, because, as this book would like to try to explain, this is exactly what happened.

## Bibliographical Guidelines

The frequent references to research on the historical Jesus and the work of Meier in particular should not mislead. In reconstructing the motivations for Jesus' death, I have resorted above all to what is now the common heritage of Christology. With this in mind, I must acknowledge my debt to **Italian Christology** which demonstrates a rare competence and balance from many points of view. In particular: M. Bordoni, *Gesù di Nazaret Signore e Cristo. Saggio di cristologia sistematica, I: Problemi di metodo*, EDB, Bologna 2016; *II: Gesù al fondamento della cristologia*, EDB, Bologna 2017; *III: Il Cristo annunciato dalla Chiesa, tomo 1*, EDB, Bologna 2018; *III: Il Cristo annunciato dalla Chiesa, tomo 2*, EDB, Bologna 2019; A. Cozzi, *Conoscere Gesù Cristo nella fede. Una cristologia, Cittadella*, Assisi 2014; N. Ciola, *Gesù Cristo figlio di Dio. Vicenda storica e sviluppi della tradizione ecclesiale*, Borla, Roma 2012. For an analysis of the emerging themes: R. Nardin, *Cristologia: temi emergenti*, in G. Canobbio – P. Coda (edd.), *La teologia del XX secolo. Un bilancio, II: Prospettive sistematiche*, Città Nuova, Roma 2003, 23–87. See also the ever classic: H. Kessler, *Christologie*, in Schneider T., *Handbuch del Dogmatik. Band I*, Patmos Verlag, Düsseldorf 1992, 241–444; W. Kasper, *Jesus the Christ*, Continuum Books, London 2011; G. O'Collins, *Christology. A Biblical, Historical, and Systematic Study of Jesus Christ*, Oxford University Press, Oxford 1995. For the **biblical** part: R. Penna, *I ritratti originali di Gesù il Cristo. Inizi e sviluppi della cristologia neotestamentaria, I: Gli inizi*, San Paolo, Cinisello Balsamo 1996; *II: Gli sviluppi*, San Paolo, Cinisello Balsamo 1999.

For the **relationship with the Old Testament**, see, among many: E.P. Sanders, *Jesus and Judaism*, Fortress Press, Philadelphia 1985; P. Beauchamp, *L'un et l'autre Testament. Essai de lecture*, Éditions du Seuil, Paris 1976; Id., *L'un et l'autre Testament. Accomplir les Écritures*, Éditions du Seuil, Paris 1990; Pontifical Biblical Commission, *De sacra Scriptura et christologia*, Libreria Editrice Vaticana, Roma 1994. I have often used "Israel" or "Hebrew" in a generic way when I did not wish to enter into the internal distinctions of the different eras and traditions; for a clarification of the various terms – Hebrew, Jew, Israelite – cf. Biblia, *Vademecum per il lettore della Bibbia*, Morcelliana, Brescia 2017, 233–236. For the different messianisms and expectations of Israel: Ciola, *Gesù Cristo Figlio di Dio*, 163–170; J. Moltmann, *The Way Jesus Christ. Christology in Messianic Dimensions*, HarperCollins Publisher, New York 1990, 1–37; P. Grelot, *L'espérance juive à l'heure de Jésus*, Desclée, Paris 1979.

An interesting investigation on the **Jewish revival** of the theme of mystical filiation can be found in M. Idel, *Il figlio nel misticismo ebraico. I. Tarda antichità, medioevo aškenazita e qabbalah estatica*, Centro Studi Campostrini, Verona 2013; *II. Zohar, qabbalah cristiana e ḥassidismo*, Centro Studi Campostrini, Verona 2014.

The **relationship between the poor and sinners is** particularly interesting. For the general theme, see: J. Sobrino, *Jesus the Liberator. A Historical-Theological Reading of*

*Jesus of Nazareth*, Orbis Books, New York 1993. Moltmann is certainly right when he states that "The liberation of the poor from the vicious circle of poverty is different in form from the liberation of the rich from the vicious circle of riches, although both vicious circles are interlinked. The justification of godless sinners is different from that of the sinful devout" (J. MOLTMANN, *The Crucified God. The Cross of Christ as the Foundation and Criticism of Christian Theology*, Fortress Press, Minneapolis 1993, 53; on the subject, cf. also C. THEOBALD *Le christianisme comme style. Une manière de faire de la théologie en postmodernité*, Les Éditions du Cerf, Paris 2007, 959–997). However, I have preferred to accentuate the condition of objective inability to escape the grip of both because I think that this is the only way to grasp one of the most explosive (and disturbing) aspects of Jesus' proclamation.

CHAPTER 5

# Towards Death (2). The Children

Law, sin and forgiveness are important in a religion. They tell of the complexity of a true relationship. However, they are not the most important thing. They are in fact functional steps to what is essential, namely, the relationship itself. Beyond rules, beyond merit, the question is about closeness to God, the possibility of knowing him and dealing with him. How? What relationship does God have with us? And we with him? These questions touch the religious heart of the Judeo-Christian tradition. Unlike other philosophical-religious perspectives that have, at their centre, the promise of a possible moral life, or peace, or social order, or prosperity, in this tradition, there is only one possible centre: the relationship with God.

## 1      Israel: The Prophet Messiah

This religious characteristic is not new to Jesus but is something he inherits from the tradition of Israel. Covenant, love, friendship, fatherhood, mercy are the words with which, in different ways, this relational centrality is recognised. Abraham and Moses were great, not because they were more righteous than the others but because "the Lord used to speak to Moses face to face, as one speaks to a friend" (*Ex* 33:11); Moses is "the man of God" (*Ps* 90:1), while Abraham is called "[God's] friend" (*Is* 41:8). The prophets, in particular, have insisted on the centrality of this relationship of love and friendship, made of awareness and care. But the wisdom tradition has also much to say: it knows the sweetness of the relationship in the *Song of Songs* and the hardness of the same relationship in the book of *Job*. This relationship involves signs, gestures and customs but, in the end, what counts is the heart: "The Lord your God will circumcise your heart and the heart of your descendants, so that you will love the Lord your God with all your heart and with all your soul, in order that you may live" (*Deut* 30:6).

On the other hand, the centrality of this relationship puts the religion of Israel in a special tension. Not that of one who has to keep a law, but that of one who is loved and wants to love. Like anyone who is involved in a relationship of love, Israel also perceives that love is on the way to its fulfilment; it is not simply given already. As with all love, Israel lives between what already is and what will be because it could be. That is why the meaning of the covenant, its fulfilment, is marked by a law written on the heart. It is the great prophetic vision of ch. 31 of *Jeremiah*: made of everlasting love (*Jer* 31:3), emotion and tenderness (*Jer* 31:20), singing and dancing with tambourines (*Jer* 31:4.12–13). It is so beautiful that perhaps it is only a dream: "Thereupon I awoke and looked, and my sleep was pleasant to me" (*Jer* 31:26). However, the perspective is clear: the law is written on the heart (*Jer* 31:33) and "they shall all know me, from the least of them to the greatest" (*Jer* 31:34). The closeness and knowledge of God – typical of the prophet – becomes accessible to all: "I will pour out my spirit on all flesh; your sons and your daughters shall prophesy" (*Joel* 2:28).

All this is not self-evident or already realised: it is a promise that raises the expectation of a messiah who is able to bring this kind of salvation. Not from some misfortune or even from our sin, but from that distance from God and the inability to love him that renders empty the gestures and practices of religion itself. Someone who envisages a new heart for us (*Ezek* 11:19), who knows how to walk humbly with God (*Mic* 6:8), like Adam who walked with God in the garden at the beginning of time. It is the prophet-messiah who makes prophets. Being the heart of piety itself, it is a perspective that is both primordial (man as he was thought of) and eschatological (man as he will be).

The enigmatic figure of the "son of man"[1] could also be read in this key. This is perhaps the strangest of the titles attributed to Jesus. There is a good chance that Jesus himself used it for himself. After him, early Christianity, as well as the following tradition, used it only rarely because it was too difficult to decipher. In earlier literature, it is a term that oscillates between designating an eschatological figure (*Dan* 7:13) and simply indicating man in general, as in the book of *Ezekiel*. It seems to me that, in this trait, there is something common to both the expectations of Israel and the preaching of Jesus: the idea that the eschatological and marvellous revelation is not outside of history, does not foresee 'another' man, but the same man who was from always, from the beginning. The figure of the "son of man" thus indicates "man in his archetypal greatness (protology) and also the future messiah (eschatology)".[2]

Cultivating this prophetic dream of original communion with God, however, is not harmless. The moment such a man were to become real, he would end up relativising the law written on stone, since he bears the law written on his heart, just as he would end up relativising temple worship itself. For, at that point, the presence of God would be so immediate that there would no longer

---

1   *Cf.* R. PENNA, *I ritratti originali di Gesù il Cristo. Inizi e sviluppi della cristologia neotestamentaria*, I: *Gli inizi*, San Paolo, Cinisello Balsamo 1996, 134–143; M. BORDONI, *Gesù di Nazaret. Presenza, memoria, attesa*, Queriniana, Brescia 2018⁸, 160–169.
2   BORDONI, *Gesù di Nazaret*, 163.

be any difference between what takes place in the Holy of Holies and what takes place at a dinner among friends:

> On that day there shall be ascribed on the bells of the horses: "Holy to the Lord", and the pots in the house of the Lord shall be holy as the bowls in front of the altar; and every pot in Jerusalem and Judah shall be holy to the Lord of hosts, so that all who sacrifice may come and use them to boil the flesh of the sacrifice (*Zech* 14:20–21).

However, it is an acceptable price when the expectation of closeness and love that lies at the heart of Israel's religious story is realised. It is about fulfilment, the reason why the law and the temple exist. It is a time of *closeness* – "For what other great nation has a god so near to it, as the Lord our God is whenever we call to him?" (*Deut* 4:7) – and of *love*, with God behaving like a mother who consoles (*Is* 66:13) and who never forgets her own son (*Is* 49:15).

This new man enables us to understand how we should feel before God: as sons, friends and lovers. Not as servants (*Hos* 2:18). "I have calmed and quieted my soul, like a weaned child with its mother, my soul is like a weaned child that is with me. O Israel, hope in the Lord, from this time on and forevermore" (*Ps* 131:2–3).

If the image of the messiah priest reminded us that God is not a merciless judge, but a father, the image of the messiah prophet reminds us how men and women must feel before him: as children.

## 2  The Near *Abba*

### 2.1  *An Awkward Nearness*

Jesus develops this image of the Father in his deeds and words. The God of whom he speaks is certainly a God who is close, as shown by his own mission which takes place in towns and villages where men and women live, not on remote desert moors. The God Jesus proclaims makes himself close to everyone: he knows no barriers of status, morality, gender, age or ethnicity (albeit with some difficulty).

There is one aspect in particular in which this God becomes accessible, and that is the very language used by Jesus to narrate. His parables are particular for the form they take, even more so than their content. A simple language, which refers to the concrete experience of everyone's life at that time – and, basically, in all times. Shepherds, farmers, trees growing, children leaving home, wage earners, women losing something. One of the favourite images of early Christianity – and of Christianity in every age – is that of the good shepherd: it points to Jesus, but also to God himself, who, having found the lost sheep, "lays it on his shoulders and rejoices" (*Lk* 15:5). This image matches another, equally memorable, which is that of the father who welcomes back his lost son with a feast (*Lk* 15:11–32). In this case, it is more evident that the father-shepherd is God himself.

Strangely, however, the third of the three images that Luke places side by side in the same chapter to indicate the same idea and which is right between the other two is never used: it is that of a woman with a broom in one hand and a lamp in the other (*Lk* 15:8–10). The same could be said of the woman kneading bread with yeast (*Lk* 13:21; *Mt* 13:33). It could be simple machismo that recoils at the idea of comparing God to a woman, but I do not think it is just that, given the examples found in the Old Testament. Rather, it seems to me to be a symptom of a difficulty inherent in Jesus' own parables: the suspicion that there is a limit to the level of familiarity and everydayness that can be used to talk about God. A limit that Jesus ignores.

## 2.2 *Excessive Love*

God, therefore, makes himself close, accessible, in simple gestures and words, and he does so by placing love at the centre. A God who loves and who asks for love. Here too, Jesus is recovering familiar things. In fact, the golden rule – which in *Matthew* seems to constitute the pinnacle of Jesus' teaching: "In everything do to others as you would have them do to you; for this is the Law and the Prophets" (*Mt* 7:12) – was and is widespread, in different variations, in almost all the cultures of the world.[3] Similarly, the centrality of the love of God and neighbour – i.e. the original juxtaposition of *Deut* 6:4–5 and *Lev* 19:18 made by Jesus[4] – is evidently something in which Israel could recognise itself. In particular, Mark emphasises this fact by reporting the figure of a scribe who agrees with Jesus – something unique rather than rare: "You are right, Teacher; you have truly said that 'he is one, and besides him there is no other'; and 'to love him with all the heart, and with all the understanding, and with all the strength', and 'to love one's neighbour as oneself' – this is much more important than all whole burnt offerings and sacrifices" (*Mk* 12:32–33). For Israel too, love is the true meaning of law and worship.

However, Jesus goes further with one of his sharp aphorisms: "Love your enemies; do good to those who hate you; bless those who curse you; pray for

---

3  MEIER, *A Marginal Jew.* 4, 551–558.
4  MEIER, *A Marginal Jew.* 4, 481–527.

those who mistreat you" (*Lk* 6:27 and, in other words, *Mt* 5:44). No culture, not even Israel, supports this.[5] And it is, indeed, untenable if one considers it a moral commandment. One can recommend forgiveness, meekness, but not love for those who wish us harm. Only, in Jesus, this is not a moral precept but the consequence of a precise image of God. If you behave like this, "you will be children of the Most High, for he himself is kind to the ungrateful and the wicked" (*Lk* 6:35 and, with other words, *Mt* 5:45). This is not a novelty but the effect of a fatherly image of God taken to its ultimate consequences, those involving us and the way we look at one another. If God is Father, I am son, and others are brothers and sisters and, therefore, cannot be hated, not even when they themselves hate me. Paul will express the same idea in other words when he calls his neighbour "one for whom Christ died!" (*Rom* 14:15).

This invitation to love one's enemies is puzzling not only because it seems to ask for something impossible, but much more so because it suggests the idea that a form of love that is typical of God is possible for human beings: "Be perfect, therefore, as your heavenly Father is perfect" (*Mt* 5:48). This really seems a bit much, not only in the result, but in the attempt itself.

## 2.3 *The Sons of* Abba

In the light of all this, one can grasp the significance of the term with which Jesus chooses to address God: abba-father-dad. What is disruptive is not – as I have already said – the traditional affirmation of God's fatherhood. Rather, what is disconcerting are the consequences for those who address him in this way, namely, daughters and sons.

To address God as *Abba* means reliance, trust, obedience, availability. From him we receive life; to him we turn for our needs. And we can do this like all the 'little ones' who have no one else to turn to. However, this is not a childish word, and the tones of passivity and minority should not be exaggerated. In fact, it is not these that are the most important aspect. The risk is to fall into the devotional image of a big fatherly hand holding a sleeping infant. What is not grasped here is what it means to be a son, from the son's point of view, that is, the aspect of *entitlement*. It is sometimes emphasised that the child is the one who receives life and sustenance from the parents *as a gift*. Being a child would then mean living in the gift. This is true, but it is only half of sonship, because, from a certain point of view, it is *not* true. A mother who breastfeeds her child or a father who provides food and clothing

---

[5] MEIER, *A Marginal Jew.* 4, 528–550.

are not making a gift, an act of generosity; they are fulfilling a duty of their own. If a mother starves her child or the father – having the means – does not take care of it, he is in our eyes a degenerate parent, liable to prosecution by law. This is true in every culture; it is part of the very concept of fatherhood. The father may have more or less rights with respect to his child, depending on the era and context, but he always has duties also. Consequently, children have rights.

Jesus' way of acting clearly reflects this filial dignity and possibility. The protagonist of the Gospels does not address the Father as the subordinate who begs for a grace, but as one who knows that he will obtain what he asks for. His relationship with the Father does not make him insecure, but decisive in his actions, counting on the Father's 'cover'. In fact, Jesus not only behaves like this; he urges his followers to behave in the same way. They too must turn to God, calling him Father and making requests: "Ask, and it will be given you; search, and you will find; knock, and the door will be opened for you" (*Mt* 7:7; *Lk* 11:9), "Ask and you will receive, so that your joy may be complete" (*Jn* 16:24), "You do not have, because you do not ask" (*Jas* 4:2). If the Father does not answer, it is enough to have the cheek to insist, and he will wake up even in the middle of the night to grant the request (*cf. Lk* 11:5–8). This kind of request clearly presupposes a right that derives from a bond that cannot be broken because it binds two subjects with their autonomy and freedom. Here, the son is not just "a weaned child" (*Ps* 131:2), but is, at least, an adolescent who turns to his father with his requests, the result of his judgements, and decides what to do. As in the Parable in *Lk* 15,11–32, the Father will agree – even to a request that takes the son far away or against him.

Indeed, the same can be said for the possibility of judgement. The son does not simply adhere to the will and judgement of another. That is what the slave does, whereas the position of the son is, by its very nature, dialogical and dialectical. The son has a right, indeed a duty, to his own thoughts: "You know how to interpret the appearance of earth and sky; but why do you not know how to interpret the present time? And why do you not judge for yourselves what is right?" (*Lk* 12:56–57). With these words, Jesus invites his own to have the same maturity of judgement that they use in everyday affairs – on which they stake the future of their crops and families – to judge the things of God also. With this, the position of the adolescent is further compelled, not to return to that of the infant but rather to assume that of the adult who brings his competence, his judgement and his freedom into play in order to decide how to move before the other, even before God.

Being a child, therefore, means having a relationship that confers rights, and not only on the register of gratuitousness but also on that of duty. First and foremost, that of carrying one's freedom with dignity.

## 3 The New Temple

The image of God can change even very radically without the gestures with which one addresses him changing in substance. There can be bowing, feasts, celebrations, prayers, as well as a moral and social system, even with very different deities, more or less anthropomorphic, more or less numerous. Much can remain essentially unchanged as long as the changing image of *God* does not affect the resulting image of *man*. Now, Jesus' stance of pressing the loving fatherhood of God ends up doing exactly that because it changes the way man can stand before him. Precisely as a son stands before his father. At this point, there are very few things that remain unchanged both in theory and in practice. A son can be expected to be respectful towards his parents but, apart from that, there are not many rules and limitations. There is no limit to the access a child can have to his or her own parents, either of condition, or of space, or of time. A humanity of children who have free access to the divine. At this point a series of 'treasures', which contemporary Judaism rightly guarded as its most precious forms, are threatened. Not in a direct way: Jesus does not lash out at these treasures; on the contrary, he may respect and appreciate them, and yet, even beyond his possible intentions, he empties them from within of their very *raison d'être*.

Think for example of the *laws of purity*. They may seem strange to us today – ablutions, penances, dedicated times and spaces – yet they do nothing more than define what is distant from and what is near to God. This is not about what is morally *pleasing* or *displeasing* to God but, rather, what is *near* to or *far* from him. Before morality, it helps people to give an objective order and value to many aspects of reality. Death is distant from God and must be treated with care; life belongs to him and must be treated with equal care. Therefore, corpses and blood are realities which need to be handled with appropriate religious circumspection and must be regulated before God. This creates a shared landscape that helps a community manage the spaces of life and regulate access to the sacred and to worship. This regulation serves not only to safeguard God, but, well before that, to ensure that man does not find himself in a condition of excessive proximity to the divine.

Contemporary sensibilities – also because of the influence of Christianity – are in danger of missing this point: getting too close to God is dangerous. Analogously, I believe that none of us would like to find the pope or the Dalai Lama at dinner on any given day. That would be a disturbing surprise. Far better that there are rules and times which allow me to invite them on the day I am in the state to do so.

This regulatory system easily becomes a minefield. Especially for those who are in a marginal condition and for those who cannot avoid coming into contact with publicans, prostitutes, pagans, menstruating women, etc. For some, the conditions for having the pope for dinner are practically never there. Too complicated and too onerous, both economically and psychologically.

Jesus does not lash out head-on against this system; the permissibility of a series of contacts with conditions considered unclean (lepers or the woman with the flow of blood) could border on being a dubious case, a matter of debate in his time. "Yet apparently, for Jesus ritual purity is not only not a burning issue, it is not an issue at all. But why should that be?"[6]

Perhaps it is because, for a son, there can be no criteria of proximity to or distance from his parents. All that the father has is accessible, as is the father himself, all the more so if this father presents himself as a shepherd with a beast on his back or as a housewife with a broom. If God is accessible and we are children, it is difficult to imagine rules of access. The door is always open.

Something similar applies to *time*. What is an appropriate time to meet a father? The answer is: 'Any'. For those in a hurry: 'Now'. But the same is also true in reverse: there is no definite time when the father can present himself to his children. Any time is good. Regulating time, on the other hand, is essential in the relationship between bosses and employees. There are hours 'due' to the employer and there are holidays when employees are free. A guarantee for both, for the bosses to have their own time, and for the employees not to be bothered at any and every hour. Not so for a child. A child can address the parent at any time, and *vice versa*. This relationship provides for a completely different level of proximity and freedom.

And hence the threat to a second central institution of Judaism, the *Sabbath*, the observance of the Lord's Day. In the case of Jesus, one must not make the mistake of focusing on 'dubious' or obvious cases where common sense would have come into play. Even the Pharisees – the social group most attentive to Sabbath observance – would probably have had no objection to transgressing the Sabbath in cases of imminent danger to life; for everyone else, the rhetorical question that Jesus addresses to his audience is significant: "If one of you has a child or an ox that has fallen into a well, will you not immediately pull it out on the Sabbath day?" (*Lk* 14:5). The answer is, of course: "No one!"[7] The disruptive aspect of Jesus' position on the Sabbath does not lie in common sense – which, in principle, is not disruptive – but in his assumption of freedom with regard to the Sabbath. Faced with a transgression that does not presuppose any danger of death or any absolute necessity, such as tearing off ears of corn in order to eat the grains while on a journey, the position is clear: "The Sabbath was made

---

6 MEIER, *A Marginal Jew*. 4, 414.
7 MEIER, *A Marginal Jew*. 4, 235–341.

for humankind, and not humankind for the Sabbath! So the Son of Man is lord even of the Sabbath" (*Mk* 2:27–28). If this son needs, or feels he must do something, he has no problem transgressing *even* the Sabbath, because he considers himself free lord of it. It is not the belonging that is questioned, but the bond. That day belongs to the father, but, if need be, a son may use it as he pleases, even without asking first – at most he will clear it with him later.

Similar, again, is Jesus' attitude towards the institution of the *priesthood*. What role did the priests play in Jesus' life? We are not talking here about the role they played in his death – where both the Synoptics and John clearly attribute to the 'chief priests' a role in the plot to kill him. Nor are we talking about the priestly function that the *Letter to the Hebrews* assigns to Jesus. The question is rather about the role the priests played in his mission and the role he attributed to them. The results are very meagre; practically limited to only one episode, which Mark places at the very beginning of Jesus' activity (*Mk* 1:40–45): Jesus heals a leper and then drives him away in a rather brusque manner, ordering him: "See that you say nothing to anyone; but go, show yourself to the priest, and offer for your cleansing what Moses commanded as a testimony to them" (*Mk* 1:44). The text refers to the role of the priests in managing the 'quarantine' for lepers and verifying their possible healing (*Lev* 13–14). In practice, a role of health officials. The role of the priests as intercessors for sin, or even less as mediators of the relationship with God, has no importance for Jesus. And yet he does not lash out at them, does not directly challenge their function. It is simply that what is really important is not this: it is independent of them.

There is, however, one point, one place, with respect to which this filial nonchalance becomes critical, and that is *the temple*. Regardless of its rather turbulent origins (*2 Sam* 7), the temple performs an essential religious function, in total harmony with what Jesus is affirming, namely, that of making God's *closeness* visible. Not in an abstract, philosophical or intimistic way. Not to the king or the prophets alone, but to all the people. In the concreteness of history, in space and time, God makes himself close to Israel and makes himself present in the temple. And Jesus seems to recognise all this: his family presents him in the temple (*Lk* 2:22–24); from his youth, he goes there to have discussions with the doctors (*Lk* 2:41–50); he returns there later to teach (to the point of being able to claim: "Day after day I was with you in the temple teaching", *Mk* 14:49); he pays the temple tax (*Mt* 17:24–27); he defends its honour before those who think they can invoke it with false oaths (*Mt* 23:16–22).

In fact, the greatest recognition of the temple lies in his whole story which points to Jerusalem, the city of the temple, as the place of fulfilment: "He set his face to go to Jerusalem" (*Lk* 9:51). How is it possible that such a man could be accused of wanting to destroy the temple (*cf. Mk* 14:57–59; *Mt* 26:60–61)? The answer lies in a particular episode which John reports at the beginning of his Gospel, as a sort of programmatic gesture, unlike the Synoptics who place it, more likely on a historical level, at the end of Jesus' ministry. An episode that deserves attention because it risks not being understood, yesterday as today.

> The Passover of the Jews was near, and Jesus went up to Jerusalem. In the temple he found people selling cattle, sheep, and doves, and the money changers seated at their tables. Making a whip of cords, he drove them all out of the temple, with the sheep and the cattle. He also poured out the coins of the money changers and overturned their tables. He told those who were selling the doves, "Take these things out of here! Stop making my Father's house a marketplace". His disciples remembered that it was written, "Zeal for your house will consume me" [Ps 69:10]. The Jews then said to him, "What sign can you show us for doing this?" Jesus answered them, "Destroy this temple, and in three days I will raise it up." The Jews then said, "This temple has been under construction for forty-six years, and will you raise it up in three days?" But he was speaking of the temple of his body. After he was raised from the dead, his disciples remembered that he had said this; and they believed the scripture and the word that Jesus had spoken (*Jn* 2:13–22).

Jesus arrives in Jerusalem during the days of the Passover when devout people, like himself, go to the temple for sacrifices in order to fulfil their religious duties. He prepares an improvised weapon and then begins to overthrow everything. He does not attack the cult directly but the simple vendors who enabled it to be practised. Why? What exactly did he want?

The reference to the "marketplace" risks leading us astray. It cannot be just a question of organisation of space: if he wanted the merchants to position themselves a little further away, there was no need to make such a fuss. Are people from the four corners of Israel – and beyond – expected to bring animals from home for the sacrifices, at the risk of them turning out to be imperfect and unfit for purpose? Much more practical to buy suitable animals directly, on the spot. And to do so, one would have to change the money, the common currency with the face of the emperor-god printed on it, to avoid introducing idolatrous images into the temple. So what is really going on here?

To understand this one could try a parallel. On an Easter Sunday, during a crowded celebration, I enter the church and, using my belt like a whip, start creating pandemonium, saying that this is rubbish and not good. Everything needs to be changed. Apart from the initial bewilderment, I could find a number of people willing to give me credit. The songs are obscene, the priest has not prepared, the people are bored and distracted, and the whole thing is more reminiscent of a market than a "house of prayer" (*Mt* 21:13; *Mk* 11:17; *Lk* 19:46).

'If you are saying that a reformation is needed to bring the whole thing back to its deeper meaning, you are indeed right. A reformation is needed.' At that point I raise the stakes: we need a radical reform, like erasing everything and starting all over again, renewing everything. The people willing to listen to me are already fewer, but someone is found. 'And then? What exactly do you have in mind?' At that point I say something, but, fortunately, no one understands much and it ends there. It will be understood later: "after ..." (*Jn* 2:22). I imagine church worship to be related to me, to my body. The very few who have grasped anything are horrified. Am I really proposing to do away with what is being done here, in the name of a new cult that is free of all this? Is the temple of stones being replaced by a temple of flesh, which would then be me? The worst thing is that, in doing this, I would be claiming to be bringing things back to their original meaning.

In essence, this is what John is describing. Acceptable, perhaps, to his Christian readers, not to Jesus' immediate audience. I say 'perhaps' to emphasise that, in its extreme consequences, this is also unacceptable to Christians. As long as the temple of Jerusalem is replaced by the new temple that is Jesus, the thing can still work. But, in the end, the idea is likely to be that the temple is replaced, not by the body of the Son but by the sons and daughters themselves, on whose hearts of flesh the law will be written, in whose bodies the "living sacrifice, holy and acceptable to God", the true "spiritual worship" will be celebrated (*Rom* 12:1). "The hour is coming when you will worship the Father neither on this mountain nor in Jerusalem. [...] But the hour is coming and is now here when the true worshippers will worship the Father in spirit and truth" (*Jn* 4:21.23), that is, *without* a temple. In this perspective, any feast, any time, any place is skipped over. Any possibility of distinguishing the places and spaces of God's presence. A passage not easy to face for anything that wants to call itself a religion.

## 4  The Son of Mary

What we have seen is, perhaps, the stamp of Jesus' religious change. The new form of relationship with God that he embodies and in which he wants to involve those who believe in him. That is why it is not easy to express it correctly. Every age – and every person, to the extent that they have been involved in this perspective – will have their own way of experiencing and narrating it, emphasising one aspect or another. At the same time, they will also have to find a way to make this position and its scandal, its structurally excessive character, sustainable. The strain of all this leads one to focus attention on Jesus and his novelty, sometimes causing one to neglect the supporting actors that enabled him to express such a way of living before God and make it real in history. Instead, it is worth asking how and with whom Jesus was able to elaborate and mature such a position.

We have already seen the case of the Syro-Phoenician woman (*cf.* above, ch. 3, § 2.4) whose role emerges more clearly at this point. In the dialogue, a decision is being made concerning 'sons and dogs'. Who is son before God? And who is dog? Who is at the table and who under the table? If one thinks of it as an abstract disquisition, one is baffled. Does the Son himself think that a little possessed child is a dog? Must he learn from a pagan woman that everyone needs to receive the daily bread that is the children's right? Here, however, it is not a matter of theory but of life in the concrete. The two protagonists of the story, Jesus and the Syro-Phoenician woman, are not the protagonists at all. In fact, at the centre is the relationship between the Father and the 'little possessed child'. Is it possible to believe that she too has a right to a place at the table? A simple word from Jesus would not be enough after all. It would be a theoretical affirmation, coming from a distant guru who can speak fine words without effort. It is only in a concrete story, in which a woman first believes herself entitled to demand bread, life, healing – a woman who *already lives as a beloved and dignified daughter* – that Jesus can affirm the salvation offered by his own conception of God. Had he been the only one to believe and live this relationship, it would have been something beautiful but useless; it would not have become history for anyone. To be able to express concrete sonship, Jesus depended on others.

This statement appears less sharp when one considers perhaps the most fundamental of the people on whom Jesus depended, for his own sonship, for his own life and, as I would like to show, for his own specifically religious ideas. Indeed, before Jesus announced to men the right to turn to God with the loving and free closeness of sons, someone had already experienced this. If this had not been the case, Jesus would not even have been born. This person is his mother, Mary.

To understand the significance of all this, one must make an effort to look at Mary *before Jesus* or *regardless of him*. This is an inappropriate operation from a theological point of view, but perfectly logical from a narrative point of view. Not only because there was a time when Mary was in the world but not Jesus, but also because, in a more radical way, Mary, like each of us, is a person *in front of Jesus*, as well as being *in*, *with* and *for* him. So who is this woman who played such a special role in the story we want to tell?

Certainly she is someone who experiences the *closeness* of God. For her, the God of Israel is close, has a relationship *with her*, so close and intimate that it takes shape in the history of her body. This relationship is visceral, even before the relationship with her son, and takes place *apart from* anything other than her love. Nothing tells us whether God checked the laws of purity related to menstruation before approaching, or even if it was on the Sabbath. He approached her, ignoring the law, his own law, which would have condemned Mary if she had not had a man beside her who could understand this closeness. Even if tradition links Mary to the temple, the Gospels certainly do not place the annunciation in a sacred place. It therefore takes place regardless, between God and her. Not *against* but *regardless of*. In fact, Mary respects the temple: she brings her son there at the appropriate time and attends the feasts. She says nothing against the law, the Sabbath or the rules of purity; yet all this is essentially irrelevant – as it will be for her son – in the face of her own body as a woman who was a temple of relationship with God before being a temple of flesh for her Son. The prophetic promise of a law written in the heart, in the bowels, was realised in Mary before it was realised in Jesus. Indeed, it was realised in Mary, thus making it possible for it to be realised in Jesus.

At the same time, however, Mary experiences this loving closeness with *the freedom of an adult person*. She is the subject of her own life, thoughts and relationships. She is so with regard to her promised husband and society, she is so with respect to the customs of her people and her religion. She is certainly so before God. Indeed, she wants to understand before agreeing: "How can this be?" (*Lk* 1:34). God is not simply within her but also before her, as many annunciations show in a plastic way in which a real dialectic develops between the angel and Mary. In Simone Martini's painting (1333), Mary seems almost to withdraw, as if to make it clear that she must first settle a series of questions of her own; even more so, in Antonello da Messina's *Annunciation* (1475), she stands before an interlocutor, whom we do not see, with a dignity that could be the manifesto of the modern subject.

It is, however, in relation to her son that this characteristic of an adult and free person takes on its most fascinating and dramatic traits. Indeed, the Gospels constantly tell us that Mary is Mary and Jesus is Jesus. They are not one function of the other, but two autonomous subjects, true interlocutors of each other. As for all true interlocutors, they too do not understand each other immediately: we see this at the moment when the son remains in the temple without alerting anyone, but also throughout Jesus' public life when this woman's strain in understanding what is happening is evident– a strain very similar to that of the Baptist. The one who was her son detaches himself from her with gestures and words that she does not always understand, just as the one who was a disciple detaches himself from the master, John the Baptist, creating problems for him. The dramatic aspect of the statement, "Mary treasured all these things and pondered them in her heart" (*Lk* 2:19), should not be underestimated; this pious gesture actually conceals all the difficulty in understanding the evolution of her own inheritance. This difficulty extends so far that, "when his family heard it, they went out to restrain him, for people were saying, 'He has gone out of his mind'" (*Mk* 3:21); the text does not say that Mary was present, but neither does it exclude it.

It is the *Gospel of John* that allows us to understand the full value of this difference, of this standing before each other, in dignified and responsible freedom. In describing the moment when Jesus has to decide to begin his public activity, unlike the Synoptics, the fourth evangelist does not tell of a Jesus who prepares for his mission alone, in the desert, in the company of angels and animals, and in relation to *Deuteronomy*. Instead, he speaks of concrete relationships. The one with the Baptist and with the circle of his disciples (*Jn* 1:35–51), but, especially, the one with his mother in Cana of Galilee, during a banquet, which sees the beginning of his miracles or, as John puts it, "signs" (*Jn* 2:1–12). After this, the evangelist goes directly to the episode in the temple (*Jn* 2:13–25). Jesus' choice to begin his ministry takes place, therefore, in connection with his fundamental relationships, not in the desert; and it will be his mother, with a disarming boldness, who will press him to begin, ignoring his reservations and prompting others to do his bidding.

As already mentioned for Joseph (*cf.* above, ch. 4, § 4.2), the features of this woman may not be historical. Again, I do not see this as a difficulty. Quite the contrary. If, historically, Mary had been a submissive and mute woman, totally moulded by the words and gestures of her son, it would be even more significant, from a theological point of view, that the evangelists wished, instead, to draw this figure of a strong, autonomous, indomitable woman, capable of looking freely at her own beauty, without arrogance but also without shame, in the wake of other women of Israel before her (*cf. Lk* 2:46–56). This – the authors of the Gospels seem to say – is the figure of Jesus' mother, one who stands before him throughout his life, in true dialogue with herself, with God, with her son and with her own religious tradition. A woman, not a function.

Describing Mary in this way does not diminish the relationship with her son, but strengthens it. In fact, a relationship only arises where there are authentic partners, dignified and free. Strong in union as in distinction. Above all, without that dependence that becomes confusion, as the Council of Chalcedon already declared,[8] and as so much psychology of the relationship between

---

8 "… to be acknowledged in two natures, inconfusedly, unchangeably, indivisibly, inseparably; the distinction of natures being by no means taken away by the union" (Council of Chalcedon, *DH* 302).

mother and child warns us today.[9] Nor is it a question of bending Christology into submission to Mariology. Rather, it seeks to pave the way for a Christology of bonds that does not feel threatened but rather enriched by the relationships that sustained and formed the fully human story of the son.

Once again, it is John who allows us to grasp the advantages of such an approach. She who has the strength to stand before her son when he has to decide whether it is better to start or wait is the same person who will later have the strength to stand before him near the cross. For John, such an autonomous woman is the one who can be proposed, in the face of her son's death, to put her own motherhood on the line for others.

> Standing near the cross of Jesus were his mother, and his mother's sister, Mary the wife of Clopas, and Mary Magdalene. When Jesus saw his mother and the disciple whom he loved standing beside her, he said to his mother, "Woman, here is your son." Then he said to the disciple, "Here is your mother." And from that hour the disciple took her into his own home (*Jn* 19:25–27).

A discipleship that is born in the spirit of this woman can never be a flat adhesion to the person and will of another but, always and only, the singular assumption of one's own dignified freedom, which resists the other, not because it does not love him, but, precisely, because it wants to offer him a true interlocutor, who can also support the atrocious spectacle of his defeat.

Once again, I like to think that the statement, "Is not this the carpenter, the son of Mary and brother of James and Joses and Judas and Simon, and are not his sisters here with us?" (*Mk* 6:3) may not only be an attempt to lead Jesus back to the humility of his origins but also the astonishment of seeing in him the son who was able to take up the extraordinary inheritance of a woman who did not preach but, in her flesh, lived a new relationship with the God of Israel, in the spirit of a visceral closeness that does not hold back but exalts the freedom and dignity of each one.

---

9  For a less idealised perspective on the mother-child relationship than that presented in H.U. VON BALTHASAR *The Glory of the Lord. A Theological Aesthetics. V. The Realm of Metaphysics in the Modern Age*, Ignatius Press, San Francisco 1991, 613–627, see: M. KLEIN, *On Observing the Behaviour of Young Infants* (1952), in ID., *Envy and Gratitude and Other Works: 1946–1963. The Writings of Melanie Klein. Vol. 3*, Hogarth Press, London 1987, 94–121; J. BOWLBY, *Attachment and Loss. 2. Separation: Anxiety and Anger*, Hogarth Press, London 1982.

## 5  Contested Sonship

We are at the religious heart of Jesus' proposal. In a perhaps somewhat unexpected way, we discover that it has to do with the definition of man, of the "son of man". Affirming the loving fatherhood of God ends up making everyone a son. This can obviously be contested, and has been contested.

If it is understood not as a generic allegory but in the proper sense, with the consequences of rights and duties it entails, it seems *far too much*.

Too much for Jesus, the Son. "By what authority are you doing these things? Who gave you this authority to do them?" (*Mk* 11:28) i.e.: Who do you think you are? What opinion do you have of yourself? Properly applying the name of Father to God, and to oneself the name of Son, means being a relative of God, able to treat him as one would treat a cousin, grandfather or aunt.

It is too much for God, who must be protected from an attitude so disrespectful of his transcendence, his holiness, his difference from human beings. To behave like this is to be blasphemous towards God; God must, therefore, be protected by Jesus. But it is also blasphemous towards man, as it takes him beyond his limits, makes him delusional, believing he can stand on a par with God. Man too must, therefore, be protected by Jesus.

For if there is anyone for whom this religious approach is *too much*, it is man himself. He who says "Be perfect, therefore, as your heavenly Father is perfect" (*Mt* 5:48) seems, in fact, to endorse that temptation that was the first temptation in Eden and which is inherent in everyone in one way or another: "You will be like God" (*Gen* 3:5). One understands that his intention is different, but who can explain this to people, individually, with their natural tendency to titanism, *hubris* and delusion? Who can manage a community in which everyone considers themselves children of God and believes they have the rights of children? One does not need to be a prophet to understand what will happen: "Sibling will betray sibling to death, and a father his child, and children will rise against parents and have them put to death" (*Mt* 10:21). In a world of siblings, there will be rebellion against the fathers, against the Father himself, and fratricidal warfare will break out because it will be impossible to come to an agreement between all these princes, the children of God.

Yet, even more than *too much*, this is *false*. How is it possible to uphold the independent dignity of adult children and total obedience at the same time? Does Jesus claim to be the one who been given "all things into his hands" (*Jn* 13:3) or is he the one who "obeys the will of the Father" (*Jn* 9:31)? As long as things go well, one can argue for an easy harmony: "My Father is still working, and I also am working" (*Jn* 5:17), but what happens if the wills do not coincide?

Either the Son wins, and sonship is crushed by independence, or the Father wins, and sonship is crushed by obedience. Even if all this were true for Jesus, it cannot be true for others: men are "worthless slaves" (*Lk* 17:10) who are asked to obey God. One runs the risk of being confused: "I do not call you servants any longer [...], but I have called you friends" (*Jn* 15:15), but, at the same time, "You are my friends if you do what I command you" (*Jn* 15:14); "Slaves are not greater than their master" (*Jn* 15:20); "If you keep my commandments, you will abide in my love" (*Jn* 15:10). Are we children, friends or servants?

Here we see the greatest risk of this approach. It is not a risk for God, but for mankind, especially the little ones who trust in God. If they really believe that they are children of God, that they can ask and obtain – with the obviousness of a rhetorical question: "Is there anyone among you who, if your child asked for bread, would give a stone?" (*Mt* 7:9), "or if the child asked for an egg, would give a scorpion?" (*Lk* 11:12) – they risk getting into trouble, getting hurt. God is not always near and does not always answer. We must say this with pain and in a whisper, but we cannot lie. It is not fair to the many who have prayed and have not been heard. "O Lord, how long shall I cry for help, and you will not listen? Or cry to you 'Violence!' and you will not save? Why do you make me see wrongdoing and look at trouble?" (*Hab* 1:2–3). To think that one can automatically rely on God's help, his closeness, his response is false and dangerous.

For, in the end, an ambiguity must be resolved. When he uses the word "son", is Jesus talking about himself or about everyone? Of his mother, of some extraordinary men and women – whom Israel always thought could be called "God's child" (*cf. Wis* 2:18) – or of human children in general?

At this point, the best thing is to accept his word and carry it through to its ultimate consequences. We are all children who can evaluate, judge and choose before God. And before God, as an adult responsible for himself and his brothers, the "high priest that year" (*Jn* 11:49) he who had to decide what to do, decided: "It is better for you to have one man die for the people than to have the whole nation destroyed" (*Jn* 11:50). If Jesus is right about sonship, Caiaphas' behaviour is justified; if he is right about fatherhood, there is nothing to fear, because the one who always answers his prayers will save him from the possible error of a zealous brother.

This is the definitive, the most tragic, objection to sonship. It leaves the whole affair hanging, to see what will happen, how the Son will behave, and how the Father will behave, in the face of these objections. A word and a gesture will not suffice. Faced with this definitive religious crossroads, the whole life of Jesus, and the very name of God, will be at stake.

## Bibliographical Guidelines

In many respects, the search for the reasons for his death is in the groove of the **phenomenology of Jesus**, or at least aspires to be a possible variation on it. For a comparison with the perspective from different angles: P. SEQUERI, *L'interesse teologico di una fenomenologia di Gesù: giustificazione e prospettive*, in *Teologia* 23 (1998) 289–329; ID., *La "storia di Gesù"*, in G. COLOMBO (ed.), *L'evidenza e la fede*, Glossa, Milano 1988, 235–275; M. SALVIOLI, *La misericordia invisibile del Padre nella compassione visibile di Gesù, il Figlio. Per una fenomenologia di Gesù in chiave anagogica*, in *Divus Thomas* 2 (2008) 22–110. Possible examples of topic development are: M. NERI, *Il corpo di Dio. Dire Gesù nella cultura contemporanea*, EDB, Bologna 2010; ID., *Gesù, affetti e corporeità di Dio. Il cuore e la fede*, Cittadella, Assisi 2007; S. DE MARCHI, *Gesù. I primi trent'anni. Un'indagine biblico-narrativa*, Cittadella, Assisi 2015. For an original variation on the theme (which presents itself as a "phenomenology" of Teresa of Avila, through Edith Stein and phenomenology): R. OTTONE, *La chiave del castello. L'interesse teologico dell'empatia di Gesù*, EDB, Bologna 2018.

More particularly, I would like to mention the work of **Giovanni Cesare Pagazzi** as an example of the attempt to put forward theological proposals that hold together this perspective and the interest in the relational dimension. Whether it be the relationship with things (G.C. PAGAZZI, *Fatte a mano. L'affetto di Cristo per le cose*, EDB, Bologna 2013), with others (ID., *C'è posto per tutti. Legami fraterni, paura, fede*, Vita e pensiero, Milano 2008), with God, or the relationship that binds Jesus to the Father (ID., *In principio era il legame. Sensi e bisogni per dire Gesù*, Cittadella, Assisi 2004; F. MANZI – G.C. PAGAZZI, *Il pastore dell'essere. Fenomenologia dello sguardo del Figlio*, Cittadella, Assisi 2001), the core of these theological insights lies precisely in being able to keep in mind simultaneously the issues of a relational perspective and the need not to impose them or simply superimpose them on the biblical-theological datum but rather to make them act from within as a stimulus and a rethink.

For the **spiritual significance of theology** (and philosophy): P. HADOT, *Philosophy as a Way of Life. Spiritual Exercises from Socrates to Foucault*, Blackwell Publishers, Oxford – Malden (MA) 1995; S. D'AGOSTINO, *Esercizi spirituali e filosofia moderna. Bacon, Descartes, Spinoza*, ETS, Pisa 2017; H. JONAS, *Gnosis und spätantiker Geist*, Vandenhoek & Ruprecht, Göttingen 1988 (I cite this text because I believe that Jonas succeeds uniquely in rendering the spiritual significance of different philosophical positions; for Gnosticism, cf. JONAS, *Gnosis*, 219–229; for a quick comparison with Christianity, cf. JONAS, *Gnosis*, 777); G. MOIOLI, *L'esperienza spirituale. Lezioni introduttive*, Glossa, Milano 1992; CH. THEOBALD, *Le christianisme comme style. Une manière de faire de la théologie en postmodernité*, Les Éditions du Cerf, Paris 2007, 389–412; E. SALMANN, *Presenza e critica. Sulle affinità elettive fra filosofia e mistica*, in ID., *Presenza di spirito. Il cristianesimo come gesto e pensiero*, Messaggero, Padova 2000,

224–256; D. BALOCCO, *Dal cristocentrismo al cristomorfismo. In dialogo con David Tracy*, Glossa, Milano 2012, 112–122. The same significance, stated in an entirely different way, is found in: G. GUTIÉRREZ, *A Theology of Liberation. History, Politics, And Salvation*, Orbis Books, Maryknoll (NY) 1973, 3–82; J.B. METZ, *Mystik der offenen Augen. Wenn Spiritualität aufbricht*, Verlag Herder GmbH, Freiburg im Br. 2011; P. CASALDÁLIGA – J.M. VIDAL, *Spirituality of Liberation*, Orbis Books, Maryknoll (NY) 1994.

CHAPTER 6

# Towards Death (3). The Brothers

Jesus took up his people's image of God and stressed the traits of a merciful *Father* over those of a just judge. This could be reassuring in one respect but disturbing in another. It is really difficult to live up to the gaze of those who love us.

From this point, Jesus also proposed an image of the human that invites everyone to consider themselves worthy of God's gaze, to live before him as *children* who can judge and ask, the free subjects of their own lives. This could be liberating, but also, ultimately, very demanding to keep up for a whole lifetime.

However, Jesus goes further. For he believes that – precisely because God is Father and he is Son – we are *brothers and sisters*. "You are not to be called rabbi, for you have one teacher, and you are all brothers and sister. And call no one your father on earth, for you have one Father, the one in heaven" (*Mt* 23:8). This is the new relationship that is proposed, even at the cost of going *against* other natural relationships.

> Someone told him, "Look, your mother and your brothers are standing outside, wanting to speak to you". But to the one who had told him this, Jesus replied, "Who is my mother and who are my brothers?" And pointing to his disciples, he said, "Here are my mother and my brothers! For whoever does the will of my Father in heaven is my brother and sister and mother" (*Mt* 12:47–50).

In the name of this new brotherhood, the very relationship with his mother Mary seems to be called into question. This change of perspective will be very clear to early Christianity. Paul, in particular, will suggest the idea that making all sons and, therefore, all brothers is the very meaning of the Son's presence: "That he might be the firstborn within a large family [brothers]" (*Rom* 8:29).

With this theme of brotherhood, things become difficult because too many relationships, too many expectations, too many interests are affected. In fact, as long as an inheritance is transmitted between *a* parent and *a* child, everything can take place with a certain composure and without disturbing the social sphere. Tensions can certainly be created, both in those who decide to (or are forced to) leave and in those who decide to (or try to) take over the inheritance. But if the inheritance concerns *many* brothers and sisters, it is a different matter altogether. Worse still, if this inheritance cannot simply be divided but must be shared. Fear, suspicion, resentment, envy, aggression in defence or attack easily emerge in these situations. For many family biographies, it would have been better if there had been no legacy at all. For many national biographies it would have been better if the king had only had one son.

But, above all, it would be better for the Son to be the only son and not to be involved with all the other stories. What is the deep root of this claim of brotherhood that exposes Jesus so dangerously?

The reason why the Son can and must regard everyone as brothers is understood in the *Letter to the Hebrews*: "For the one who sanctifies and those who are sanctified all have one Father. For this reason, Jesus is not ashamed to call them brothers and sisters, saying, 'I will proclaim your name to my brothers and sisters, in the midst of the congregation I will praise you'" (*Heb* 2:11). To be able to stand before God as a Father, the Son must recognise that it is the Father who is *the origin*, his as much as anyone else's. The same origin that makes him Son also brings him closer to all others, "firstborn within a large family [brothers]" (*Rom* 8:29), but also "firstborn of all creation" (*Col* 1:15). There are no limits to God's fatherhood and, therefore, no limits to brotherhood.

This means, however, affecting the relationships that bind people to one another, the forms that life takes on a social and public level. It is a political statement. It is crucial to grasp the connection between brotherhood and politics because it is often not very evident. Forgiveness and the relationship with God can indeed – within certain limits – remain confined to the private sphere. Not so brotherhood, which affects real relationships and is structured in public and institutionalised forms. In a word, it changes reality.

At this point, things become worthy of attention even for the powers that rule this world, as they do with some success if we consider that Jesus lived in the time that history remembers as the *pax romana*, which lasted more than two hundred years (29 BC – 180 AD). A priest or prophet messiah could be ignored by the Romans; not a king messiah.

## 1 Israel: The King Messiah

This idea of concrete brotherhood, which touches on social relations, is also not original to Jesus. He received it as Israel's promise and dream. Understanding its contours and significance can be complex, however, since, like any social dream, it depends very much on the specific context of the society to which it is addressed. More recent eras may have expressed this, for instance, in the *fraternité* of the French Revolution or in the equality of communism.

For Israel, the dream was of a kingdom led by a messianic king. God's paternity, his care for the people and for each person, risks being something abstract and distant. Instead, this fatherhood can be embodied by a concrete person, capable of effectively liberating personal, social and political relationships. Intimistic, individualistic or eschatological perspectives give way to the historical relevance of God, a God who liberates and governs, who makes himself present to the earthly needs of his people. The eschatological perspective must also yield to this earthly evidence: the living God gives satisfaction and makes the heart and flesh of the living rejoice (*Ps* 84:3), not those of the dead.

Hence the hope for a messiah king, modelled on David, the king *par excellence*.

> I will be a father to him, and he shall be a son to me. When he commits iniquity, I will chasten him a rod such as mortals use, with blows inflicted by human beings. But I will not take my steadfast love from him, as I took it from Saul, whom I put away from before you. Your house and your kingdom shall be made sure for ever before me; your throne shall be established forever (*2 Sam* 7:14–16).

Someone who can make the people free from foreign domination and slavery, and thus be a new Moses. Someone who can enable them to inhabit the land that has been given to them, and thus be a new Joshua.

Above all, however, someone who liberates from the injustice that characterises human relationships. Someone who brings true peace, who enables one to live with others fully and justly. A desire that is valid for everyone, and for all times, but which takes on dramatic tones in the face of those who are crushed by injustice and the normal difficulties of politics. Those who for so many reasons are poor, sick or have been struck by misfortune – as is the case with widows. Those who are unjustly accused by someone who is more powerful than they are, or who are forced to become servants or slaves in order to repay a debt or to be able to feed themselves and their children.

For all these, the hope is that from the root of Jesse, that is, from the Davidic lineage, a new ruler may arise:

> He shall not judge by what his eyes see,
> or decide by what his ears hear;
> but with righteousness he shall judge for the poor,
> and decide with the equity for the oppressed of the earth;
> he shall strike the earth with the rod of his mouth,
> and with the breath of his lips he shall kill the wicked.
> Righteousness shall be the belt around his waist,
> and faithfulness the belt around his loins (*Is* 11:3–5).

A kingdom of justice, especially for those who cannot take justice into their own hands. This ideal is embodied by the king, but it is not directly his work, nor is it the response to a legitimate demand. Indeed, the concreteness of life teaches that if justice is only a demand, even if legitimate, it will be disappointed (*Qoh* 3:16; 5:7; 7:15). The biblical peculiarity is that "the defence of the weak, of the poor does not arise from a right that comes from below, but is the explication of a demand that comes from God, who is by definition just and liberator".[1] This is why the very boundaries of this hope do not coincide with the boundaries of human possibilities but with those of the creative hand of God.

> The wolf shall live with the lamb,
> the leopard shall lie down with the kid,
> the calf and the lion will feed together,
> and a little child shall lead them.
> The cow and the bear shall graze,
> their young shall lie down together;
> and the lion shall eat straw like the ox.
> The nursing child shall play over the hole of the asp,
> and the weaned child shall put its hand on the adder's den (*Is* 11:6–8).

The hope expressed in the idea of the messiah-king is the government of God, a direct theocracy over all creation or, if you prefer, the return of God to walk in his garden. That is why whoever embodies this figure, whether a historical king or a future one, will be nothing but a servant.

Of course, Israel is well aware that, in reality, this is a dream. This is why the monarchical institution always remains veiled in a shadow. The request to have a king "like other nations" (*1 Sam* 8:5) risks being a refusal to answer to God directly: "They have rejected me from being king over them" (*1 Sam* 8:7). As for the king, one can well imagine how he will behave in reality:

> He will take your sons and appoint them […] to plow his ground and to reap his harvest […] He will take your daughters to be perfumers and cooks and bakers. He will take the best of your fields, your vineyards and olive orchards and give them to his courtiers (*1 Sam* 8:11–14).

One must, therefore, hope for a strong king – otherwise he will not have the power to change anything – but, at the same time, one capable of not turning into a dictator. The prophet Zechariah's image of a king who is "triumphant

---

1   CIOLA, *Gesù Cristo Figlio di Dio*, 170.

and victorious [is he], humble and riding on a donkey, on a colt, the foal of a donkey" (*Zech* 9:9) is meant to hold out hope for someone who embodies power and meekness together. Power to do something, meekness not to do too much or do it too badly.

One could object that this is a dream of paternity or paternalism and not of brotherhood, but that would be an error in perspective. In fact, the content of this dream does not lie in the relationship with the monarch-father. Precisely because of its constitutive ambiguities, this figure must remain in the background, guarantee the conditions and step aside. What emerges in the foreground, instead, are the concrete relationships between the persons – or between all the creatures – that must have those characteristics of respect, freedom and debate that characterise a proper fraternity. In the end, for this to succeed, it is not God who must change: we must change, reality must change.

## 2     A Changing World

### 2.1    *The Thaumaturge*

The most powerful sign of a real change brought about by Jesus were his miracles. In the last two centuries, the culture of Modernity has not been comfortable with Jesus' activity as exorcist and thaumaturge. Miracles tend to be set aside or interpreted as symbols. A large proportion of Christians today believe *in spite of* miracles, not *because of* miracles. A smaller number, on the other hand, still regard them in the manner described in the *Acts of the Apostles*: "Jesus of Nazareth, a man attested to you by God with deeds of power, wonders, and signs" (*Acts* 2:22). Much more polarised than in the 1st century, when it comes to miracles, believers today are divided between sceptics and enthusiasts. In the Gospels, on the other hand, there are no sceptics. There is hardly any discussion of Jesus' miracles; if at all, whether they came from God or Satan. A problem that no one seems to ask today with respect to extraordinary works. Instead, there are the enthusiasts, who are interested in Jesus precisely because he performs signs. They range from those who, "believed in his name because they saw the signs that he was doing" (*Jn* 2:23), to Herod Antipas who "had been wanting to see him for a long time because he had heard about him and was hoping to see him perform some sign" (*Lk* 23:8). Jesus is cautious about this enthusiasm: "Unless you see signs and wonders, you will not believe" (*Jn* 4:48).

It is essential to place Jesus' activity as a thaumaturge and exorcist in the context of his time. Not only for historical reasons, but also because it plays a strategic role in understanding the reasons that led to his death.

> Any historian who seeks to portray the historical Jesus without giving due weight to his fame as a miracle-worker is not delineating this strange and complex Jew, but rather a domesticated Jesus reminiscent of the bland moralist created by Thomas Jefferson. […] His miracle-working activity not only supported but also dramatized and actuated his eschatological message, and it may have contributed to some degree to the alarm felt by the authorities who finally brought about his death.[2]

Precisely because the ancient world was not sceptical about miracles, it was inclined to grasp an aspect of them that is in danger of being overlooked today, even by enthusiasts. In a society without ophthalmologists, dermatologists, orthopaedic surgeons and psychiatrists, in a world without hospitals or centres for the care of the disabled, without painkillers or anti-psychotics, the only possibility for many was a miracle. This is the most straightforward attitude to Jesus' reputation as a healer: people in need, for themselves or for others, and who come to him hoping that their situation might change. They are not looking for the extraordinary that will bring some excitement to the ordinary; instead, they are looking for the extraordinary that will bring the ordinary back to its normality. They seek something that will take away the deformity, the pain, the difficulty in living. Knowing whether the cause of the evil is a demon, a psychic (or psychosomatic) illness, a tumour or whatever, is unimportant. The diagnosis is of interest to the doctor, much less to the patient. And, actually, Jesus does not seem to mind. He does not ask first what the origin of the evil is. He eliminates it, whatever kind it is, and returns the person to his strength, his dignity, his home: to his normality. The normality of seeing, of walking, of being able to "sitting there, clothed and in his right mind" (*Mk* 5:15) in the midst of others.

Remarkably, Jesus also shows the same attitude towards an 'evil' that we tend to put in a different category from physical evils, namely, sin. This too is treated by Jesus in the same way. It must be removed so that the person can return to life. An attitude that is difficult for a judge to understand but very evident to one who is weary with being the evil person that he or she is. Even when it is someone's *fault*, evil is still evil that prevents one from living. And it must be removed. Emblematic of this attitude are the case of the sinner (*Lk* 7:36–50), but even more so of the paralytic (*Mk* 2:3–12): Jesus does not distinguish physical evil and moral evil – forgiving sins or making people walk seem to him the same thing. If anything, one senses that what he is really interested in is forgiveness, and that the patient must be put in the condition to receive it, physical, mental and moral, and go on his or her way.

---

2  MEIER, *A Marginal Jew.* 2, 1235.

What is remarkable about Jesus, however, is not the fine words, but the fact that what he says happens. "For he taught them as one having authority and not as their scribes" (*Mt* 7:29). "What is this? A new teaching – with authority! He commands even the unclean spirits, and they obey him!" (*Mk* 1:27). Jesus' authority does not consist primarily in the fact that he is morally authoritative, a consistent and trustworthy person, but in the fact that he demonstrates the ability to change reality. This is what is extraordinary; whether he achieves it with kind words or by putting dirt and spit in someone's eyes is irrelevant: "I do not know whether he [Jesus] is a sinner. One thing I do know, that though I was blind, now I see" (*Jn* 9:25).

Jesus is not first and foremost one who speaks, but one who acts, who is able to change reality. This is the main reason why he has a following, in a world of people who need and hope to see their lives changed in practical terms.

## 2.2 The Kingdom is Here

This point is crucial. In Jesus, the new world, where there will be no injustice, no pain, no evil – Isaiah's dream of a universal brotherhood – is claimed to be real. "The blind receive their sight; the lame walk; those with a skin disease are cleansed; the deaf hear; the dead are raised; the poor have good news brought to them" (*Lk* 7:22). The future Kingdom is powerfully present, and Jesus is the mighty one who announces and realises it. John the Baptist awaited the Kingdom brought by one more powerful than himself. Now the Kingdom has arrived, and the powerful one is Jesus.

This is an eschatological assumption that was as difficult to accept yesterday as it is today. For those who believe in God, it can be taken for granted that God *will* reign. Tomorrow, elsewhere. And it can also be taken for granted that God does reign, *in general*. After all, he made the world and it is in his hands. It is another thing to believe that the fullness of God's rule over the world is realised *now, here*, in this specific house.

Yet, without this homespun eschatology, one cannot understand some of Jesus' more original positions, or one is forced to turn them into moralistic and vague appeals. We have already seen Jesus' view on divorce (*cf.* above, ch. 4, § 3). If interpreted as a moral project, it is untenable and also false: one who leaves one woman and marries another is not always an adulterer – in the sense of morally reprehensible. This is something our age perceives clearly. And, indeed, it is not a moral appeal but an eschatological consequence. *If it is* true that *we are* in the Kingdom, I can even think of living with this woman, no matter how unbearable she seems to me at the moment. But, in the Kingdom, many things can happen. ...

The same applies to the beatitudes. The tension between the eschatological appeal and the attempt to reduce it to a moral perspective is so strong that one finds traces of it in the Gospels themselves. The clearest example is that relating to poverty. In *Matthew*, we find: "Blessed are the poor in spirit, for theirs is the kingdom of heaven" (*Mt* 5:3). In *Luke*, on the other hand: "Blessed are you who are poor, for yours is the kingdom of God" (*Lk* 6:20). *Matthew* turns this, like the other beatitudes, into exhortations to attain one or other moral virtue: meekness, mercy, purity, etc. (*Mt* 5:3–10). *Luke*, on the other hand, reports the domestic, eschatological proclamation: this poor man, this hungry man (for bread, not for justice), this one who weeps: all these are already blessed *now* because the Kingdom is here and it will change their lot. Now, immediately. Even for sinners, as in the case of Zacchaeus: "Today salvation has come to this house" (*Lk* 19:9).

The Kingdom is, therefore, very close. I do not think it is worth wasting too much time figuring out how much is present and how much is future. "The precise relationship between the coming and the present kingdom remains unspecified".[3] Much more interestingly, however, is that this presence has consequences; it does not go unnoticed. It evidently has positive results for those who are healed or liberated. Already, for the relatives and friends around, things can be complicated. In the episode – curious enough – of the legion of demons driven out into a herd of swine and drowned in the lake (*Mt* 8:28–34; *Mk* 5:1–20; *Lk* 8:26–39), which results in a possessed person finally being able to return home among his own people, the reaction is fear: "Then all the people of the surrounding country of the Gerasenes asked Jesus to leave them, for they were seized with great fear" (*Lk* 8:37). Every sick person who used to sit at the city gate begging for alms will have to find a job once he is cured.

So there are practical relationships that change when reality changes, and new relationships – personal, economic, social – have to be redesigned. Morality enters a new perspective. The Kingdom present in the everyday requires a very different relationship with one another. And this is not a joke or a future appeal.

> You have heard that it was said to those of ancient times, "You shall not murder", and "whoever murders shall be liable to judgment". But I say to you that if you are angry with a brother or sister you will be liable to judgment, and if you insult a brother or sister, you will be liable to the council, and if you say, "You fool," you will be liable to the hell of fire (*Mt* 5:21–22).

One can understand that, at first, many admire the effectiveness of Jesus' word, but then, as soon as they realise the consequences it would entail, they begin to hold back. So are you then sure you want to enter this new world?

---

3  MEIER, *A Marginal Jew.* 2, 451.

## 3 Complex Inheritances Again

### 3.1 The Heir of the Poor

Jesus, however, does not give in. His conviction is, indeed, that the Kingdom is present and is being made effective in his own person and action.

In this royal perspective, Jesus enters Jerusalem as the promised messiah on the back of a donkey to testify that the Kingdom of justice and fraternity is present and that he is its king, meek and powerful at the same time (*Mt* 21:1–11). He is a true descendant of David, a true heir to the throne of power, because if, in the end, fraternity and justice do not become realities in law, powerful and effective realities in history, they are just a joke.

The triumphal entry into Jerusalem is, perhaps, an account that can claim little historical verisimilitude, yet, in its essence, this is how Jesus perceived himself – and this is how he died. As an (alleged) king.

But why? Why did he have to claim a royal function? To understand this, we must look at what is, perhaps, the most precious of the inheritances that Jesus collects and embodies. For Mary and Joseph, maybe, he might not even have been a king. That was fine. Not so for the poor.

Jesus chooses to share the inheritance of the little ones, the poor, the sinners. Their problems are his problems, their view of reality is his. All people for whom the world is no good if it remains as it is. They would remain poor, sick, sinners.

Especially for sinners, however, the coming of the Kingdom is as necessary as it is disturbing. Something must change radically for them to live a good and beautiful life again, and yet the appearance of this newness may turn out to be a catastrophe, a condemnation. Like warmth for hands and feet that are too cold, like light for those who have been too long in the dark. If the coming Kingdom does not take on their demands radically, it would be better if it did not come at all.

### 3.2 The Heir of His Disciples

The prophet of Nazareth has a following; he has chosen a following of people representing the twelve tribes of Israel, an eschatological symbol of the final reconstitution of a people. Only, the twelve are not a symbol at all in the same way that the rotten belt (*Jer* 13:1–11) or the broken jug (*Jer* 19) had been for the prophet Jeremiah; they are concrete people who bring with them expectations and perspectives. This, too, Jesus will have to take on, willingly or unwillingly.

The disciples are people who have followed a powerful one: one capable of changing reality. He has humble origins, yet can apparently boast of Davidic descent; he speaks with simplicity, yet seems to know and do great things. In the fourth Gospel, Nathanael is sceptical of the peripheral prophet and is then astonished when Jesus tells him that he has 'magically' seen him under the fig tree. The scene is emblematic and very realistic. Those who follow him are impressed by his miracles, his powers, his wisdom, and Jesus promises even greater things: "Do you believe because I told you that I saw you under the fig tree? You will see greater things than these!" (*Jn* 1:50).

They are people who follow one who changes reality and who have themselves changed their own reality, abandoning family or profession, the fishing nets or the customs post, embracing an itinerant lifestyle – albeit, for most of them, not much harder than the one they came from. They expect great things; that is why they follow him. They expect nothing more than what he promises, although each, as is normal, interprets this in his own way. They are convinced that they share the same power, we might say the same sonship as that of Jesus, or a similar one. The Father who gives Jesus the power to perform great deeds will also give them something similar.

> Then Jesus called the twelve together and gave them power and authority over all demons and to heal diseases, and he sent them forth to proclaim the kingdom of God and to heal the sick (*Lk* 9:1–2).
> After this the Lord appointed seventy-two others and sent them on ahead of him in pairs to every town and place where he himself intended to go [...]. The seventy-two returned with joy, saying, "Lord, in your name even the demons submit to us". He said to them, "I watched Satan fall from heaven like a flash of lightning. Indeed, I have given you authority to tread on snakes and scorpions and over all the power of the enemy, and nothing will hurt you. Nevertheless, do not rejoice at this, that the spirits submit to you, but rejoice that your names are written in heaven" (*Lk* 10:1.17–20).

They have legitimate expectations; nothing strange there. They have left much, or at least what little they had, to follow one who has power, and they expect a reward. Jesus openly supports their expectation:

> Truly I tell you, there is no one who has left house or wife or brothers or parents or children, for the sake of the kingdom of God, who will not get back very much more in this age, and in the age to come eternal life (*Lk* 18:29–30).
> You are those who have stood by me in my trials, and I confer on you, just as my Father has conferred on me, a kingdom, so that you may eat and drink at my table in my kingdom, and you will sit on thrones judging the twelve tribes of Israel (*Lk* 22:28–30).

James and John are not simply naive when they ask: "Appoint us to sit, one at your right hand and one at your left, in your glory" (*Mk* 10:37). They express a legitimate expectation, and not to understand this is to fail to understand the concrete expectations that Jesus nurtured.

At the same time, it is normal for the disciples to ask what the limits of this 'sharing' of power and sonship are. "Master, we saw someone casting out demons in your name, and we tried to stop him, because he does not follow with us" (*Lk* 9:49). Does this stranger also share Jesus' power? Or is he to be treated as a stranger, as an enemy?

Things become disconcerting, however, when we see *the mighty one* who, until the end, will expressly interpret his own figure with the texts of *Daniel* as the one who comes "in clouds with great power and glory" (*Mk* 13:26 and *cf. Mt* 26:64), looking more and more like the suffering *servant* of *Isaiah*, one whose beard is pulled off and whose face is spat in (*cf. Is* 50:6), "from whom others hide their faces" (*Is* 53:3).

This too is an inheritance, a burden of expectation before which Jesus cannot simply shrug his shoulders but to which he must respond. In this sense, Judas is not only the traitor, the one who did not understand, but represents an open, complex question that remains addressed to the Master. We do not know what motivated him to betrayal. The Gospels seem to point to greed. Yet even the Gospels cannot hide that this motivation is insufficient. Judas will return the money he received; this was not what he was looking for.

Jesus approaches his destiny, therefore, as the one who bears a multiple inheritance. That of a merciful and paternal image of God, bequeathed by the prophets, underlying the whole religious vision of Israel and embodied in many of the people closest to him, but also that of a poor, sick and treacherous people who naturally distrust that there can be anything for them, any hope, much less a concrete reality. He is also the heir of his own disciples in whom he himself has raised expectations that he will then have to honour or disappoint.

All this can only alert him to the fact that things can end very badly. There are too many complex bonds that bind him. Loyalty to an imminent, indeed present, eschatological dream in which he will be the one to whom are given "dominion and glory and kingship" (*Dan* 7:14). And yet, in this dream, great upheavals and afflictions are foretold which leave the prophet who has seen them disturbed (*Dan* 7:15–28). He is also heir to a prophetic tradition always at risk, compelled to announce salvation to the "descendants of those who murdered the prophets" (*Mt* 23:31). His own master, the Baptist, the last of the prophets, ended badly. And not for having announced conversion and the Kingdom in the abstract, but for a few words spoken against Herod Antipas, the last of the reigning kings and, in his own way, the meanest. When the word of the eschatological prophet claims not to be just a vague appeal, but to affect the flesh of reality, this flesh rebels like a wounded animal or gets aroused like an animal in springtime. And it kills.

But, above all, Jesus makes the claim to collect the inheritance owed to a mass of poor and sinful, marginalised, people who might have had a chance to change their condition, and did not. He wants to do it for them, to take charge of them. The brotherhood he demands for each one is first and foremost a necessity for him: considering even the unpresentable as brothers.

Everything suggests that, when the time comes, they will be the ones who will judge what he is doing as excessive and turn against him.

## 4    Contested Fraternity

The claim of our universal brotherhood is so patently false that it is not worth contesting. At the same time, however, it is difficult to contest Jesus on this point because of the miracles, i.e. because of his power. "This man is performing many signs" (*Jn* 11:47). Jesus' authority and power were not considered objectionable in his time: he was, indeed, able to change reality. All the evidence says that we are *not* brothers – except in a poetic sense or as a vague wish – and yet he seems to have the power to create a world of brothers and sisters.

Precisely because it is about power, however, the question immediately becomes one of limits and sharing. Is this power yours or will you give it to others? Even to us? And what will be the limits of this supposed brotherhood? Our group? Our people? Everyone? The fact that in the *Acts of the Apostles* and in Paul the word 'brother' refers to *Christians* is a clear sign of the difficulty of extending brotherhood concretely beyond the boundaries of the small group of followers.

The contestation on brotherhood is the most serious as it cannot be considered a dream. It touches too closely on concrete relationships, the way of being in the world. Affirming and practising it puts at risk many things – more or less serious.

Firstly, it puts everyone's own power at risk. If we are all brothers, every right of superiority, of supremacy, of order, simply leaps away. Fraternal relations require that we call no one master, no one father (*cf. Mt* 23:8). It skips every right of kings, of priests, of the rich. But it also skips any right of fathers or elder brothers. All brothers and no more. Or rather: every kingship, priesthood or wealth, every paternity or right is subjected to fraternity. And so it is rescaled and distorted. It is not only the great of this world who are bothered; there is hardly anyone who is so miserable that he does not have his own little power, a street corner in which he is lord and not brother. Many in Jesus' time may have perceived that his action endangered their power, as high priest, as soldier, as smallholder, as king.

However, this is not just a petty revolt of the powerful, big and small. Behind it there is a greater risk and objection. These small powers, in fact, represent the rights of this world that see themselves threatened by the proclamation of the Kingdom. 'You announce a new world. What about the old, the present, ours? In the name of the Kingdom, you blow it up! What you would like to save, you are actually destroying ... You are our enemy!' This is perhaps the most powerful and painful objection addressed to Jesus.

*You are the enemy of life.* What real relationships are possible if the only form you envisage is that of fraternity? Real life does not work that way. It remains exposed and vulnerable. It does *not* work. One cannot be a brother to the poor and the Roman invader, to Herod and Caesar, who for that matter have no intention of being brothers, much less to Jesus, as will be seen. The result of a world of equals would be pale, sad, resentful of all flair and superiority. It is a classic accusation that will be levelled at Christianity over the centuries. To be the enemy of life in the name of exalting misery.[4]

*You are the enemy of this world.* The same force that changes the world destroys it, challenges it, at the same time. The Kingdom is the judgement of this world. But this world also has rights to the Kingdom. The world is not all bad, all to be changed. It is not all sin and all sinners. The frequent use of the word 'world' – in *John* in particular – as that which is simply opposed to God speaks volumes about the esteem that Jesus' message induces towards reality. To be able to hand over the bill of repudiation and thus be able to divorce – instead of killing one's wife – is one of the rules we have found to live by; to pluck out one's eye instead of killing the whole family and setting fire to the house is one of the compromises we have found to manage social relations. Jesus proposes a ban on divorce and invites us to do good to those who do us harm. It is a radical challenge to the most basic rules of coexistence. In the name of what? Of *another* world, which no one has ever seen, of which it is not clear whether it has arrived, is coming or will arrive. The history of Christianity shows many of the nuances that can be given to this hypothetical Kingdom: it is already realised, it is us, and whoever does not conform is done away with; it will arrive shortly and it will be the end of the world; it is the other world, future, and it is opposed to the vale of tears that is this present life. Too many possible interpretations. And then one can

---

4 *Cf.* F. NIETZSCHE, *The Anti-Christ, Ecce Homo, Twilight of the Idols, and Other Writings*, Cambridge University Press, Cambridge New York 2005, 1–68.

already see where this will lead. A world of brothers will be a world that, deprived of its powers and lords, will set one against the other: "brother will betray brother to death" (*Mt* 10:21), each with his own dream of a future or present world. Fratricidal war will no longer be an aberration but a right of all these sons and brothers who have the possibility of choosing and living in the name of a world that does not exist.

*You are an enemy of God.* Finally, is God at least safeguarded himself from the spread of brotherhood? Or does he too become the friend and brother of men? This is not a provocation. The God of Jesus does indeed seem to put himself on a dangerously equal level with his creatures, face to face, heart to heart. Ambiguity can be maintained up to a certain point. Then it will have to be clarified whether brotherhood is really the criterion for every relationship – which means reciprocity, equality, dialogue, dialectics and conflict. Even for God, who will end up involved and entangled in our human relationships. Too high for man and too low for God.

But let us even assume that things are as Jesus seems to suggest. To the extent that brotherhood has indeed to be the guiding principle, a tough stand by the brothers against Jesus himself becomes inevitable. Not the revolt of the petty, but the autonomous voice of brothers who, at this point, have the right to speak and judge.

*A word of law for the leaders* – one for all, Caiaphas. He brings the reasons of a society and a world in balance, the reasons of one who cares for his brothers and fears that the new world will simply destroy the old, dragging it into chaos. Of course, he also brings the reasons of his own power, which is, however, legitimate – he did not kill anyone to become high priest! His reason overwhelms Pilate because it confronts him with a simple choice – and a just and well expressed one at that. The choice is between two social and political orders: one is Caesar – the paternal and hierarchical, but existing – the other is Jesus – the fraternal and equal, but only a dream. Caiaphas has chosen, perhaps to defend himself and the *status quo*, perhaps to defend his people; in practice, Pilate has nothing to choose from.

*A word of law for the righteous* – elder brothers who have laboured and toiled. Will they really be treated equally with sinners and the lost? Will everyone really receive an equal share in the inheritance, as among brothers? This is like saying that their lives, their efforts, count for nothing.

*A word of law for sinners.* In truth, these had already spoken their word. They had decided that they did not want to treat *anyone* as a brother. Are they to be treated as brothers too, against their own will? One can save a *partial* brotherhood by excluding the wicked. But if they too are to be involved in the inheritance, one will find oneself taking into one's house the very ones who want to destroy it.

The call to brotherhood is a call to involvement, to the sharing of power and right. To the extent that Jesus really wants to give others the right to speak, to listen to their voice, he exposes himself to the risk that this word will become a chorus of death – a risk which will become a reality. The dignified and free brothers agree in their condemnation.

At this point, rather than questions about Jesus, questions remain about God. Did God really give this man all this power? Did God really give the brothers power over this man? Jesus will use the last days of his life to try to answer the questions and contestations that have been put to him by men.

Before listening to his answer, however, I would like to consider one last cause that might have led to his death, very different from these previous ones, in that it is a faceless motive, a murder without a killer.

## Bibliographical Guidelines

The **contestations** addressed to Jesus are not destined to go away, and the history of Christianity can be read as a continuous re-emergence of some of these insoluble knots. Perhaps the most interesting perspective for re-reading the occurrence of these tensions and challenges is to look at them from the point of 16th century Europe. Here, in the confrontation with the birth of the modern subject, the same difficulties had to be re-addressed under new conditions.

This certainly applies to the knot that links God's **fatherhood** to forgiveness, freedom and grace. On the one hand, there are those who, starting from God the Father, tend to emphasise trust and abandonment to the point of making human freedom evanescent and the whole of humanity sinful (i.e. the Augustinian-Lutheran line), and, on the other, those who, starting from God the Father, tend to stress filial dignity to the point of leaving the suspicion that they save themselves (the Thomist-Ignatian line). The clash between Augustine and Pelagius seems to have no possible solution in the history of Western Christianity. In order to put an end to the sixteenth-century dispute between Báñez and de Molina, after ten years, Pope Paul V ordered the parties to discuss their own perspectives without censuring their neighbour (cf. DH 1997; R. OSCULATI, *La teologia cristiana nel suo sviluppo storico. II. Secondo millennio*, San Paolo, Cinisello Balsamo 1997, 315–320); in 1748, Benedict XIV (like Paul V before him) was to support Augustinianism, although setting as a principle the lawfulness of the different theological schools in the name of a church that "favours the freedom of schools [and] up to now has not reproved any of the ways proposed to reconcile human freedom and divine omnipotence" (DH 2565; J.-Y. LACOSTE (ed.), *Histoire de* *la théologie*, Éditions du Seuil, Paris 2009, 340). Rather than being a symptom of the contentiousness of the Christian fraternity, it seems to me to be the sign of a conflict of freedom that, starting from the proclamation of God's paternity and his forgiveness, has no solution: for a parent, the balance between gift, prevarication, respect and violence is always provisional and susceptible to being evaluated at the same time, in different ways.

The discussion on the limits of **sonship** is also endless. It can be summed up in one question: for whom are the beatitudes (the children's law) intended, and to whom do the Ten Commandments remain? It is clear that the solution whereby the sons of the beatitudes are priests and monks while the commandments suffice for everyone else does not work, even though it is, in fact, the medieval solution (cf. G. LAFONT, *Histoire théologique de l'Église catholique. Itinéraire et formes de la théologie*, Les Éditions du Cerf, Paris 1994, 128–129). Even the Reformation, however, which would make opposition to these divisions its banner, would find its difficulties in applying the beatitudes to the government of the city, and, above all, in managing its limits. "Zwingli soon found himself confronted with the most radical interpretation of Christian and evangelical ethics, according to which the communion of goods of the primitive Jerusalem community is the only social context consistent with the spirit of Jesus, and the public violence of law and arms and oaths is to be rejected. Then, with a very convoluted interpretation of the New Testament message, he will highlight, as had already been the case for Luther, the impossibility of fully realising the gospel in today's world, which must stand on a lower moral plane. […] Zwingli's ethics thus assume a dual aspect of valorisation of the social commitment to order, harmony and collaboration, referring a more effective imitation of the human life of Christ back to personal intimacy. The humanity of the vagabond and crucified master could be elevated against the pompous and hypocritical Roman system, but then it became incapable of effectively guiding the public and private interests of a flourishing community, dominated by an industrial, commercial and banking bourgeoisie, loving order and alien to revolutionary and pauperistic follies. When, therefore, the hated preachers of the invalidity of infant baptism and the need for a new baptism that implied the literal acceptance of the evangelical ethic [Anabaptists] appeared in Zurich, Zwingli also considered the application of the Old Testament and Roman law of the death penalty to be necessary, thus also placing his reform in a very ambiguous light" (OSCULATI, *La teologia cristiana nel suo sviluppo storico. II*, 238–239). Here, too, it cannot just be a matter of the personal inability of individuals. There is something in the initial message, in the very possibility of a sonship open to all, that dramatically impacts reality.

The real challenge, however, lies in **fraternity**. A Christian Europe which basically shared the bulk of ideas about Christ and the Trinity was to end up torn by division in the Thirty Years' War. The 16th and 17th centuries seem to have been a theatre where all against all is staged. And all Christians, all brothers. Without understanding the link between this violence and the claim of Christian filial dignity and freedom, one cannot understand the Enlightenment and deist reaction of the following century. In the face of violence between Christians, it seemed a possible way out to appeal to something less free and aligned, such as reason. In this sense, the 19th century accusations that define Christianity as the 'enemy of life' must also be grasped in their complexity. There may be the challenge of Christian weakness, a religion of infants, women, the weak and slaves; all resentful of every manifestation of strength and life (Nietzsche). But there is also the trace of the massacres that these weak and resentful people have been able to perpetrate, sometimes in the name of order (Marx), sometimes in the name of their rights. Indeed, what happens if the servant/master dialectic does not find an agreement that defines one as master and the other as servant (Hegel)? The permanent civil war between brothers: no one slave and no one master, but also no one in peace, ever.

For **fraternity**: PONTIFICAL BIBLICAL COMMISSION, *What Is Man? A Journey Through Biblical Anthropology*, Darton, Longman & Todd Ltd, London 2021, cap. III.3 and IV.3; G.C. PAGAZZI, *C'è posto per tutti. Legami fraterni, paura, fede*, Vita e pensiero, Milano 2008; S. DIANICH – C. TORCIVIA, *Forme del popolo di Dio fra comunità e fraternità*, San Paolo, Cinisello Balsamo 2012; A.M. BAGGIO (ed.), *Il principio dimenticato. La fraternità nella riflessione politologica contemporanea*, Città Nuova, Roma 2007; G. OSTO, *Come olio profumato. Scorribande sulla fraternità*, Cittadella, Assisi 2018; *La fraternità*, in Parola Spirito e Vita 77 (2018).

Interesting paths could be pursued in this sphere in the monastic rules, for example (C. FALCHINI (ed.), *Abitare come fratelli insieme. Regole monastiche d'Occidente*, Qiqaion, Magnano 2016) and in the life and work of the 'universal brother', Charles de Foucauld (CH. DE FOUCAULD, *Oeuvres spirituelles. Antologie*, Éditions du Seuil, Paris 1959; J.-F. SIX, *Itinéraire spirituel de Charles de Foucauld*, Editions du Seuil, Paris 1958, 272–303; MD. SEMERARO, *Charles de Foucauld. Esploratore e profeta della fraternità universale*, San Paolo, Cinisello Balsamo 2016), as well as the proposal to read Pope Francis' Evangelii gaudium and much of his magisterium through the lens of fraternity (E. CASTELLUCCI, *Una «carovana solidale». La fraternità come stile dell'annuncio in Evangelii gaudium*, San Paolo, Cinisello Balsamo 2018; C. THEOBALD, *Fraternità. Il nuovo stile della Chiesa secondo papa Francesco*, Qiqaion, Magnano 2016 and, in a different vein, J.C. SCANNONE, *La teología del pueblo. Raíces teológicas del papa Francisco*, Éditions Lessius, Bruxelles 2017, 181–274). The entire theme of fraternity should be taken up in the light of Pope Francis' very recent encyclical *Fratelli tutti* (2020); this text has the merit of not unbalancing itself on the theological foundation of the concept of fraternity in order to keep open the horizon of Pope Francis' fundamental interest, that is, the hope that fraternity can be the way that, for all, makes it possible to face the current social and cultural urgencies: communication, technology, migration, marginalisation, populism, tension between local and global, coexistence between religions and cultures. Against any attempt to relegate fraternity to an intimistic and private concept.

CHAPTER 7

# Towards Death (4). Chance

## 1   A Faceless Enemy

### 1.1   *A Contemporary Demand for Salvation*

The attempt to consider *chance* among the possible causes of Jesus' death certainly places what is being attempted here within the framework of a contemporary theological operation. This question interests us, much more than it did the early Christian authors. Indeed, their effort was often to deny that something like chance, fate or destiny existed. It was an effort to affirm both man's freedom and God's providence. As will be evident, it is not my intention to deny either one or the other but, rather, to try to respond to a need for salvation that seems to me very acute in our time. In a world where scientific explanations cover such a large part of our experience, the first result is that of greater security. We know the causes of what happens to us. Yet, as this security is extended, a spectre also arises: one which insinuates the idea that, within all this ordered mechanism, there is no room for what concerns the individual, me. In the end, an armoured mechanism. The reasons for my life and my attempt to make sense of what happens to me are in danger of being overwhelmed. The space for my story is reduced to zero.

A few examples are worth more than a definition, a difficult one at that. The fact that someone runs me over, that I suddenly fall ill, that I meet an old love at a party, that it is fine weather on the day I could go skiing, but also the place where I was born or the current laws on retirement: these are random facts, not because they are without causes – there are causes, and today we can identify them better than yesterday – but because, on the whole, these facts *reach me by chance*. Their consequences *for me*, especially in the negative examples, seem so disproportionate to the causes or to their own reality that it is difficult to identify their *meaning*. The guy driving the car is a good person; he just got distracted by his mobile phone, and yet I am now lying on the ground.

A situation such as this, which grows with the advance of scientific knowledge, poses a specific soteriological problem. What is to be done? How should such situations be dealt with? It is a very different landscape from the one faced by, say, a man in the Middle Ages. At the risk of caricaturing him, we can say that, for him, almost everything was inexplicable. He had no explanatory and predictive theory of the development of diseases or of the reproduction of plants and animals or of the formation of clouds in the sky. With so many uncertainties, what remained was really only the power of freedom and trust in God's providence. This is not the case today.

For this reason, i.e. for theological-soteriological reasons, it seems to me important to leave the hypothesis of chance open and try to take it seriously. Like many of our lives and deaths, Jesus' too may have encountered that particular phenomenon we call 'chance'. How did he deal with it? How did he judge it? In the end, the weightier question is: how did he *redeem it*? How is his style in living and taking charge of the whole human experience still significant for all those biographies that chance has blessed or cursed, exalted or destroyed?

All of us have witnessed events in which chance has turned against someone. Sometimes we have looked away because we have seen a life, which, until then, had been great and worthy, end in a miserable way, bent and humiliated by events. At other times, on the other hand, we have been moved to admiration: we have seen how one can bear the blows of fate with dignity, with grit and with beauty. In Italy, the cases of Bebe Vio or Alex Zanardi remain remarkable examples of how a woman and a man, a young girl and an adult, were able to face disaster and emerge from it with courage, flair and beauty, whatever the outcome. The same applies to the opposite cases, those that fate did not bring down but raised. Not everyone reacts well to a great fortune – be it an unexpected inheritance or a fabulous sum on a scratch card. Lives can be devastated by good luck as well as misfortune, and this raises a soteriological question. How does one save one's humanity in such events? The risk is that, for this specific request for salvation, so typical of our times, Jesus simply has nothing to say.

### 1.2  *Unexpected Aid*

At the risk of inserting a digression into the discourse, I would like to point out that one of the possible ways of tackling the challenge of chance is through the observation that unexpected help can come, precisely from the scientific disciplines that have raised the perception of this problem. Before being soteriological, in fact, the question was posed to other disciplines as a biological one. 'How does life handle the randomness that invests it? What does it do with it?'

This is neither to deny any randomness nor to overestimate it but to recognise its specific role and the specific way in which life interacts with it. The result is rather interesting on the whole when one can see chance in action, in relation to the formation and functioning of the human brain, for example.

## 1.2.1   Chance and Genetics

Sexual reproduction makes important use of chance. The DNA of each of us is a random mix of that of our parents – not counting mistakes and *crossing-overs*[1] which increase the randomness of the process even further. One could define sexual reproduction as a refined *generator of diversity*,[2] thus emphasising that this randomness is not useless but is put at the service of increasing the internal diversity of the biological population and the species, helping to improve its resilience and adaptability.

## 1.2.2   Chance and Brain

Even more interesting – and perhaps less obvious – is the observation that our brain is restless, i.e. it spontaneously produces fluctuations. This is because important regions of the brain function with activation thresholds; a relatively insignificant fluctuation can be the straw that breaks the camel's back and spontaneously activate a brain circuit.

> By spontaneously generating fluctuating patterns of activity, even in the absence of external stimulation, the global workspace allows us to freely generate new plans, try them out, and change them at will if they fail to fulfil our expectations.[3]

## 1.2.3   Chance and Experience

The place, however, where chance plays the most decisive role is not with what is inside us, our genes and brain, but with what is outside us. For our brain is not a computer that comes out of the factory with a preinstalled programme; it creates its own connections and develops itself through interaction with the environment. This is something we have evidence of in the development of children: they become what they are – and so does their brain – through genetic endowment and through interaction with the outside world. And it is here that chance intervenes in the most massive way. Indeed, even the best educator cannot plan or predict the series of events that will contribute to shaping a child. It is the concrete history of that individual that will shape him or her. In fact, every biological life has a history,[4] is born, grows in a context,

---

1   *Cross-over* refers to the genetic recombination mechanism that allows the exchange of DNA segments between homologous chromosomes during meiosis.
2   *Cf.* G.M. EDELMAN, *Second Nature. Brain Science and Human Knowledge*, Yale University Press, New Haven – London 2006, 27; ID., *Wider than the sky. The Phenomenal Gift of Consciousness*, Yale University Press, New Haven – London 2004, 32–47.
3   S. DEHAENE, *Consciousness and the Brain. Deciphering How the Brain Codes Our Thoughts*, Viking Penguin, New York 2014, 204.
4   To describe the relationship between genetics and experience, Seung uses the happy image of the reciprocal relationship between the land and the flow of water to shape the course

makes encounters and dies. Wine, dogs and people are not indifferent to what 'happens' to them, precisely because they are alive.

In these examples, one can see how, from a biological point of view, a certain degree of randomness is not only tolerated but, indeed required in order to make the population of individuals richer and more resilient.[5] By integrating chance, one is also able to grasp how the uniqueness and historicity of the biological individual grow, along with their dependence on context, on interactions with the natural and social environment. From a biological point of view, a certain dependence on the context is always present, and yet, in the construction of the self, some living beings have the characteristic of being much more bound than others to the characteristics of what interacts with them; rather than being a limitation, this often turns out to be an evolutionary advantage as it allows the individual to construct the *patterns* of his or her own adaptive responses from the contextual specificity in which he or she lives.

This is certainly not a soteriological proposal; yet here we are offered a promising perspective on the singularity, uniqueness and historicity of a living creature. If nothing else, it allows us to make of these characteristics something that binds us to other living beings rather than merely differentiating us. In fact, it reminds us that history – with its share of risk and drama[6] – was born well before us, with life itself; the same goes for the need to come to terms with the possibilities and limits of one's own personal history.

## 2   What is Chance?

The question remains, however, as to what chance actually is. It is precisely the scientific disciplines, in fact, that would lead us to think that chance does not exist. I will not attempt to give an account of the different philosophical

---

of a river: "'Earth tells water how to move' […], 'Water tells earth how to move.' I believe the stream inside our brain works in much the same way. The flow of neural activity through our connectomes drives our experiences of the present and leaves behind impressions that become our memories of the past" (S.S. SEUNG, *Connectome. How the Brain's Wiring Makes Us Who We Are*, Houghton Mifflin Harcourt, Boston (MA) 2012, 349).

5   This is the basic thesis of the classic, J. MONOD, *Chance and Necessity. An Essay on the Natural Philosophy of Modern Biology*, Vintage Books, New York 1972, 98: «Randomness caught on the wing, preserved, reproduced by the machinery of invariance and thus converted into order, rule, necessity.» For Monod, chance and necessity are not antithetical, but both contribute to evolution in different ways.

6   *Cf.* G. EDELMAN, *Bright Air, Brilliant Fire. On the Matter of the Mind*, Basic Books, New York 1992, 131–136 and 165–172.

or theological perspectives that can be taken on this but only to offer some insights into the phenomenon I am trying to describe.

## 2.1 A Theological Voice

Dealing with chance is always problematic in theology. Especially when one tries to apply this category to the central event of Christianity. The theologian who was perhaps most courageous in dealing with this issue in the last century was Romano Guardini. In *The Lord*, he repeatedly returns to the idea that the story of Jesus *did not have* to end as it did.

> Intellectual habit has made the fact that Jesus lived to be little over thirty almost self-understood. Automatically we think of him as one crucified after a short period of public activity. Actually, the prematureness of that death was not nearly as self-understood as we may suppose. True, he did say: "Did not the Christ have to suffer these things before entering into his glory?" (*Lk* 24:26). But this was a 'must' of love-God's love. From the human point of view, Golgotha was anything but 'necessary.' It was a monstrosity terrible beyond conception that this vessel overflowing with divine potentialities should have been broken so soon! [...] still it should have been otherwise, and it is incomprehensible that things went the way they did.[7]

Guardini grasps very well that, when we speak of chance, we are not talking about a specific or abnormal cause but about the effect that a set of causes have on the singularity of someone's life. "It goes without saying that there is no such thing as absolute chance. That would mean that something happens that is based neither on relations of necessity of things nor on the responsibility of freedom. Yet the feeling of chance exists".[8] What is missing is not a specific explanation but rather something that helps me place this fact within my own history. It is, precisely, a 'feeling' that has the power to question the meaningfulness of the world, of my world.

> The character of chance can be accentuated. It can reach absurdity, when an irrelevant cause, e.g. a small oversight, causes fatal events; or injustice, when an action gives rise to consequences that contradict the sentiment of morality, e.g. a misfortune from an action performed with the best of intentions; or wickedness and perfidy, when a petty thing destroys a great thing.[9]

---

7  R. GUARDINI, *The Lord*, Gateway Editions, Washington DC 1996, 36–37; 201.
8  ID., *Freiheit Gnade Schicksal. Drei Kapitel zur Deutung des Daseins (1948)*, Kösel Verlag, München 1956, 183.
9  ID., *Freiheit Gnade Schicksal*, 184.

Chance, therefore, moves to the edge of the absurd. This is why it is so dangerous for theology. It induces a specific temptation, that of using the absurd to deny chance itself. In order not to fall into nonsense, one denies chance. Instead, the effort should be to look into the face of this particular form that events can take, taking the strain from the shadow they cast over the feeling of our lives.

### 2.2  *The Word to Literature*

This aspect that is so difficult to deal with in theology or philosophy finds its form of expression *par excellence* in literature. The stories worth telling always incorporate this dimension because they force the protagonists to come to terms with it, to bring their choices and the concreteness of their actions into play in a framework where, at every turn, an unpredictable combination of events can overwhelm or save them. In the case of Carlo Emilio Gadda's unfinished novel, *Quer pasticciaccio brutto de via Merulana*, the random and entangled nature of events becomes the very theme of the tale, which – like the tale of the passion of Jesus – is the story of a murder with an open ending. In the very first pages of the novel, Doctor Ciccio Ingravallo is the spokesman for this random plot.

> He sustained, among other things, that unforeseen catastrophes are never the consequence or the effect, if you prefer, of a single motive, of *a* cause singular; but they are rather like a whirlpool, a cyclonic point of depression in the consciousness of the world, towards which a whole multitude of converging causes have contributed. [...] The opinion that we must "reform within ourselves the meaning of the category of cause," as handed down by the philosophers from Aristotle to Immanuel Kant, and replace cause with causes was for him a central, persistent opinion, almost a fixation. [...] The apparent motive, the principal motive was, of course, single. But the crime was the effect of a whole list of motives which had blown on it in a whirlwind (like the sixteen winds in the list of winds when they twist together in a tornado, in a cyclonic depression) and had ended by pressing into the vortex of the crime the enfeebled "reason of the world." Like wringing the neck of a chicken.[10]

With a beginning like that, it is already clear that the ending cannot be the solution to a riddle, as is often the case in mystery novels. Because life almost never goes like this; it does not offer a definitive and clear solution, which allows for closure and relaxation. Everything remains confused, even after the mystery is, to some extent, solved.

It is another police commissioner who speaks out for the complex reasons of reality against the simplifications of crime writers in a novel by

---

10   C.E. GADDA, *That Awful Mess of Via Merulana*, New York Review Books, New York 2000, 5–6.

Friedrich Dürrenmatt, significantly entitled *Das Versprechen. Requiem auf den Kriminalroman* [*The Pledge. A Requiem for the Crime Novel*]. It reflects on a crucial aspect of contemporary storytelling: without integrating chance, the tale will turn out to be contrived, more like a riddle than the narrative of true or plausible events.

In discussion with a mystery writer, the commissioner blurts out:

> No, what really annoys me is the plot in your novels. Here the fraud gets to be too raw and shameless. You build your plots up logically, like a chess game; here the criminal, here the victim, here the accomplice, here the mastermind. The detective need only know the rules and play the game, and he has the criminal trapped, has won a victory for justice. This fiction infuriates me. [...] but the factors that bollix up the works for us are so common that all too frequently only pure professional luck and chance decide the issue for us. Or against us. But in your novels chance plays no part, and if something looks like chance it's represented as some kind of destiny or divine dispensation. [...] An event cannot ever be solved like an equation because we never know all the necessary unknowns. We know only a few, and usually unimportant ones. Chance, the incalculable, the incommensurable, plays too great a part. Our rules are based only on probabilities, on statistics, not causality; they apply only in general and not in particular. The individual stands outside our calculations. [...] Drop the perfection if you want to get anywhere, if you want to get at things, at reality, which is what a man ought to be doing. Otherwise you'll be left way behind, fooling around with useless stylistic exercises.[11]

The talk will be resumed by the two protagonists at the end of the novel. The mystery will be solved, but there will be no peace for anyone. Precisely because chance will still have had a hand in things. And yet, in these final considerations, Dürrenmatt also opens up new perspectives for analysis.

> It is so ridiculous, stupid, and trivial that it would have to be suppressed if this story were to be set down on paper. [...] For the very fact that this gruesome point unfortunately does exist, that there is this element of incalculability, of chance, if you will, exposes his genius, his plans and actions as all the more painfully absurd in hindsight than was the case when in the opinion of everyone at headquarters he was mistaken. Nothing is grimmer than a genius stumbling over something idiotic. But when such a thing does happen, everything depends upon the attitude that the genius takes toward the ridiculous thing that has brought him to a fall, whether or not he accepts it. Matthäi could not accept it. He wanted his calculations to accord with reality. Therefore he had to deny reality, and end in a void.[12]

---

11   F. DÜRRENMATT, *The Pledge*, Signet Book, New York 1960, 13–14.
12   DÜRRENMATT, *The Pledge*, 122.

Dürrenmatt's perspective has the advantage of pointing out both the problem and an intriguing avenue for a solution: what makes a story fascinating is not the absence of chance, but witnessing the protagonist's genius in dealing with it. In the novel in question, the protagonist's drama lies precisely in being caught up in chance and not knowing how to deal with it, thus collapsing the whole affair into tragedy.

### 2.3   *An Attempt to Circumscribe the Chance*

What I am trying to describe, therefore, is something that, as Guardini argues, may well have one or more causes but whose effects are disproportionate to each person's feeling about his or her own life. It is something that has a close connection with the fact that animals, as biological beings, have a specific interest in their own lives. For an animal, the events that happen are not neutral but are positively or negatively connoted *for each one*. I have no problem with the fact that one can be distracted while driving – even I am sometimes –, I have a problem with the fact that a guy hit *me* today because he was distracted.

What then is chance? What are its boundaries? Wanting to place this concept within a broader semantic landscape and offering references to classical themes that touch on the history of Western thought, one could say the following.

As for its *modality, chance is not necessary*. In this sense, it maintains relations with terms like 'accidental', 'possible', 'contingent', 'random'. There is nothing metaphysical about being run over; it would have taken only a second and nothing would have happened.

As for *freedom, chance is unpremeditated*. Even if there is a freedom in what happened, the effects outweigh the intentions. The boy behind the wheel did not 'intend' to run me over, and God did not create the world 'for the purpose' of running me over, yet both are involved: too much to be excused, too little to be responsible. If they had intended it, the meaning would be recovered: there is nothing random about someone who, hating me, runs me over in order to kill me, nor would there be anything random about a God who wanted to punish me for my faults.

As for *knowledge, chance is (often) indeterminable*. The cause is there, yet I could not control or predict it. Hence a certain familiarity with terms like 'indeterminate', 'chaotic', but also 'complex' or 'statistical'.

As for *reality, chance is factual*. It is not merely possible, it is 'actual'. From this point of view, chance retains all the unique characteristics of individual, historical and biological facts.

It follows from all this that I cannot make sense of this event *a priori*, but, if at all, only *a posteriori*.

Something happened, therefore, without its being immediately attributable to a horizon of meaning for me, for us, for God or for anyone. All this becomes more evident in a world rich in scientific explanations, as ours is. The more we know about the causes and mechanisms that regulate reality, the more we have the feeling that all this is beyond us. The more everything has its own cause, the more the result is an inexplicable tangle with potentially devastating – or wonderful – consequences for me, from which I seem to be excluded.

## 3   The Chances of a Lifetime

Chance is not directly and systematically denied in the Gospels. Yet the atmosphere, both narrative and theological, that envelops the life of Jesus is such that chance does not seem to exist. Everything happens in its own time; every action is matched by a reaction, positive or negative, which seems to be part of a coherent framework, a plan. The theological reasons for this framework are clear. If the world is governed by the Father's presence, by his care, there is no room for the fortuitous: the hairs of the head are numbered (*cf. Lk* 12:7) and, like the crows and the lilies of the field (*cf. Lk* 7:22–32), those who live in his care need not worry about the future because it is in his hands. "Your Father knows what you need before you ask him" (*Mt* 6:8).

Chance appears on just a few occasions, as if in passing, and only to avoid the fact that, in a world where everything makes sense, an injustice or a misfortune ends up becoming proof of who knows what hidden guilt:

> At that very time there were come present who told Jesus about the Galileans whose blood Pilate had mingled with their sacrifices. He asked them, "Do you think that because these Galileans suffered in this way they were worse sinners than all other Galileans? No, I tell you, but unless you repent, you will all perish as they did. Or those eighteen who were killed when the tower of Siloam fell on them – do you think that they were worse offenders than all the others living in Jerusalem? No, I tell you, but unless you repent, you will all perish just as they did" (*Lk* 13:1–5).

Looking for traces of chance in Jesus' life, we might note that what appears orderly is much less so in the lives of the other protagonists. Trying to show that chance is not there for Jesus is one thing; trying to show that it is not there for anyone else is more problematic. Why precisely Joseph? Perhaps some other 'righteous man' could have been chosen, since he will not have been the only one. For what reason was Lazarus resurrected? Surely there must have been some other deceased young man nearby who was not fortunate enough to be Jesus' friend. However, even here, one can push in the direction of a grand paternal plan that covers and foresees everything.

With the events of Jesus' passion and death, things become more problematic. He who did not have to worry about a single hair on his head will find himself crowned with thorns. Among the many involved in the final scenes of the drama, no *one* responsible, no *one* reason, no *one* motive can be found. The protagonist is caught in the whirlwind of a mess and comes out slaughtered. Everyone is involved and, somehow, everyone is acquitted, or almost.

It is here that it seems appropriate to summon chance too among the possible perpetrators of Jesus' death. Among those involved in the whirlwind is also this faceless enemy. With respect to this possibility, however, both the theology of the Gospels, as well as much of later Christian sensibility, defend themselves.

How do the evangelists deal with the possible presence of chance as a contributory cause of Jesus' death? As I have already pointed out (*cf.* above, at the end of ch. 2), the space for chance is not lacking in the Gospel narrative: it is kept open precisely by the gap of information the evangelists demonstrate over the real reasons for Jesus' death. However, they – and among them John in particular – tend to use and accentuate this gap in order to move the clash that leads to Jesus' death on to a different plane from that of the contingent political-religious quarrels of those days, one which constitutes the plausible motive for the events. For them, it is important that there is no specific human motive precisely because the confrontation that takes place is not between Jesus and Pilate or Caiaphas; these actors would not bear the weight of the event. The confrontation is theological and involves evil – Satan – giving this death the eschatological weight that makes it the centre of the story. In this, they align themselves with the interpretation that Jesus himself presumably attributed to his own death: "Jesus in fact shares the apocalyptic conception of history as the theatre of the struggle between God and Satan. And [...] the liberation of Israel is for him liberation from the dominion of Satan, not from that of the Romans".[13]

The value of this move is undeniable as it turns the story of a murder into a religious story, which is the intention of the evangelists. However, there are also risks involved. The first of these is narrative and appears particularly striking in a time such as ours that is so sensitive to the plot and to the script. The problem is that of having theological motivations that are not narrative motivations. The most problematic aspect is, secondly, that, in this way, chance is denied in favour of a general theological plan that covers every aspect, even the tragic.

---

13   JOSSA, *Voi chi dite che io sia?*, 151.

This is a strategy that will find much favour among Christians: either chance is denied – forgetting that 'non cade foglia che Dio non voglia' [a leaf does not fall without the will of God] is *not* a biblical quotation – or it is considered a *locus* of God's action – 'Chance is God when he wills not to leave his signature'.

Thus, the scandal of chance, of its meaninglessness and the difficulty we have in dealing with it, is evaded. In practice, by evading the problem, one does not see it and does not offer a word of salvation to it. From a Christological point of view, however, it is decisive not that Christ evaded death or denied it, but that he saw it, passed through it and redeemed it. The same applies to chance. For those who, today, face a cultural context that stresses the perception of the randomness of life, with its risk of meaninglessness in the background, it is a matter of having a word that does not deny this condition but, rather, grasps its real challenge, confronting it and redeeming it.

## 4   Dead by Chance?

What advantage could be gained, then, from including chance among the murderers? To ask whether Jesus also died *by chance* is not to suggest the idea that he died *without meaning*. Rather, it is a matter of approaching chance without causing it to collapse immediately either on to theological interpretations – which remove the scandal by evading the question – or on to simple non-sense. It is necessary, therefore, to identify the theological reasons that enable and oblige us to leave this front open in the reading of Jesus' death.

I take up here what I have proposed in the attempt to circumscribe chance (*cf.* above, § 2.3). For each aspect, insights and suggestions emerge that do not close the story but, rather, try to make it more complex, more painful perhaps, but also truer.

As for *the modality*, it emphasises that this death does not happen out of necessity. This was *not* how this affair *should have* ended. It was a chance. Jesus is not the victim of necessity but is the active actor of his own passion, precisely in the confrontation with this mess. This allows us to highlight more clearly both the evil absurdity of the affair and the role of filial freedom that acts in the constitution of the plot, as much on the side of human actions as on that of Jesus' response.

As for *freedom*, chance reminds us that this death is not the result of a direct choice by God – who as such does not want the death of the Son but the salvation of his children – but neither is it the result of a choice by men. Contemporary sensitivity, both historical-critical and narrative, acutely perceives this fact. Nobody simply wants the death of Jesus. For all of them, this ends up being an unpremeditated effect linked to other motivations, not always so clear: Caiaphas wants to save the people; Peter and the disciples want to save their own skins; Pilate wants to solve a problem – to please the Jews and not get into trouble with Rome; Judas ... it is not clear what he wants. Yet the result is the cross.

The only freedom that appears consciously at stake in the story is that of Jesus himself who moves on the scene showing that he knows and has chosen what he is going to encounter, bearing the burden of the consequences for others as well.

As for *knowledge*, it becomes important to emphasise that such a contingent tangle of associated causes means that Jesus himself may not know exactly why he is condemned to death. This is not because he does not know something or misses something but, rather, because of the opposite: he is confronted with the hypothesis that there is, at least in part, something that cannot be known because it lacks a determinate and sufficient cause. Therefore, the greatness of Jesus, the genius of Jesus, consists, not in having understood more than others but in being able to face and live even that which, in its crudeness and banality, produces effects disproportionate to the causes. He does not *know more* than others, but *lives more* than others. His superiority is not in knowledge but in living.

> If mankind went straight to any particular goal, that would be not history but logic; mankind would stop ready for immediate *status quo*, like animals. [...] For there exists no ready *libretto* to follow. And if it did, history would become dull, unnecessary, and ridiculous. [...] And where [the road] none exists, genius will pave it.[14]

As for *reality*, this death is first and foremost a fact. It could have been otherwise, but that is how it is. The protagonist could evade reality precisely because it is not necessary but only actual, and, instead, makes it the place for the fulfilment of his freedom and his faithfulness to the Father and his brothers. Even from this alone, the interest of this perspective emerges: a large part of the fidelity that is required in the following of Jesus must be able to be implemented in the face of the banal occurrence of events. Otherwise, a motive can always be advanced that, by appealing to the randomness of the situation, enables the appeal contained therein to be evaded.

---

14    A. HERZEN, *From the Other Shore*, in ID., *Selected Philosophical Works*, Foreign Languages Publishing House, Moscow 1956, 364–365. *Cf.* I. BERLIN, *Russian Thinkers*, Penguin Books, London 1978, 186–209.

To the extent that one tries to keep in mind the weight of chance in the death of Jesus as a factor at play – not the only one –, the power of Jesus' action that imposes meaning on what, in itself, does not have enough to justify the enormity of the consequences will emerge more clearly. This affair simply has no meaning *a priori*, and, for this reason, it remains a scandal before which to cover one's face; in the proper sense it has no meaning even for God. Rather, it is the Son's action, his way of living it and of managing the relationships that bind him to his brothers and sisters and to the Father, that makes a particular fact, partially senseless, largely fortuitous, the centre of history and the place where God's manifestation is accomplished. Starting from a mess, Jesus manages to make it the place of the manifestation of God's paternity, of his own sonship and the sonship of his murderers.

## 5  Heir to Chance?

Chance cannot be inherited. It happens, precisely, by chance. But one can inherit a style of action in the face of chance. One can learn behaviours, postures, reactions to assume when faced with what, without warning, strikes one's life for better or for worse.

To the extent that his story was touched by chance, Jesus was able to cope with it, or, at least, this is what I would like to show. However, I would not want to leave Jesus alone in this endeavour. He may also have inherited this aspect: a learned style of how one behaves when 'something' happens.

In some sense, his father, Joseph was one to whom a disaster happened at a certain point. His betrothed was pregnant. And not on his account. Nothing strange there; a few giggles, a few pats on the back. It can happen. The *Gospel of Matthew* describes the scene by placing Joseph in exactly this psychological condition:

> Now the birth of Jesus the Messiah took place in this way. When his mother Mary had been engaged to Joseph, but before they lived together, she was found to be pregnant from the Holy Spirit. Her husband Joseph, being a righteous man and unwilling to expose her to public disgrace, planned to divorce her quietly (*Mt* 1:18–19).

What does one do when such a misfortune occurs? Joseph does two typical things – before the dream allows him to read events differently (*Mt* 1:20–21).

First: he "planned to divorce her". If you have a misfortune, you must not let it ruin your life. You don't keep it. You prevent a misfortune from becoming a catastrophe, as it would be to live a whole life alongside a woman you cannot trust. Jesus seems to have learnt this style. He does not jump headlong into trouble if it can be avoided – as when "… they tried to arrest him again, but he escaped from their hands" (*Jn* 10:39).

Second: "quietly". If a misfortune happens, it is good to avoid it becoming a condemnation, even for the alleged perpetrator. These things happen; they don't have to ruin my life … but not even yours either. Chance intended me to be here; I don't get crushed, but neither do I throw it back on to the first culprit who shows up. This too is something Jesus seems to have learnt: "Father, forgive them, for do not know what they are doing" (*Lk* 23:34). Jesus uses the excuse of chance, lack of premeditation, so that the guilt of his death does not overwhelm the guilty. The history of the Jewish people has shown us that the Christians of later centuries did not learn this lesson. Once the Jews were identified as the guilty ones, the blame fell, precisely and intentionally, on the children's children.

Joseph is the example of an apparently negative chance. Mary, on the other hand, is that of a strikingly positive one. In this, she is herself the heir and image of the whole of Israel, which, without merit, had been chosen by God as the chosen people: "it is you the Lord has chosen out of all the peoples on earth to be his people, his treasured possession" (*Deut* 14:2). God must have had his reasons. Yet, it is important for the people to consider this event as 'fortuitous'; it is not meritorious; it does not depend on Israel's being 'greater than the other nations':

> It was not because you were more numerous than any other people that the Lord set his heart on you and chose you, for you were the fewest of all peoples. It was because the Lord loved you and kept the oath that he swore to your ancestors (*Deut* 7:7–8).

Just as it is not the merit of Abraham, Moses or David.

If anything, the point is to understand what to make of this election. Mary is the example of how a great unexpected fortune, that of being the mother of the Redeemer, must be lived in such a way as to be a blessing for all. Right from the start. Mary will not carry her 'fortune', still fragile and in swaddling clothes, away from the foreign gazes of the Magi and the dirty hands of the shepherds. The traditional nativity scene shows a woman who is not afraid to expose her treasure to great risks in order to make it accessible to all. She will be like this throughout her life, right up to the last tragic exposure. Her blessing will always be an involving blessing. Herein lies the key to unlocking the ambiguous statement of the Hail Mary: 'Blessed art thou amongst women." This can be read as a privilege that separates Mary from all the others: a mass of useless women 'from/among' whom emerges one who is different from them, who is 'blessed'.

This is not what the prayer is about. Rather, it is about a beauty that infects, that becomes beauty 'for/among' all women. In the same way, the blessing of Israel is such as to become a blessing for all peoples.

One of the major soteriological concerns of the problem of chance is shown here. If an adequate way of dealing with it is not found in Jesus, there is a risk of being overwhelmed, both for those for whom chance is misfortune – and they are crushed by this misfortune, feeling cursed – and for those for whom chance is favourable. The latter are perhaps the most at risk. They may indeed keep this good fortune for themselves, like a jealous treasure, thus turning their own blessing into a curse.

Jesus will have much to learn from this couple. He, more than anyone, will have to confront the extraordinariness of his own privileges and the extraordinariness of the mortal events that will befall him. He will have to have shoulders strong enough to bear the weight of his own misfortune, without turning it into condemnation for those involved. He will have to have hands strong enough to accept the gift he has received, and even stronger not to keep them closed but to share his inheritance even with those who are not worthy to receive it.

## Bibliographical Guidelines

The subject of **chance** is difficult to deal with. One can consult E. DURAND, *Évangile et Providence. Une théologie de l'action de Dieu*, Les Éditions du Cerf, Paris 2014, 131–150; M. RIONDATO *In un mondo non-necessario. Scienze della natura, filosofia, teologia a confronto sulla nozione di «contingenza»*, EMP, Padova 2021; E. JÜNGEL, *The World as Possibility and Actuality. The ontology of the Doctrine of Justification*, in ID., *Theological Essays*, Bloomsbury T&T Clark, London – New York 2014, 95–123; E. SALMANN, *Il tragico dietro le quinte del testo. Postille sulla persistenza impertinente del destino*, in ID., *Presenza di spirito. Il cristianesimo come gesto e pensiero*, Messaggero, Padova 2000, 138–150. See also A. MAGRIS, *Destino, provvidenza, predestinazione. Dal mondo antico al cristianesimo*, Morcelliana, Brescia 2016², C. MALABOU, *Ontology of the Accident. An Essay on Destructive Plasticity*, Polity Press, Cambridge 2012; É. NOËL, *Le hasard aujourd'hui*, Éditions du Seuil, Paris 1991. A philosophical insight that well highlights the breadth of the implications of the theme of chance in relation to the contemporary world is: E. SEVERINO, *Legge e caso*, Adelphi, Milano 2020, 11–59.

For some unusual **approaches**: M. MUGNAI, *Possibile necessario*, il Mulino, Bologna 2013; C. BADANO, *Il possibile fra l'essere e il nulla. Il ritorno della questione ontologica fondamentale nella filosofia del Novecento*, Unicopoli, Milano 2009. In this sense, one can also read H. ARENDT, *Eichmann in Jerusalem. A Report on the Banality of Evil*,

Penguin Classics, London 2006; it is, in fact, the engagement with history – and in particular military history – that forces one to confront the role of chance in human affairs. Arendt highlights well how it is precisely the relational character of the human being that makes human reality fragile (EAD., *The Human Condition*, The University of Chicago Press, Chicago 1998, 188–191).

One possible track is that of **complexity**, in particular biological complexity: G. BOCCHI – M. CERUTI, *Caso/necessità*, in U. TELFENER – L. CASADIO (edd.), *Sistemica. Voci e percorsi nella complessità*, Bollati Boringhieri, Torino 2003, 150–153; C.S. BERTUGLIA – S. VAIO, *Complessità e modelli. Un nuovo quadro interpretativo per una modellizzazione nelle scienze della natura e della società*, Bollati Boringhieri, Torino 2011, 13–60; J. MONOD, *Chance and Necessity. An Essay on the Natural Philosophy of Modern Biology*, Vintage Books, New York 1972; E. MORIN, *Le Méthode. 1. La Nature de la Nature*, Éditions du Seuil, Paris 1977, 33–154; S.J. GUASTELLO – M. KOOPMANS – D. PINKUS, *Chaos and Complexity in Psychology*, Cambridge University Press, New York 2009.

Even more difficult is the treatment of chance in the death of Jesus, that is, the idea that it did **not have to end this way**; one path is to read the Lucan perspective of δεῖ/ἔδει (dêi/édei, "one must/it is necessary"; cf. R. PENNA, *I ritratti originali di Gesù il Cristo, II: Gli sviluppi*, San Paolo, Cinisello Balsamo 1999, 367–369) not as a theological necessity but as a factual necessity that Jesus did not shirk. The key is the active character of Jesus' passion, as expressed in J. MOLTMANN, *The Trinity and the Kingdom. The doctrine of God*, Fortress Press, Minneapolis 1993, 75–82; H.U. VON BALTHASAR, *Theo-drama. Theological dramatic Theory. III. Dramatis Personae: Person in Christ*, Ignatius Press, San Francisco 1992, 191–201.

CHAPTER 8

# The Heir

## 1 At the Test of the Contestations

Jesus received much and did much to contribute to, to interpret creatively the inheritance of Israel, of his relatives and of those he considered his travelling companions. All this, however, was contested. For many, it was unrecognisable, doubtful or wrong. At this point, Jesus is alone. Alone before all and against many, he will have to face the last act of his life in which he will have to answer the objections he received. Here it will be seen whether and how he will know how to remain faithful to what he has upheld until now, and, at the same time, it will be seen whether and how he will know how to give satisfaction to those who have contested him. It is at this point that an inheritance comes to the fore, the one in the light of which he interprets all the others. It is the inheritance of the Father, his relationship with him.

What is striking during the events of the passion is the feeling that everyone is against everyone. Up to this point, actually, many could have walked together on the same paths. The Son's demands were matched by the Father's action, and both corresponded to the expectations of a wounded people asking for salvation. As long as the Son's request is bread for a hungry crowd or healing for a blind man, and the Father agrees to this request, it can be hoped that everyone will be satisfied. This agreement, however, is broken with the passion. Each actor plays for himself, and the interests of each are pitted against those of the others.

Even more disconcerting is the feeling that this confusion creeps into the relationship between Jesus and the Father. During his preaching and itinerant activity, in fact, being the beloved Son who was heard was something relatively easy for Jesus. He asked and the Father answered. The extraordinary affirmation of his sonship was supported by the Father's powerful voice and action. With the passion, everything changes. Being the Son suddenly becomes something painful, where what stands out most is the absence of the Father's words and actions to support Jesus. The whole load of his life and words weighs on him. Indeed, the whole load of the Father weighs on him as well. He literally remains alone to bear the burden of naming a distant God 'Father', himself 'Son', and 'brothers and sisters' those who want him dead.

This experience of role reversal is common to everyone. There is a time when, even with all the possible quarrels, being a child guarantees unquestionable

© BRILL SCHÖNINGH, 2024 | DOI:10.30965/9783657794539_010

advantages. Someone pays for the food I eat and the clothes I wear; someone takes care of changing me if I get dirty or forgiving me if I make a mistake. Yet, there comes a time when being a child becomes burdensome. I am the one who has to provide food for an old man who no longer supports himself; I am the one who has to clean him if he gets dirty or feed him.

It is here that the category of inheritance becomes interesting. If one looks at one's relationship with one's parents from a static, ontological point of view, there is no difference between being an infant, looked after by one's parents, a slightly rebellious teenage child, or an adult child caring for one's elderly parents. One is always a child, from conception to death. Yet, in everyone's experience, it is very clear that the first time we stood up to our father or the first time we had to feed him with a spoon were defining moments, both of our being children and of his being a father. They were turning points where sonship was no longer just a fact but a choice, and we had to make it our own. They were dynamics of inheritance.[1] What might have seemed to be moments when we were *less* children, because we acquired autonomy or power against and over the one who gave us life, turned out instead to be the moments when we became *more* children, because we made the relationship our own, asserting the uniqueness of our person or assuming the debt of what we had received.

Of all these transitions, however, there is one that surpasses them all and represents the very fulfilment of inheritance. It is the moment when we, in our turn, become fathers or mothers. At this turning point, our parents are absent; it does not concern them, and, at the same time, they are absolutely present. We are in fact fulfilling, in reverse, the relationship that made us live. What had once made them fathers and mothers now makes us fathers and mothers of others. It is the ultimate test of their inheritance. If they have left us a sick fatherhood, this will be the time to reject it or heal it, so as not to repeat the evil they have done to us. If this fails, the fruit will be seen: sterile children or future bad fathers. If, on the other hand, their paternity has been sufficiently good, this is the moment when it can flourish even beyond their action and possibility.

That is, during the passion, at the very moment when he is truly alone, Jesus is also accompanied by all the fathers and mothers who generated him, he is accompanied by all his inheritances. Now, however, he must take them on as an *adult son*, as a *father*. This applies first and foremost to the Father's inheritance. Without this relationship, Jesus, his words and his work so far are not

---

1 *Cf.* P. ROTH, *Patrimony. A True Story*, Simon & Schuster, New York 1991, and the commentary on it by M. RECALCATI, *Cosa resta del padre? La paternità nell'epoca ipermoderna*, Raffaello Cortina, Milano 2011, 119–153.

comprehensible. Will it prove to be a bond that can sustain his life and death? That can withstand even the Father's absence? Even more so, however, are the other inheritances, those of all the people he encountered. These are in fact ambiguous and multiform relationships, some positive, some perplexing, some openly oppositional, right up to relationships that try to kill him. So far, even without these, Jesus is not comprehensible. What will he do with them? Will he simply set them aside to affirm his belonging to the Father? And how will he involve them at the very moment when they challenge and kill him?

With these questions I would like to address the central moment of Jesus' story, namely, his passion, trying to use the category of inheritance as a key to interpretation. In order to understand how he who was Son also showed himself to be heir, capable of making the gifts he received his own, capable of bearing them even in the solitary and adult form that characterises every inheritance worthy of the name.

To do this, in this chapter, I shall first try to clarify certain aspects of the concept of inheritance, as I intend to use it. In fact, the concept possesses: its *own logic* (§ 2) – that is, it requires a grammar and particular characters in order to function; a *present-day specificity* (§ 3) – that is, it is culturally characterised; and an *evangelical specificity* – that is, the nature of the *object of inheritance* in the New Testament needs to be understood (§ 4) as do the main *texts* are on which I have tried to base this proposal (§ 5). At this point, it will be possible to deal with the two great figures of inheritance – the *testator/father* (§ 6) and the *heir/son* (§ 7) – who, in the concrete events of the passion, dramatically enact the dynamic of inheritance. Finally, it will be necessary to emphasise both the *claim* (§ 8) of these events and their substantial *failure* (§ 9).

## 2      Inheriting

### 2.1     *Grammar*

What does inheritance mean? Inheritance occurs when someone leaves something to someone else. In the grammar of inheritance, we can say that there is a passive subject, the one who leaves, and a more active subject, the one who receives. An old man at the end of his race and a young man with the strength of the beginning. Usually, the old man is the parent and the young man is the child. It may be otherwise, but the institution is designed for these protagonists. In this way, everyone wins: the son wins by receiving a fortune to invest, but the parent also wins by being guaranteed that what he has sweated over in a lifetime still remains in his possession somehow by being passed on to his blood.

Unlike in a dynamic of *gift*, where the active subject is the giver and the passive subject is the receiver, in a dynamic of *inheritance*, the focus falls on the receiver, not the giver. In the life of a parent, the moment of inheritance is, indeed, important, but, fundamentally, because it coincides with his own death; the importance lies in the death, not in the inheritance. In the life of a child, on the other hand, the moment of inheritance is decisive: he becomes what he is by receiving it from another who bequeaths.

At the centre of the inheritance, therefore, is the son/heir, who is the real protagonist of the action. Hence one of the most interesting aspects of the category of inheritance: it expresses the dynamic, active aspect of sonship. One is a son from birth, but only becomes an heir with time – in the challenge of living up to the inheritance received. Thus, inheriting is an action that, peculiar to the son, occurs in a non-spontaneous way, as the famous expression in *Faust* underlines: "The inheritance of your fathers, if you want to have it, you have to earn it".[2]

The New Testament is familiar with this dynamic sonship *for us* who become children insofar as we are redeemed and adopted. In his *Letter to the Galatians*, Paul expresses this dynamic that begins from a merely virtual sonship ("Heirs, as long as they are minors, are no better than those who are enslaved", *Gal* 4:1) and involves the son in his becoming an adult ("So you are no longer a slave but a child, and if a child then also an heir, through God", *Gal* 4:7) thanks to the gift received and made his own ("God has sent the Spirit of his Son into our hearts, crying, '*Abba*! Father!'" *Gal* 4:6). One is an heir and one inherits; the two things do not coincide, so much so that the heir who has not yet inherited is assimilated to a slave. In the same way, one *is* a son and one *becomes* a son.

In the *Letter to the Hebrews*, however, this dynamic is also extended to Jesus who, "although he was a son, he learned obedience through what he suffered" (*Heb* 5:8). His sonship involves him and, like the sonship of each of us, knows moments of trial and evolution.

The concept of inheritance thus focuses on *the dynamics of the adult assumption of sonship as a prospective relationship of origin*. One opens oneself to the future, becoming what one is from one's provenance. The adult son is the one who is not only a son according to the flesh but who has assumed this origin of his by making it part of his own path of subjectivisation. The adult son is one who inscribes his provenance in his own name. Thus, as children, we are called by our first name while, as adults, in many cases, we are called by our surname. Our name has become that which once belonged to others.

---

2   J.W. von Goethe, *Faust,* Act I, Scene I, vv. 682–684.

Inheritance is thus shown as a *qualifying* and *dynamic* moment of sonship. He who had to say 'I am Armando's son' will be able to say, if he can live up to it, 'I am Armando's heir'. He who was always 'the Son of the Father' will have to prove that he is 'the heir of the Father'.

## 2.2   *Characters*

If we try to define the characters who move about the theatre of hereditary action, two co-protagonists emerge in the forefront: they are the *son/heir* and the *father/testator*. When we widen our gaze, however, we catch sight of two other characters that allow us to define the contours of this dynamic in more precise terms. In the first place, we must note that while father and son are self-sufficient,[3] testator and heir naturally give rise to the theme of inheritance, that is, of the *patrimony* that is passed from father to son. Precisely because the act of inheriting takes place in the absence of the testator – who is dead – the inheritance that is constituted as the middle term between those who are no longer there and those who must continue on their own becomes central. In an inheritance, there is always something passing on, whether material or ideal. This makes more explicit a question that risks remaining in the shadows: what is it that passes between the Father and the Son? What is it that they pass on?

A second figure that risks remaining in the shadows but is, instead, central and qualifying to the entire inheritance process are the *siblings*.[4] They may, in turn, be co-heirs, i.e. participate in the process of the son's inheritance, or be excluded from the inheritance. Anyone who has experienced an inheritance, even from afar, cannot fail to have noticed that it is precisely from the consequences that the patrimony exerts on the dynamics involving the heirs that the nature and amount of the inheritance itself can be assessed. Both the father – as the person responsible for (his) patrimony – and the son – as the person called upon to assume it – are judged by the effects that this passage will have on the siblings/heirs.

Many of Shakespeare's plays focus on precisely this tragic dynamic: the kingdom is passed on to the sons so carelessly, with such a load of unresolved issues, that it becomes a tragedy for the sons. The latter are incapable of handling what they have received. Yet, it is well understood that the fault is not theirs alone, but, to a large extent, falls on the ineptitude or meanness of their

---

[3] If we leave out, of course, the problem of the mother and the role that the female figure takes on precisely in the Age of the Son (*cf.* M. CACCIARI, *Generare Dio*, il Mulino, Bologna 2017).

[4] G.C. PAGAZZI, *L'identità custodita. Il Primogenito e i suoi fratelli*, in L. CASULA – G. ANCONA (edd.), *L'identità e i suoi luoghi. L'esperienza cristiana nel farsi dell'umano*, Glossa, Milano 2008, 125–162; *cf.* ID., *C'è posto per tutti*.

fathers. If the sons are tragic figures, like Hamlet, the fathers are, instead, guilty or insane, like Lear.[5]

The judgement involves everyone because, when the process of inheritance fails, it is the heritage that will be overwhelmed. In Shakespeare's plays, as in the drama of Christ, this heritage is called the 'Kingdom', that is, the set of people who, if the inheritance fails, will lose the chance to live in peace. Here then, another question arises: how and in what terms are we, the adopted children, involved in the transmission of the patrimony? Are we merely spectators, subjects of a Kingdom that belongs to the Son, or are we more radically involved, as co-heirs?

At this point several important aspects are on the table: the centrality of the figure of the son as a central agent; the importance of the inheritance as a reality bequeathed and assumed; and the dynamic of inheritance as it emerges in the complex interweaving involving the co-heirs. We shall focus on these aspects in order to see how the passion of Jesus can be considered a dynamic of inheritance and how it can illuminate and redevelop this experience, just as the actual life of Jesus.

## 3   Inheriting in the Age of the Son

Several objections can be raised against the choice of the category of inheritance, and I would like to address them before proceeding.

The first is that it is a *legal category*, and our age already seems far too inclined to read everything in a legal light. At least, this is a rather strong impression for an Italian. At the same time, the tradition of Western Christianity has paid a very high price for choosing legal categories to interpret the story of Jesus. We have already noted (*cf.* above, ch. 1, § 1.2) how the events of the passion, if interpreted with the categories of *expiation* and *satisfaction*, read through a juridical lens, have had the effect of giving us a distorted image of Jesus and God. The passion as the 'payment' by Jesus of the price of our ransom to the Father, the exactor-kidnapper. However, one must avoid a perspective error. It is not necessarily that it is these concepts that favour this drift; rather, it could be that a legalistic attitude favours the centrality of these concepts and their distorted interpretation. The category of inheritance itself, if read in a purely legal sense, risks being very reductive and dangerous when applied to the passion. By contrast, it can be acknowledged that, if read outside the legalistic straitjacket, even *expiation* and *satisfaction* can turn out to be much richer categories than

---

5  *Cf.* M. CACCIARI, *Re Lear. Padri, figli, eredi*, Saletta dell'uva, Caserta 2016.

we tend to hold to be true today, ones which seek to account for the aspiration towards an ascending soteriology – that is, a concrete involvement of humans in the salvation that reaches them.

The second objection has to do with the *centrality of the son/heir*. Is our age not already too busy reflecting on itself and its own dynamics, unable to recognise that what it has, it has received?

I respond to these objections by emphasising that the choice to read the passion in the light of inheritance stems from the perception that, today, a series of epochal cultural transitions have expanded this category, making it take on a weight and potential that were largely unexpressed in the cultural context in which the New Testament was written and initially received.

With regard to the first objection, this cultural shift has meant that inheritance is no longer primarily a legal phenomenon but, rather, a philosophical, existential and psychological one. It becomes possible to use it without immediately having to refer to guardians, notaries and lawyers.

For the second objection, things are more complex. It is certainly true that our age risks being focused on the self-image, with the danger of drowning like Narcissus in the effort to contemplate it more closely. However, I do not believe that we can escape this lethal risk simply with a pious appeal to altruism. We shall not be able to escape the Narcissus trap without taking seriously and examining thoroughly the reasons why this individual is looking at his own image, and without providing tools that can hold together the attention to self – typical of the modern subject – with the presence of the other. This is a strategic step for Christianity in general and for Catholicism in particular. Many of the current difficulties that prevent the person of Christ from being a convincing figure for contemporary men and women derive, in my opinion, precisely from our never having taken seriously the challenge that Modernity has posed to Christianity – let's say since the 17th century. It is a question of a centrality of the subject that cannot just be condemned, as if it were possible to return to the man or woman of the Middle Ages,[6] or resolved by appealing to altruism. Either we shall succeed in finding a soteriology that really knows how to involve the human being – a being that today presents itself with the hypertrophic subjective traits of modern people – or Christianity will condemn itself to being a form of life of the past, destined for the men and women that we are no longer.[7]

---

[6] *Cf.* D. BONHOEFFER, *Prisoner for God. Letters and Papers from Prison*, The Macmillan Company, New York 1959, 145–149 and 161–164.

[7] Just as a footnote, I would like to emphasise that the real problem with the role of women in the church lies at this level. It is not a question of justice, power or gender equality, or not

## 3.1 Three Contributions

Among the many that could be analysed, therefore, I would like to mention, if only in passing, three important components of the process that has led to the redefinition of the category of inheritance.[8] These are major theoretical and existential contributions that have emphasised the dynamism of the assumption of subjectivity and filiation, and so provide suitable words and conceptual tools to talk about it.

A first contribution, of an eminently speculative nature, is made by *German Idealism*. In fact, it is in Idealism that the effort is made to describe metaphysics beginning from the subject. This requires thinking about its historicity and dynamism, finding categories that are less static and more capable of integrating freedom as a structuring moment. In the exponents of Idealism, the process of subjectivisation becomes a founding model for thinking about reality, history and God. Regardless of the outcomes, which may be more or less agreeable to and compatible with the Christian perspective, this is an epoch-making philosophical contribution, precisely for Christianity. Indeed, a starting point so radically linked to the subject offers challenges, contributions and a vocabulary particularly suited to those who, as in Christianity, consider a subject – Jesus Christ – the centre of history and reality. For many of these authors, it is precisely the debate with Christianity, the need to rethink it under the conditions of the modern subject, that constitutes the starting point and the heart of the philosophical enterprise.

In this sense, Friedrich Schelling's proposal[9] to think of the whole of our time as beginning from the specific relationship between Father and Son is significant. According to this author, the action of Jesus has such a philosophical weight that it draws everyone into a new epoch which can thus be defined as the *Age of the Son*. Its fundamental characteristic lies precisely in the new weight that falls on the figure of sons and their dynamics. After what has happened in the historical story of the Son, it becomes clear that what requires

---

primarily. Instead, it is a question of the fact that women living Christianity today are, at the very least, modern women. Even when they are nuns. That is why there is an urgent need to design modern – and then also post-modern – figures that can be taken on by *these* women. Otherwise, there will simply be no place for them in the church. This goes far beyond the albeit important issues of the priesthood or diaconate for women (S. Noceti (ed.), *Diacone? Quale ministero per quale Chiesa*, Queriniana, Brescia 2017). If, at the end of this debate, we were to end up with a few women playing a role in a medieval church, the result would be far too poor. For everyone.

8  P. Ricœur, *The Conflict of Interpretations. Essays in Hermeneutics*, The Athlone Press, London 1989, 481–497.
9  *Cf.* F.W.J. Schelling, *The Ages of the World (1811)*, State University New York Press, New York 2019.

attention is no longer the rights and actions of fathers but the freedom and dignity of children. Within the fundamental father/son relationship, the focus has now shifted to the children's possibilities of adult subjectivisation. Therefore, the fundamental turning point of our age – which began over two thousand years ago and has not yet ended[10] – deals with the possibility of providing convincing figures to interpret and experience this relationship.

Perhaps the text that most marks this transition, however, is Hegel's *Phenomenology of the Spirit*. Here, the story of the absolute subject is described as a *Bildungsroman* of the divine and the human, of the subject in all its forms. Here, a fundamental development for our theme takes place, namely, the possibility of describing the process of subjectivisation as a process of desire. Indeed, this term undergoes a profound mutation. It no longer describes the passing cravings of an already formed subject, but rather the fundamental dynamic with which one turns to another in order to constitute oneself. The bonds of origin, and bonds in general, become the weft on which the warp of subjectivisation is woven. These can be positive, loving bonds, as in the *Philosophy of Spirit*[11] or, more radically, bonds of fear and power, as in the servant/master dialectic of the *Phenomenology of Spirit*.[12]

At this point, it is not so important whether the inheritance received is positive or negative, whether it is accepted or rather leads to the affirmation "That is not me".[13] What is important is that one can no longer think of describing a subject philosophically apart from the bonds that constitute it.

A second contribution, of an eminently psychological nature, is made by *psychoanalysis*, which offers tools to address the inheritance relationship beyond its purely economic-legal aspects. One could start from the centrality that the Oedipus complex assumes in Freud's approach to the point of being able to affirm that "with the Oedipus complex, psychoanalysis stands or falls [...]. The Oedipus complex is in a certain sense the crucial question posed by psychoanalysis to its public".[14] It is not a question of wanting to uphold the absoluteness of a description of an evidently mythological-metaphorical character but,

---

10   Here we can see the difference from Joachim of Fiore († 1202) for whom we have already passed into the Age of the Spirit. The European events of the eight hundred years that separate us from the speculations of this Calabrian abbot with apocalyptic overtones make us, I think, sceptical about the possibility that our *children's* problems are now behind us.
11   *Cf.* G.W.F. HEGEL, *Gessammelte Werke. Band 6. Jenaer Systementwürfe III*, Felix Meiner Verlag, Hamburg 1976, 185–288.
12   *Cf.* ID., *The Phenomenology of Spirit*, Cambridge University Press, Cambridge 2018, 102–136.
13   J. BUTLER, *Subjects of Desire. Hegelian Reflections in twentieth-century France*, Columbia University Press, New York 1987, 29–30.
14   RICŒUR, *The Conflict of Interpretations*, 470.

rather, of recognising, at the heart of the psychoanalytic theoretical construct, the structuring and subjectivisating function of the Oedipus complex: *psychoanalysis has as its substance the idea that identity-subjectivisation is constructed from its own relational origin*. In this sense, psychoanalysis offers tools to talk about inheritance as a structuring moment of recognition of one's own provenance and of the symbolic debt-patrimony that binds us in the relationship with those who precede us.

This idea can now be supplemented and expanded with contributions from neuroscience. Our brain becomes what it is thanks to the contribution – positive or negative – of the encounters and clashes we have with a reality that precedes us and which forms our history. Studies on memory and brain-functioning allow bridges to be built between psychoanalytic theories and neuroscience, and the encounter takes place precisely with respect to this *constitutiveness of dependence*. In essence, it is a question of giving Freud and his successors credit for having identified the fundamental process of the constitution of the human subject and having, at the same time, provided the images to describe it. A relationship of creative, individual, painful and inevitable recovery of what others have left us, in a plurality of forms. Language, feelings, concepts, social structures, examples, accusations and promises.

Lastly, there is a third contribution, an epoch-making event that risks remaining underestimated, namely, the centrality assigned to *childhood* in the 20th century.[15] Childhood underwent an extraordinary metamorphosis in the last century, going from being a provisional condition of minority to being, instead, the fontal and decisive moment of the adult condition. Hence the focus on children and how they become adults, more or less successful, unsuccessful or wounded. This shifts the social focus from the adult/father to the children/heirs and the dynamics of subjectivisation they go through.

These various contributions have arisen to interpret a process that has lost those attributes of automatism and naturalness that characterised other eras. The centrality that the figure of the son/heir has assumed indicates the complexity of the act of transmitting and receiving, of becoming oneself, at both the individual and social levels. Therefore, the Age of the Son is not a simple time in which one is freed from one's fathers. To think this would, basically, demonstrate that one has not grasped what is at stake in this process, namely,

---

15   *Cf.* E. BECCHI – D. JULIA (edd.), *Storia dell'infanzia*, II: *Dal Settecento ad oggi*, Laterza, Roma – Bari 1996, 332–407. See also, as a demonstration of the extent to which this change was grasped as it developed, E. KEY, *The Century of the Child* (1906), The Knickerbocker Press, New York 2020.

the patrimony: something that is left behind in the hope that it can be maintained or increased but which can also always be squandered or lost.

## 3.2    Fathers and Sons

The problem of inheritance in danger of being lost is particularly evident in all those institutions that are not able to rely on blood and so have to rely on transmission-tradition in order to exist: churches, parties, associations. Indeed, fathers and mothers have the advantage that, as long as they are parents and generate other parents, at least their blood – their genes, we would say today – has a future. In institutions, however, the rapidity and fluidity of the contemporary world throws into crisis the balance between adherence to and detachment from the inheritance received, to the point of forcing children to ask themselves whether the inheritance they have received is not more of a ballast than a gift, and making fathers no longer to recognise in the inheritance received that same inheritance which must be delivered.

The action of the son must, therefore, be thought of more deeply and, with it, the figure of the father must be rethought. The revolt against the fathers of the anti-Oedipus of 1968[16] intensifies and re-enacts the Oedipus itself without succeeding in getting out of it, while the current situation seems, rather, to describe a society without fathers or, better, a society in which children completely disregard their fathers since, as soon as they are teenagers, they already realise they cannot inherit anything useful from them.

*Bewilderment of the fathers, then.* To describe this, one can share Recalcati's analysis which sees in two figures from Nanni Moretti's cinema the icons of the crisis of contemporary fatherhood: on the one hand, the frightened pope of *Habemus papam*[17] and, on the other, the gibbering leader of the Italian Communist Party of *Palombella rossa*.[18]

> At the intersection between *Habemus papam* and *Palombella rossa*, the two great symbols of the Ideals that have guided the lives of the masses in the West (the leader of the Holy Roman Catholic Church and the secretary of the glorious Communist Party) are no longer able to speak, they can no longer carry the symbolic weight of their public role. They appear lost, evaporated.[19]

---

16    G. DELEUZE – F. GUATTARI, *Anti-Oedipus. Capitalism and Schizophrenia*, Penguin Books, London 2009.
17    N. MORETTI, *Habemus papam*, Italy, 2011.
18    ID., *Palombella Rossa*, Italy, 1989.
19    M. RECALCATI, *The Telemachus Complex. Parents and Children after the Decline of the Father*, Polity Press, Cambridge 2019, 23. *Cf.* also ID., *Cosa resta del padre? La paternità nell'epoca ipermoderna*, Raffaello Cortina, Milano 2011.

*But also bewilderment of the children.* To remain in the cinematic sphere, one can look at the large number of teenage heroes and semi-heroes that populate films and television series. What is most striking is not so much their age – which could be explained by the youthful audience at which such films are aimed – but rather the fact that their fathers are hardly ever figures to whom these heroes can refer. If at all, grandfathers or uncles, but not fathers and mothers. One thinks of the *Hunger games* saga[20] or *The 100*,[21] like many American comic book superheroes[22] in their contemporary incarnation. For them, adolescence becomes the place of the self-creation of an impossible inheritance in which they have to respond to the challenges and ambiguous complexity of the world with no other reference than themselves and their peers. Or, at least, that is the issue presented.

The very grammar of inheritance shows how, although it is apparently the fathers and their inheritance that are experiencing the greatest difficulties, it is precisely the analysis of filial dynamics that is at the centre of change. When it comes to inheritance, in fact, it is always more interesting to see how the heirs are moving than to dwell on the depression or the affairs of the testators.

Reflection on these dynamics, therefore, is topical and urgent. With the baggage of these tools and challenges, we can now turn to the New Testament to see if and how this category can come into play. More than definitions or titles, however, it is the dynamics that will be the focus of attention. It is not so important to *say that* Jesus was heir but, rather, to *see how* he was able to realise this process in the concrete unfolding of events.

---

20  G. ROSS, *The Hunger Games*, USA 2012; F. LAWRENCE, *The Hunger Games: Catching Fire*, USA 2013; Id., *The Hunger Games: Mockingjay 1*, USA 2014; ID., *The Hunger Games: Mockingjay 2*, USA 2015.

21  J. ROTHENBERG, *The 100* (TV series), USA 2014–2020.

22  Batman is an orphan, as is Spider-Man who is raised by his uncles, one of whom dies at the beginning of the saga. Superman's parents, are even from another planet … As for the Disney classics, the discourse becomes more complex and reflects the needs of products that have children as their primary target audience. Some films explicitly themed the question of inheritance – *Bambi* (1942), *The Lion King* (1994), *Mulan* (1998), *Moana* (2016) –, but many maintain the testimony of an impossible inheritance – *Snow White and the Seven Dwarfs* (1937), *Pinocchio* (1940), *Peter Pan* (1953), *The Jungle Book* (1967) up to *Lilo & Stitch* (2002). This long list of orphans that stretches throughout Disney's production, making the first viewers of *Snow White* now in their nineties, alerts us to the epochal character of this theme.

## 4   Patrimony

As we have seen, one of the 'characters' or 'problems' of inheritance is the inheritance or heritage itself, i.e. the patrimony. *What*, exactly, does the Father hand over and the Son receive? Looking at the story of Jesus, it can be difficult to understand what this is all about. This is because the subject of inheritance understood as tangible patrimony does not emerge in the New Testament primarily with respect to the one who is the heir *par excellence* – that is, Jesus – but with respect to the co-heirs, those whom Jesus involved in the inheritance he received and passed on. We are 'heirs' (κληρονόμοι, *klēronómoi*)[23] as 'co-heirs' (συγκληρονόμοι, *synklēronómoi*).[24] But what exactly do we inherit? In a brief review, we can find mentioned the blessing,[25] the earth,[26] the kingdom,[27] eternal life.[28]

However, the most interesting aspect of the inheritance of which we are co-heirs in Christ is *sonship itself*:

> And because you are children, God has sent the Spirit of his Son into our hearts, crying, "*Abba*! Father!" So you are no longer a slave but a child, and if a child then also an heir, through God (*Gal* 4:6–7).
> For you did not receive a spirit of slavery to fall back into fear, but you have received a spirit of adoption. When we cry, "*Abba*! Father!" it is that very Spirit bearing witness with our spirit that we are children of God, and if children, then

---

*Cf. Acts* 20:32: "And now I commend you to God and to the message of his grace, a message that is able to build you up and to give you the inheritance among all who are sanctified"; *Gal* 3:29: "And if you belong to Christ, then you are Abraham's offspring, heirs according to the promise."

[24] *Cf. Eph* 3:6: "... the gentiles have become fellow heirs, members of the same body, and sharers in the promise in Christ Jesus through the gospel"; *Rom* 8:17: "And if children, then heirs: heirs of God and joint heirs with Christ, if in fact we suffer with him so that we may also be glorified with him".

[25] *Cf. 1 Pet* 3:9: "Do not repay evil for evil or abuse for abuse, but, on the contrary, repay with a blessing. It was for this that you were called – that you might inherit a blessing".

[26] *Cf. Mt* 5:5: "Blessed are the meek, for they will inherit the earth".

[27] *Cf. 1 Cor* 15:50: "What I am saying, brothers and sisters, is this: flesh and blood cannot inherit the kingdom of God, nor does the perishable inherit the imperishable"; *Mt* 25:34: "Then the king will say to those at his right hand, 'Come, you that are blessed by my Father, inherit the kingdom prepared for you from the foundation of the world'"; *Jas* 2:5: "Has not God chosen the poor in the world to be rich in faith and to be heirs of the kingdom that he has promised to those who love him?".

[28] *Tit* 3:7: "... that, having been justified by his grace, we might become heirs according to the hope of eternal life"; *Mt* 19:29: "And everyone who has left houses or brothers or sisters or father or mother or wife or children or fields for my name's sake will receive a hundred-fold and will inherit eternal life"; there is also the rich young man's request in *Mk* 10:17: "Good Teacher, what must I do to inherit eternal life?"

> heirs: heirs of God and joint heirs with Christ, if we in fact suffer with him so that we may also be glorified with him (*Rom* 8:15–17).
> He destined us for adoption as his children through Jesus Christ ... In Christ we have also obtained an inheritance, having been destined according to the purpose of him who accomplishes all things according to his counsel and will ... for the praise of his glory (*Eph* 1:5.11–12).
> To the thirsty I will give water as a drink from the spring of the water of life. Those who conquer will inherit these things; I will be their God and they will be my children (*Rev* 21:6–7).

What is inherited in Christ is the right to call God 'Father', i.e. the dignity of sons. Every other aspect of this inheritance – from land to eternal life – is included in the rights of the paternal-filial bond. For those who are sons, everything else is gratuitous. Sonship itself is gratuitous, for while one can extort blessings (*cf. Gen* 27:1–40), conquer land or aspire to eternal life (*cf. Mk* 5:25–34), no one can do anything to become the son of another. Hence Paul's insistence that inheritance cannot be the fruit of the law. The inheritance of things can indeed be extorted by laws or violence, but the inheritance of sonship can only come by grace.[29]

At this point, the advantage of the category of inheritance becomes clear. If we understand sonship in a static, we might say genetic, way, we risk a stalemate: someone is a son and someone is not. Instead, the very category of inheritance speaks to us of a dynamic sonship to be made to flourish, of an offering to which to correspond as sons. The name of sons is given to us, but the possibility of making this name become flesh, blood and history cannot be separated from the dynamics and concrete relationships of our lives.

Jesus is also involved in this filial dynamic. By this, I do not mean to suggest that Christ 'becomes' a son during the passion, in an adoptionist perspective, as if he had not been one before. Rather, it is to focus on how he who was true God and true man was also and always the Living One (*cf. Rev* 1:18) and so lived what he was. Jesus is the one who, as a son, inherited his own sonship, opening the way and the possibility for co-heirs to be sons in him. From an exegetical point of view, this makes it possible to account for a series of more dynamic perspectives present in the New Testament, ones which risk being dismissed as naïve by a gaze only interested in declaring the dual nature of the divine and human. One need only think of the New Testament expressions in which it is

---

29  *Cf. Rom* 4:16: "For this reason it depends on faith, in order that the promise may rest on grace, so that it may be guaranteed to all his descendants [...]"; *Gal* 3:18: "For if the inheritance comes from the law, it no longer comes from the promise, but God granted it to Abraham through the promise".

claimed that Jesus receives the *name*[30] or the *glory*,[31] or even in which it is said that he is *constituted Son* or *Lord*.[32]

It will, therefore, be a matter of looking to Christ to understand what it means to become "mature" sons (*cf. Heb* 5:11–14), to inherit one's sonship and take on one's name, at the culminating moment of the passion where Jesus' actions and relationships are most clearly delineated.

To understand what is at stake, it is appropriate to address a burning question, namely, the one that asks about the difference between our sonship and that of Jesus, the distinction between "my Father and your Father … my God and your God" (*Jn* 20:17). The most natural response is indeed to highlight the difference between these two sonships: Jesus' is 'by nature', ours is 'by grace'. He is the Son, we are the *adopted children*.

> For all who are led by the Spirit of God are children of God. For you did not receive a spirit of slavery to fall back into fear, but you have received a spirit of adoption [sonship]. When we cry, "*Abba!* Father!" it is that very Spirit bearing witness with our spirit that we are children of God. […] and not only the creation, but we ourselves, who have the first fruits of the Spirit, groan inwardly while we wait for adoption [sonship], the redemption of our bodies (*Rom* 8:14–15.23).
> … so that we might receive adoption as children [sonship] (*Gal* 4:5).
> He chose us in Christ before the foundation of the world to be holy and blameless before him in love. He destined us for adoption as his children [sonship] through Jesus Christ, according to the good pleasure of his will, to the praise of his glorious grace that he freely bestowed on us in the Beloved (*Eph* 1:4–6).

The patrimony perspective can, perhaps, help to unravel an ambiguity that risks undermining the meaning of Jesus' entire work, which is not that of reaffirming the adoptive character of our sonship but that of affirming its reality: "See what love the Father has given us, that we should be called children

---

30   *Mt* 1:21–25: "She will bear a son, and you are to name him Jesus. […] She had borne a son, and he called his name Jesus"; *Phil* 2:9: "Therefore, God also highly exalted him and gave him the name that is above every name"; *Heb* 1:4: "… having become as much superior to angels as the name he has inherited is more excellent than theirs".

31   *Jn* 17:22: "The glory that you have given me, I have given them, so that they may be one, as we are one"; *1 Tim* 3:16: "[*He* was] believed in throughout the world, taken up in glory"; *Heb* 5:5: "So also Christ did not glorify himself in becoming a high priest, but was appointed by the one who said to him, 'You are my son, today I have begotten you'" (*cf.* (cf. also 2:9); *1 Pet* 1:21: "… through him you have come to trust in God, who raised him from the dead and gave him glory, so that your faith and hope are set on God".

32   *Rom* 1:4: "… declared to be Son of God with power, according to the Spirit of holiness, by resurrection of the dead, Jesus Christ our Lord"; *Acts* 2:36: "Therefore let the entire house of Israel know with certainty that God has made him both Lord and Messiah, this Jesus whom you crucified".

of God, and that is what we are!" (*1 Jn* 3:1). My intention here is not to enter into a discussion as to whether the Greek word υἱοθεσία (*hyiothesía*) should be translated as "sonship" or "adoption",[33] but to understand whether this condition – which often appears associated with the idea that we are heirs – serves to emphasise similarity or difference. The grammar of inheritance can help us in two senses. Firstly, it reminds us that the Son also possesses his own natural sonship as something received: "If I glorify myself, my glory is nothing. It is my Father who glorifies me" (*Jn* 8:54). In his eternal origin, as much as in his earthly life, as much as in his resurrection, the Son is the one who receives himself from another and who becomes what he is in dialogue with the one who generated him. Secondly, he reminds us that, insofar as sonship is the patrimony received, this patrimony is the same for all because one is the Father of all. Being an adopted child, therefore, does not mean being *less* of a child but, rather, living the same sonship in a different way, as happens in every successful experience of adoption. Identical is the relationship, identical is the inheritance received, because identical are the paternal bowels from which the desire for the other comes. "For the one who sanctifies and those who are sanctified all have one Father. For this reason Jesus is not ashamed to call them brothers and sisters" (*Heb* 2:11).

To fail in this perspective is to turn Jesus into the one who keeps the inheritance for himself, as the only-begotten rather than the first-born. Jesus is the first-born because every generation finds its own possibility and destination in his eternal generation. The meaning of his whole life was precisely to reveal the space of generative love from which he himself came. The endeavour of his entire life was to make us feel as sons like him, not to mark the difference so it goes to our head – which is always possible but should not be feared to the point of obscuring the uniqueness of our heritage.

If, therefore, what the Son leaves in co-inheritance to his brothers and sisters is what he himself has inherited, the brothers and sisters will have to look to him to know that they too are sons and daughters and to learn from him what it means to be children, heirs of their own sonship.[34]

---

[33]  G.F. Hawthorne – R.P. Martin – D.G. Reid, *Dictionary of Paul and His Letters*, InterVarsity Press, Downers Grove (IL) 1993, 47–49.

[34]  *Cf. Eph* 1:17–19: "I do not cease to give thanks of you as I remember in my prayer, that the God of our Lord Jesus Christ, the Father of glory, may give you a spirit of wisdom and revelation as you come to know him, so that, with the eyes of your heart enlightened, you may know what is the hope to which he has called you, what are the riches of his glorious inheritance among the saints, and what is the immeasurable greatness of his power for us who believe, according to the working of his great power."

## 5 The Name of the Heir in the New Testament

The use of the category of inheritance is based on its use in Scripture. For this reason, I would like to point to some specific passages that enable its use to be anchored in the very language of the New Testament, and perhaps of Jesus himself.

The *first text* is the parable of the wicked tenants and is significant precisely because it has a good chance of being historically attributable to Jesus.[35] After having cited it on several occasion, it is time to quote it in *Mark*'s version.[36]

> Then [Jesus] began to speak to them in parables. "A man planted a vineyard, put a fence around it, dug a pit for the wine press, and built a watchtower; then he leased it to tenants and went away. When the season came, he sent a slave to the tenants to collect from them his share of the produce of the vineyard. But they seized him, and beat him, and sent him away empty-handed. And again he sent another slave to them; this one they beat over the head and insulted. Then he sent another, and that one they killed. And so it was with many others; some they beat, and others they killed. He had still one other, a beloved son. Finally he sent him to them, saying, 'They will respect my son'. But those tenants said to one another, 'This is the heir; come, let us kill him, and the inheritance will be ours.' So they seized him, killed him, and threw him out of the vineyard. What then will the owner of the vineyard do? He will come and destroy the tenants and give the vineyard to others. Have you not read this scripture: 'The stone that the builders rejected has become the cornerstone; this was the Lord's doing, and it is amazing in our eyes'?" When they realized that he had told this parable against them, they wanted to arrest him, but they feared the crowd. So they left him and went away" (Mk 12:1–12).

One of the strongest reasons in favour of the parable's historicity lies in the fact that, in its original form, the parable is disturbing. As they had done with the previous emissaries, symbolising the slain prophets, the tenants kill the son too and dispose of his body.

---

[35] *Cf.* MEIER, *A Marginal Jew.5*, 240–252, where that of the wicked tenants is one of the five parables that are saved from Meier's 'massacre' on the authenticity of the parables.

[36] *Cf.* Mt 21:33–46; Mk 12:1–12; Lk 20:9–19. The parable is also found in the apocryphal Coptic *Gospel of Thomas*, 65 (*cf.* J.K. ELLIOT, *The Apocryphal New Testament. A Collection of Apocryphal Christian Literature in an English Translation*, Clarendon Press, Oxford 1993, 143–144); for an analysis, *cf.* B. STANDAERT, *Évangile selon Marc. Commentaire, Troisième partie Marc 11,1 à 16,20*, J. Gabalda et C$^{ie}$, Pendé 2010, 840–853; A. LANDI, *Figlio diletto o ultimo dei profeti? Identità e missione cristologica in Mc 12,1–12*, in *Rivista biblica* 56 (2008) 199–219, from which the relationship with *Heb* 1:1–4 also emerges.

> This is *the* end, period. There is no resolution or reversal of this tragic injustice within the story world of the parable proper; all attempts at rectification of the injustice come from later hands and lie outside the story world of this puzzling *māšāl* (parable).[37]

A significant aspect of the parable is that it is readily understood by the listeners, so much so that it provokes their homicidal reaction, as if the story immediately causes the content it announces. A further point of interest is that here, without ambiguity or need for interpretation, the son – who comes to a sticky end and is clearly Jesus himself – is designated as the heir. It is, however, in the two additional interpretations that conclude the parable that the category of inheritance becomes red-hot. Faced with the absurd killing of the son, what is the father's reaction? Two are proposed: the slaughter of the servants ("He will come and destroy the tenants and give the vineyard to others" *Mk* 12:9) and the extraordinary rehabilitation of the dead son ("The stone that the builders rejected has become the cornerstone" *Mk* 12:10). In this second interpretation, the perspective of the resurrection appears clearly for the readers of the Gospel. This would seem to go quite well, both for the patrimony-vineyard, which will be given to others, and for the wonderfully restored son. Yet there remains a dramatic question about the fate of the tenants. They expected to become heirs and this ruined them. In the story, they had not actually been threatened with being deprived of the vineyard – the master does not send the servants and the son to *withdraw* the inheritance-vineyard but only to *ask for its fruit*. They could have stood by, as servants, without claiming to become heirs, whereas, in the end, there will be no salvation for them. They will be exterminated. Their presence casts a heavy shadow over the affair in which death is added upon death. Is this really the Father's ending? It risks becoming a condemnation not only of the ways to become heirs but of the very fact of claiming such.

The *second text* appears as a theological exegesis of this first one, focusing on the character of the son who, in the parable, was almost completely passive, sent absurdly by his father to collect the rent, and then sent to his death by the tenants.

> Long ago God spoke to our ancestors in many and various ways by the prophets, but in these last days he has spoken to us by a Son, whom he appointed heir of all things, through whom he also created the worlds. He is the reflection of God's glory and the exact imprint of God's very being, and he sustains all things by his powerful word. When he had made purification for sins, he sat down at the right hand of the Majesty on high, having become as much superior to angels as the name he has inherited is more excellent than theirs (Heb 1:1–4).

---

37    MEIER, *A Marginal Jew.* 5, 251.

In this passage, as in the *Letter to the Hebrews* in general, the theme is that, in carrying out his priestly function, Christ is an active and dialogical subject in relation to God's action and comes to his function in a dynamic manner. He *inherits* his own name, which also belongs to him from the beginning. Reality, created in him, is inherited by him in his own name as Son, precisely through the events of the passion.[38]

The *Letter to the Hebrews* itself strives to point out that it is not by means of a rite that this inheritance is manifested and passed on but through the concreteness of self-offering.

> Consequently, when Christ came into the world, he said,
> "Sacrifices and offerings you have not desired,
> but a body you have prepared for me;
> in burnt offerings and sin offerings
> you have taken no pleasure.
> Then I said, 'Here I come.
> See, I have come to do your will, O God'
> (in the scroll of the book it is written of me)" (*Heb* 10:5–7).

As can be seen, this name of heir has a solid foundation in the texts. Yet it cannot be denied that many questions that need answering are left open. Both about the Father, who is not clear what he really wants in this whole story, and about the way in which he who was also Son takes on his sonship in a new way. Yet both texts clearly indicate where to look. To answer the questions one must pay attention to the dynamics of the passion, and – according to the *Letter to the Hebrews* – focus on the concreteness of Jesus' body rather than on ritual interpretation.

---

38   It can be debated whether the name inherited in *Heb* 1:4 is that of 'Son' or 'high priest', or whether this name corresponds, rather, to a new general identity (*cf.* PENNA, *I ritratti originali di Gesù il Cristo*, II, 273–274); it should be noted, however, that even if, in the context of the letter, the inheritance assumed through suffering is closely linked to the acquisition of a priestly function (*Heb* 5:7–9; 7:27; 9:12–28; 10:1–8; 13:12), it is nevertheless clear that "the one who becomes the 'high priest' is precisely 'the Son'" (F. MANZI – G.C. PAGAZZI, *Il pastore dell'essere. Fenomenologia dello sguardo del Figlio*, Cittadella, Assisi 2001, 111) in a process that is not only functional, but involves his deepest filial identity (*Heb* 1:1–4; 2:9–14). It is basically a matter of not believing that one must obsessively define the static-essential aspect (filial) from the dynamic-functional one (priestly), as if to secure the theological dimension from the economic one. Identity as such is dynamic and is made in the functions it assumes; and Jesus, *in his theological identity*, cannot be secured from his economic mission precisely because it is only in this that he reveals himself and the Father.

## 6 The Testator

It was necessary to justify the plausibility and appropriateness of the category of inheritance. After these preliminary remarks, it is now possible to turn to the two main protagonists of the story, the one who bequeaths the inheritance and the one who receives it.

### 6.1 Handing Over

If the name of the person who inherits is the *heir*, it is more difficult to identify the name of the person who leaves the inheritance: the *testator*, the *de cuius*, or, more properly, the *dead*. In fact, one inherits when one's father dies.[39] However, the inheritance in the New Testament has the characteristic of being an inheritance that takes place with the testator still alive, since no text suggests the idea that God the Father is dead. Yet, if we look at several passages in the New Testament, we find that one who entrusts his patrimony to a third party may do so for other reasons. Sometimes because he goes away, sometimes because he yields to demands, more generally because he hands it over:

> A nobleman went to a distant country to get royal power for himself and then return (*Lk* 19:12).
> A man planted a vineyard, and leased it to tenants, and went to another country for a long time (*Lk* 20:9).
> The younger [of the two sons] said to his father, 'Father, give me the share of the wealth that will belong to me'. So he divided his assets between them (*Lk* 15:12).

It is precisely the more classical version of the theme of the 'delivery/surrender' and the act of "handing over" (παραδιδόναι, *paradidónai*), which sees the Father as the subject of the action, that has the merit of reminding us that the Father who leaves is not the passive subject of the event, even at the risk of reading into this a handing over *into the hands of men* rather than *in favour of them*.[40] The idea of the Father's being involved in the handing over of Jesus remains a strong challenge that increases rather than diminishes the dramatic

---

[39] *Cf. Heb* 9:16–17: "Where a will is involved, the death of the one who made it must be established. For a will takes effect only at death, since it is not in force as long as the one who made It is alive".

[40] *Cf. Rom* 8:32: "He who did not withhold his own Son, but gave him up for all of us, will he not with him also give us everything else?"; *Rom* 4:24–25: "… Jesus our Lord … who was handed over for our trespasses and was raised for our justification". *2 Cor* 5:21 can also be read in the same light: "For our sake God made the one who knew no sin to be sin, so that in him we might become the righteousness of God".

charge. In fact, the events of the passion would be more explicable if the Father's absence derived from his death; since he is still alive, however, the question of his absence becomes dramatic. If he is also involved in these events, it becomes essential to understand his role in the drama.

Alongside the role of the Father who hands over, however, there is a second handing-over role, namely that of Jesus himself:

> For this reason the Father loves me, because I lay down my life in order to take it up again. No one takes it from me, but I lay it down of my own accord. I have power to lay it down, and I have power to take it up again. I have received this command from my Father (*Jn* 10:17–18).
> And the life I now live in the flesh, I live by faith in the Son of God, who loved me and gave himself for me [hand over] (*Gal* 2:20).
> And walk in love, as Christ loved us and gave himself up [hand over] for us, a fragrant offering and sacrifice to God. [...] Husbands, love your wives, just as Christ loved the church and gave himself up [hand himself over] for her (*Eph* 5:2.25).
> Christ Jesus, himself human, who gave himself a ransom for all (*1 Tim* 2:5–6).
> He It is who gave himself for us that he might redeem us from all iniquity and purify for himself a people of his own who are zealous for good deeds (*Tit* 2:14).

The Son hands himself over to men, and, in doing this, he also hands himself over to the Father ("After Jesus had taken the wine, he said: 'It is finished'. Then he bowed his head and gave up his spirit", *Jn* 19:30);[41] he faces his destiny actively, not as one chained.[42] Jesus is not offered, he offers himself; he is not stripped, he undresses. The idea is powerfully expressed by the infrequent but significant depiction of Jesus climbing up the cross by a ladder and nailing himself to it. In some cases, nails and hammer are passed to him from underneath.[43]

Reading these events in terms of handing over has the advantage of enhancing the dramatic charge of the event in that it places everyone in an extremely active condition: the men who hand over/betray act, the Father who hands over acts, and the Son who hands himself over acts. However, this risks focusing attention on Jesus as the 'object' of the handing over, even of his own

---

41   See also – even though the Greek verb used is not παραδίδωμι (*paradídōmi*), but παρατίθημι (*paratíthēmi*) – *Lk* 23:46: "Then Jesus, crying out with a loud voice, said, 'Father, into your hands I commend my spirit'. Having said this, he breathed his last".
42   *Cf.* GUARDINI, *Freiheit Gnade Schicksal*, 173–192 and 213–284.
43   In this regard, one can observe the altar frontal of Badia Ardenga by Guido da Siena (ca. 1280), the miniature by Pacino di Buonaguida (ca. 1320) and the fourteenth-century fresco in the monastery of S. Antonio in Polesine (A. EÖRSI, *Haec scala significat ascensum virtutum. Remarks on the Iconography of Christ Mounting the Cross on a Ladder*, in *Arte cristiana* 85 [1977] 151–166).

handing over. Instead, introducing the theme of the inheritance helps us to ask *what exactly is being handed over*. The inheritance as such cannot be Jesus himself, if only because, as an inheritance, he could not simultaneously be an heir. In that case, it is a question not of the handing over *of the Son*, but of the handing over *to the Son*.

What then does the Father deliver into the hands of the Son? The texts that allow an interpretation in these terms have to do with the idea that Jesus was given *everything*, which is what typically happens when a father dies: during his life he grants something, but when he dies he has to leave everything.

> All things have been handed over to me by my Father, and no one knows the Son except the Father, and no one knows the Father except the Son and anyone to whom the Son chooses reveal him (*Mt* 11:27).
> Jesus, knowing that the Father had given all things into his hands, and that he had come from God and was going to God, got up from the table, took off his outer robe, and tied a towel around himself (*Jn* 13:3–4).

There are two interesting aspects that emerge when trying to identify this 'all' that Jesus receives. The first is related to the handing over of the name. What Jesus has in his hands is the very name of the Father, that is, the very identity of God: "Holy Father, protect them in your name that you have given me, so that they may be one, as we are one" (*Jn* 17:11). This fits well with the central insight of Christianity: that in Jesus and in his death and resurrection is the revelation not of an aspect of God but of his name, the centre of his identity. In this sense, between the Son/heir and the Father there is no longer any possibility of distinction as to inheritance, as to patrimony: "All that the Father has is mine. For this reason I said that [the Spirit] will take what is mine and declare it to you" (*Jn* 16:15). This is exactly what happens to a company when a transfer of inheritance takes place, i.e. the name and possession of the company passes from a father to a son, so that what was previously in the hands of one passes into the hands of the other. Obviously, if this happens before the death of the testator, he will find himself in the strange condition whereby his name, his honour, is in the hands of another. If I leave to my son the company that bears my name, it will be my name that will be exposed to the management of my heir, so that my honour or dishonour will depend on his action.

A second aspect emerges if we reflect on the fact that the name delivered into the hands of the Son is not only the name *of the Father* but is the name *of Father*, that is, it indicates the relationship to care of the children. If it can actually be said that by handing over his own name the Father hands *himself* over to the Son, it can also be said that by handing over his own name as Father he hands *us* over to the Son:

[Father,] I have made your name known to those whom you gave me from the world. They were yours and you gave them to me, and they have kept your word. Now they know that everything you have given me is from you, for the words that you gave to me I have given to them, and they have received them and know in truth that I came from you, and they have believed that you sent me (*Jn* 17:6–8).

The *content* of the Father's name is the care of the children, and the care of the children, particularly in the passion, is entrusted to the Son. Not only is the name of the Father in the hands of the Son, but also the name of the children is kept in the same place. When that name is put to the test by the events of the passion, what is at stake are the names of all. Not only his name of Son is at stake, but also the name of the Father and the name of the children. Of us all.

Under the pressure of torture and death, Jesus will have to resolve the ambiguity and decide whether to be "the firstborn within a large family [brothers]" (*Rom* 8:29) or the "only Son of God" (*Jn* 3:18). In themselves, these two names are not in conflict: "For God so loved the world that he gave his only Son, so that everyone who believes in him may not perish but may have eternal life" (*Jn* 3:16). Yet this is precisely what the events of the passion will provoke: an unnatural tension in the identity of Jesus which only he can cope with.

## 6.2   *Absences*

At this point the question shifts to the Father. At this moment of inheritance, nothing suggests that he is dead. If, however, the Father is not dead, what has happened to him?

The absence of the Father is not new in Jesus' preaching. In several parables, the idea of the 'leader' going away emerges. This is the case in the parable we saw above, where "a man planted a vineyard, put a fence around it, dug a pit for the winepress, and built a watchtower; then he leased it to tenants and went away" (*Mk* 12:1). But the same happens in the case of the parable of the talents, where "[...] a man, going on a journey, summoned his slaves and entrusted his property to them" (*Mt* 25:14). In that case, too, the servant has to cope with the master's remoteness. Needless to say, these absences are almost always the cause of disasters. They are, however, also the time when servants can show who they are, prove themselves worthy or not worthy of the trust placed in them. Somehow the master's distance is the space for their autonomous identity, for their name. Luke will make the dynamic even more explicit by making the departure an explicit and active gesture of the son ("He travelled to a distant region" *Lk* 15:13). Not like a coin or a sheep that is lost, but like a son who decides to leave home. A common experience at that time, as well as today.

However, at this point things, move out of parable and into reality, and absence is no longer a schoolyard example but dramatic existential evidence.

During the passion, in fact, the Father is absent. Jesus is abandoned. He who was always with him, acted with him and gave him concrete testimony of his closeness both in the actions he performed for his brothers and sisters and in the words confirming his affection, is now still and mute. Now "there is nothing that shows God acting on Jesus".[44] There are many ways to be alone, and, in some of these ways, aloneness expresses a positive fact. It allows us not to be consumed by the presence of others but to remain ourselves, in our uniqueness, even in the deepest relationship. In this sense, it can be said that even Jesus was alone,[45] to express the fact that whether in front of the disciples, or in front of his mother, or even in front of the Father, he always remained a subject, unique, with the need to explain himself to others in order to make himself understood, and with the need to pray to keep alive a relationship that was never a flat identity. Here, however, things are different. Now God's silence is deafening. This aloneness has the contours of abandonment and betrayal.

The image evoked by the parables could have been fascinating, that of a God capable of stepping aside, of stepping back to allow each one to show his worth, of trusting in the management of his own property. Much less so is the image of a man who has put his whole self at stake in trusting a God who, at the most dramatic moment, decides to do nothing. He who gave Jesus the power to turn water into wine as a worthy end to a wedding feast now gives nothing: neither words nor actions. Beginning with Jesus' arrest, the story continues without any divine intervention; everything happens according to the rules and logic we know. He who is struck bleeds, he who is afraid runs away, he who looks sees. One does not need to believe in miracles to hear this tale.

### 6.3 Mockery

This absence should not be underestimated. It takes its most bitter form in the words of those who see it and draw the most natural conclusion: if the Father is not close to him now, it means that he was not close to him before either. Not only was he not his Father, he was not even his friend. It would take a friend to be close to a man in such difficulty.

> Those who passed by derided him, shaking their heads and saying, "You who would destroy the temple and build it in three days, save yourself! If you are the Son of God, come down from the cross!" In the same way the chief priests, also, along with the scribes and elders, were mocking him, saying, "He saved others; he cannot save himself. He is the King of Israel; let him come down from the cross now, and we will believe in him. He trusts in God; let God deliver him now, if he wants to, for he said, 'I am God's Son'" (*Mt* 27:39–43).

---

44   BROWN, *The Death of the Messiah. Vol. II*, 1046.
45   *Cf.* PAGAZZI, *In principio era il legame*, 30–54.

# THE HEIR

One should not be hasty in judging the gaze of these men negatively. They are doing what Jesus himself had invited them to do: look at the signs, recognise in historical events the manifestation of God's presence. "If I am not doing the works of my Father, then do not believe me. But if I do them, even though you do not believe me, believe the works, so that you may know and understand that the Father is in me, and I am in the Father" (*Jn* 10:37–38). Now what you see is *nothing*. It is not they who are angry with him; it is God himself.

Their tone may take on the features of mockery, but all they are doing is telling the truth. The climax of this dynamic occurs just before his death. Jesus shouts,[46] and those who hear this shout believe he is calling Elijah and mock him.

> At three o'clock, Jesus cried out with a loud voice: "Eloi, Eloi, lema sabachthani?" which means, "My God, my God, why have you forsaken me?" When some of the bystanders heard it, they said, "Listen, he is calling for Elijah". And someone ran and filled a sponge with sour wine, put it on a stick, and gave it to him to drink, saying, "Wait, let us see whether Elijah will come to take him down." Then Jesus gave a loud cry and breathed his last (*Mk* 15:34–37).

Was he not the prophet similar to Elijah, or even Elijah himself, the never-dead, returned to earth? But above all, if this man is Elijah's friend – if not God's – he will not be able to complain that he is being treated in the same way as Elijah himself had treated the prophets of Baal (*cf. 1 Kings* 18). They too had cried out, they too had bled. But the reality was that no fire had come down from heaven, either to burn the offering or to save them from Elijah's fury. "Cry aloud! Surely he is a god; either he is meditating, or he has wandered away, or he is on a journey, or perhaps he is asleep and must be wakened" (*1 Kings* 18:27).

Yet these mockeries hide something true. This man is alone. And that is why one cannot and should not look away. The challenge of inheritance is to read this absence in its rawness as the moment when one must not look away. One must not look to heaven, one must not look to the Father. This is the moment of the heir, when to understand something one must look to him because he alone is on the stage.

At the same time, the destiny of all depends on this one actor. If there is a heritage, a possibility of inheritance, this is the decisive moment.

It is the essential moment for the *Son*, who remains alone to carry on the cause/name of the Father. In this hour, Jesus inherits his own name as Son by taking upon himself the name of the Father and the children-siblings.

---

[46] *Cf.* S. ZENI, *La simbolica del grido nel Vangelo di Marco. Aspetti antropologici e teologici*, EDB, Bologna 2019.

It is the defining moment of the *sons'* identity. The fact that Jesus persists in placing at the centre, not his own received inheritance as Son, not his divinity and sonship – as if they were a possession – but the heritage of God's own fatherhood: this is what makes us sons beyond all our possible actions; it is what makes us co-heirs of an inheritance secured by another.[47]

Finally, it is the essential moment for the action of the *Father* who shows that he is the one who risks to the full all that he has and is, entrusting it into the hands of another. Here, his name of Father shows all the risk of not having in himself the centre of his own identity, but of possessing it only insofar as entrusted to another, dependent on his action.

## 6.4   Excursus: *Everyday Inheritances*

When an inheritance is at stake, it is never easy to know where to look. Who holds the patrimony? The old man or the young man? And which one is willing to hand over something to us as well? We risk addressing our request to the one who has nothing left, or to the one who has nothing yet. At the risk of interrupting the thread of reasoning, I would like to insert a story here, which I think may clarify what this change of direction in outlook means.

About ten years ago, I bought a chainsaw which I used at the time, and then it sat in the cellar gathering dust. The Vaia storm, which swept through the forests of north-eastern Italy, mowing down millions of trees, prompted me to put it back to work in order to play my (small) part in this cataclysm. I, therefore, went back to the shop to have it resharpened, buy the additive for the fuel and a few other things. At the cashier-desk was still the shop-owner who had sold it to me back in the day, but it was his 25-year-old daughter who was in the workshop. It was she who – with a certain righteous disdain for the way I had neglected the tool – fixed everything and, just to be sure, also wanted to re-explain to me how to start it. I'm afraid I didn't look as if I knew how to do it very well. When it was time to pay, I went to the till, and the man whom I took to be the owner told me: 'Hold on, I have to ask the boss for the bill'. The boss was the daughter. This man, who was not old, had left everything in the hands of his daughter, including the right to decide whether or not to give me a discount. However, he had not gone away. He had remained there, becoming his daughter's subordinate. I was looking at the wrong person.

To know about the 'boss' now, one must look in the right direction, and understand to what extent everything is now in the hands of the Son.

---

47    *Cf.* PARIS, *Teologia e neuroscienze*, 285–310.

# 7   The Heir

The place to look is certainly the passion. Looking at the Risen Jesus, one can risk mistaking him for a gardener (*Jn* 20:15) or not recognising him despite walking with him for some kilometres (*Lk* 24:13–27). Instead, the cross is the image that Christianity has chosen to represent itself and that, from a certain point in its history, it has relentlessly reproduced. This is the place of God's ultimate manifestation to mankind.

But what did those who were present at this sad spectacle see? There must indeed have been something visible, not only for the gaze of a mystic or for those versed in his theology, symbolism and spirituality. Not even necessarily for the gaze of those who loved and followed him, but for everyone. Something visible to a 'secular' and disenchanted gaze, a gaze that can be good or bad, as long as it has its eyes open to look at what is happening. It must be something that has the same raw historicity as the events we live through every day.

Precisely because it is something so common, it can escape the eye – it can go unnoticed because, in this complex event, the eyes are turned to the wrong time or in the wrong place.

Precisely for this reason, it seems to me that our gaze must remain wide, to grasp the general dynamics at work in the event and then converge on their culminating point, *the death of a man*. Our gaze will therefore try to focus on the dynamics, on the attitudes that Jesus assumed in this tragedy. In his way of behaving in these few hours is contained, according to Christianity, the possibility of understanding who God is. Not so much in his words, which in the end say nothing different from what he had said before; what must be grasped are his movements, his attitudes. Whoever does not see here will not see anywhere.

## 7.1   *The Name of the Father*

The first attitude to look at concerns Jesus' relationship with the Father. All his life he assumed that the name of God was 'Father'. Now the Father is silent. What will Jesus do? Will he remain firm in this idea?

I would like to read one moment in particular through the lens of this question. It is the Jewish trial, the one that takes place before the authorities of the Sanhedrin. The scene is somewhat reminiscent of certain court-room films in which the trial is blocked by a stalemate. Decisive testimony cannot be found: "Now the chief priests and the whole council were looking for false testimony against Jesus so that they might put him to death; but they found none, though many false witnesses came forward" (*Mt* 26:59–60). Moreover, the accused, whom everyone wants dead for one reason or another, is reticent: "But Jesus was silent" (*Mt* 26:63). It would be necessary to make him fall into a trap, to find a question that provokes him on a sore point which he will answer against his own interest. Eventually, someone has an idea and puts it into practice with theatricality and cunning.[48]

> Then the high priest said to him, "I put you under oath before the living God, tell us if you are the Messiah, the Son of God." Jesus said to him, "You have said so. But I tell you,
> From now on you will see the Son of Man
> seated at the right hand of Power
> and coming on the clouds of heaven."
> Then the high priest tore his clothes and said, "He has blasphemed! Why do we still need witnesses? You have now heard his blasphemy. What do you think?" They answered, "He deserves death" (*Mt* 26:63–66).

The question is the right one. It is not about this or that interpretation of the temple or the law but about the core of his identity: "Are you the Son of God?" Which is like saying: 'Tell us, finally, if you believe God is father or not; tell us if you believe you are son or not'. The defendant answers. At this point, the trial is over. The fate of the guilty party is sealed.

This dramatic moment, from which it is no longer possible to escape as from an unfortunate event, is the sum of what happens. Jesus is tortured, humiliated and at last killed. Yet the onlooker must admit that no matter what is done to him, he remains convinced that God is Father. Everything is against the evidence, yet he, alone, continues to stand firm in this idea.

He does so while remaining *consistent* with what he had always maintained and taught. He does so *gratuitously*, precisely because the evidence of the absence of any action on God's part could legitimately allow him to admit 'I was wrong', or at least to acknowledge that if this paternity was true once, it is not true now. That is why he also does it in a *new, adult* way, carrying the weight of this statement *alone* against everyone and everything. Even for and against God. It had not been so in the past. That is why, now, the Son needs a shot in the arm: the ability to bear the enormity of this name alone. He believes that this is the kind of son the Father wants, and in this lies the answer to those who had challenged him over the claim that he could treat God as a family member. Only a free and adult son can be asked to bear the full weight of another's name. It is not something that can be asked of or imposed on a child. When the master no longer has the strength to assert himself, the slave regains his

---

48 Something similar to what we saw in R. REINER's master scene, *A Few Good Men*, USA 1992, in which Tom Cruise manages to get Jack Nicholson to confess his own crime.

freedom. If the boss does not pay, an employee goes elsewhere to work. The son stays. There is a bond of affection, of identity, a definitive attachment, so close that it cannot be dissolved even when it leads to disaster.

Will Jesus be able for this? Will he be able to feel himself a Son and not curse the Father to the end? Jesus' last words on the cross may leave the reader perplexed. Does it all end in confident abandonment – "Father, into your hands I commend my spirit" (*Lk* 23:46) – or in the despair of one who is forsaken – "My God, my God, why have you forsaken me?" (*Mt* 27:46 and *Mk* 15:34)?

## 7.2   *The Name of the Brothers and Sisters*

The question of Jesus' holding on to the paternal name of God is not rhetorical. Here and there, one can find hints of failure, hints that he may have been tempted to break down. Just think of the contrast between "my will" and "your will" (*Lk* 22:42) which was to give so many problems later to the Fathers. It was even to be used by the Arians to argue that Jesus was not divine, i.e. to undermine the heart of Christian theology. Such hesitations are not worthy of a God.

On the second relationship that binds Jesus – in a non-figurative sense – there is no doubt. No matter what you do to him, you cannot dissuade him from the fixed idea that others are also children and siblings. In the face of torture, he forgives; in the face of complaining about himself, he invites you to extend the complaint to the other oppressed children; in the face of mockery, he promises salvation. Here, the evidence is even more overwhelming. If the Father seems absent, the brothers, on the other hand, are very present, but they are killing him. Yet, one cannot find a single harsh word addressed by him to his executioners, his accusers or those who have abandoned him.

This could be a phenomenon we are familiar with today. When a person is completely crushed, he may not rebel against his persecutors but surrender, giving up fighting them. When a person is overwhelmed by a destiny of death, he may eventually be swept away by the current.

However, this does not seem to be the case here. In fact, Jesus seems convinced that his destiny is not sealed, that things could still turn out differently.

Right at the beginning of the drama, in the Garden of Olives, when one of his own tries to change the course of events by drawing his sword and starting a micro-revolt, Jesus stops him with these words:

> Put your sword back into its place, for all who take the sword will perish by the sword. Do you think that I cannot appeal to my Father, and he will at once send me more than twelve legions of angels? But how then would the scriptures be fulfilled, which say it must happen in this way? (Mt 26:52–54).

This short passage says many things. Firstly, that Jesus does not want his story to set brother against brother. The result would only be a massacre. But even more, and in a breathtakingly moving way, he believes that there are twelve legions of angels ready to intervene to save him. At any moment, his fate could change. Normally quite neglected by exegesis, these twelve legions increase the dramatic charge of the passion out of all proportion. In practice, they never leave. All subsequent events will take place under the astonished gaze of an army that could intervene but, instead, does nothing. And they will take place for a man who, at any moment, can hope to be freed from torture, humiliation and death.

But, then, why do they not intervene? Why 'must it happen this way'? Just to confirm some prophecy in the ancient sacred texts, and one not easy to trace at that? No. What is at stake is not one or another passage of Scripture, but its general meaning, namely, the very name of God.

Here we also see the extent to which the name of Jesus and that of the Father are different, concern different persons and can also be asserted *against each other*. For if the legions of angels had intervened – which means: if the power of the Father had saved the Son by exterminating the murderers – the name of Jesus would have been saved. His name as Son and heir would have been manifested powerfully. The Only-Begotten of the Most High, the heir of his glory, would have been saved by the power of the Father. Or rather: by the power of God. For what would have become of the name of God? He would then have manifested himself as Father, but only of Jesus. Not of everyone. A father who saves his own son and slaughters all the others. In line with the parable of the wicked tenants.

Jesus cannot allow this, because this is not what he wants. He does not want to be simply the Son; he wants to be the heir, that is, to make his own the Father's paternal capacity, the care for every creature. In order for God to be called Father, *all* others must be sons, and they cannot be killed. For in the name of the Father are enshrined the names of all. In order to be the Father's Son/heir, Jesus must *want* the salvation of his brothers.

Therein lies the final temptation of Christ. The one that recognises him as Son and asks: on what does your name as Son depend? On your nature, on your prowess, on your love? Jesus has all this and yet he must answer: no. For his name is not derived from him, but from the name of the Father. If sonship is the title that belongs to those who are worthy of it, like Jesus, it is inevitable that his story is our condemnation. No one else will be found equal to him. If, on the other hand, sonship depends on the name of the Father, everything and everyone become children, since this is his *only* form of relationship. The name of Jesus does not depend on himself but on another; it is an inheritance. Receiving it, he also finds inscribed in it the names of everyone else. He cannot save his own name without saving the Father's, and to do this he cannot invoke any angelic legion or, in the end, expect it. It is ultimately a matter of deciding whether the name of Son depends on himself or on God.

Jesus had always had this dynamic well in mind. For why would the Pharisee in the parable, who, standing up, gives thanks to God – "God, I thank you that I am not like other people: thieves, rogues, adulterers, or even like this tax collector" (*Lk* 18:11) – return home condemned? Did he not speak the truth? It cannot just be a question of humility, as if one who has some merit – "I fast twice a week; I give a tenth of all my income" (*Lk* 18:12) – should pretend he is not who he is. Instead, *the* question is *theological*. If God is Father of *all*, it is unthinkable to make oneself look good in the eyes of the Father by denigrating one's brother. The right of both to enter the temple, to stand in the presence of God, depends not on them – no one is so beautiful that he can force God to look at him – but on God – no one is so ugly that he does not attract his fatherly gaze.

Here we also show the power of the commandment of love, in which love of God comes before love of neighbour. The neighbour is loved not because he deserves it or because of my own goodness. It is only because God is Father, as much mine as his, that I cannot help but recognise that the proper bond with him can only be to see him as a son-brother. In God's paternal name.

Here, everyone's name is on different sides, and the clash is deadly. Here, none of the bonds suits Jesus. It does not suit him that God is Father, much less that others are brothers. In the end, it does not suit him to be Son either. He bears all these names by virtue of the name of freedom he has received, in a difference that allows him to take on all *against all* and *for all*.

> Therefore God exalted him even more highly
> and gave him the name
> that is above every name,
> so that at the name given to Jesus
> every knee should bend,
> in heaven and on earth and under the earth,
> and every tongue should confess
> that Jesus Christ is Lord,
> to the glory of God the Father (*Phil* 2:9–11).

## 7.3 The Manifested Heir

All this risks being speculation. Something that uses a theological key to add to events that speak of something else. Instead, the challenge lies in the possibility of all this being visible. In essence, it is about the possibility of seeing the *relationships* that bind Jesus to others. This is a strategic step. As long as the focus is on the 'natures' of Jesus, divine and human, the possibility of seeing them is, in principle, only indirect. One does not see a nature; if at all, one deduces it from actions and potentialities. One who performs miracles must be able to draw on a more than human nature, just as one who weeps or dies shows his humanity. This has been the interest and strategy of the great Fathers. If, however, what we are looking for is not natures but relations, things are different, provided we have eyes to see.

It is therefore a matter of fixing our attention in the right place to see what we can see. The four evangelists help us to identify what this place is, namely, the cross and death of Jesus. At the same time, they have different approaches and ways of presenting the event and suggesting how it should be viewed.

I shall try to go through these different gazes in search of the possibility of seeing, from beneath the cross, the relationship of inheritance that binds Jesus to the Father.

### 7.3.1 John and the Question (Jn 19:16–37)

Faced with the questions 'what to look at?' and 'how to look?', John has no doubt that one must look and look here, at the Crucified One: "(He who saw this has testified so that you may also believe. His testimony is true, and he knows that he tells the truth.) [...] They will look on the one whom they have pierced" (*Jn* 19:35.37).

If it, therefore, shows us *where to look*, it does not, however, help our eyes to move between the events of Jesus' death because it assumes that we already know at and how to look. The most interesting aspects of John's account focus on characters who are too involved, with a gaze too 'biased' to help our own, such as that of the mother or the beloved disciple. Those who would have a more detached gaze are too intent on dividing his clothes or checking that he is dead to help us. Jesus' death thus takes on an almost private aspect; it becomes an affair between him and the Father – in line with John's theological approach. The symbolic aspects that envelop every section of the story – the seamless tunic, the blood and water from the side, the unbroken bones – presume a gaze that has already been informed, already a believer. A Roman soldier cannot be expected to *see* anything from these subtle connections between banal facts and learned references to the Old Testament. Instead, it is precisely this gaze that we are looking for.

John, therefore, shows us where to look, but it is the Synoptics that will lead us into the dynamics of this gaze.

### 7.3.2 Matthew and the Earthquake (Mt 27:45–54)

The dynamic expressed by Matthew is the clearest. What happens at the death of Jesus is astounding:

> Then Jesus cried again with a loud voice and breathed his last. At that moment the curtain of the temple was torn in two, from top to bottom. The earth shook, and the rocks were split. The tombs also were opened, and many bodies of the saints who had fallen asleep were raised. After his resurrection they came out of the tombs and entered the holy city and appeared to many. Now when the centurion and those with him, who were keeping watch over Jesus, saw the earthquake and what took place, they were terrified and said, "Truly this man was God's Son!" (Mt 27:50–54).

The *events* are clear. A group of people – "the centurion, and those with him" – witness a series of extraordinary events accompanying the death of the prisoner (an ugly death). What catches their eye is not Jesus and how he dies; it is "the earthquake and what took place": this is what shocks them. It is no coincidence that none of the films about Jesus that I know of ever film the scene of these *zombies* coming out of the tombs and then, three days later, entering Jerusalem. It is just too much.

Thus, one can easily understand the *dynamic* described. A group of soldiers do their duty and kill someone reputed to be some kind of local prophet. Upon his death, there is such a cosmic reaction that they are stunned. Truly this was a son of the gods. They do not need to believe in him or convert; they simply register what the events suggest.

It is a dynamic that, even in a less cosmic and magical way, can happen at any time. If half a million people showed up at my funeral, I think many of my colleagues would be amazed, thinking: 'Maybe we underestimated him'. Matthew tells something like this.

### 7.3.3 Luke and Goodness (Lk 23:1–49)

The story told by Luke has radically different emphases. For the author of the third Gospel, the one who goes to die is the same Jesus whose parables and miracles have been recounted. He is a good man. His entire passion confirms this idea. Jesus forgives those who kill him because they "do not know what they are doing" (*Lk* 23:34); he offers salvation to the good thief, without insulting the bad one; and finally dies entrusting himself to the Father: "Father, into your hands I commend my spirit" (*Lk* 23:46).

> When the centurion saw what had taken place, he praised God and said, "Certainly this man was innocent." And when all the crowds who had gathered there for this spectacle saw what had taken place, they returned home, beating their breasts. But all his acquaintances, including the women who had followed him from Galilee, stood at a distance, watching these things (*Lk* 23:47–49).

In *Luke*, too, the gaze is collective, focusing on something that anyone can see. Only, in this case, it is not the earthquake but the faithful goodness of Jesus.

The *events* are clear here too. What is needed, however, is a broad view, one that embraces the whole affair and is able to see the way in which the prisoner dealt with beatings and insults. He coped with all this with an attitude that is astonishing.

This is also a *dynamic* one can imagine. Neither the acquaintances nor the crowd nor the centurion is necessarily evil. And precisely because of this, it is not strange that they may recognise that they have witnessed something surprising. Their own reaction is significant. Having realised what has happened – that "this man was innocent", good – they are left beating their breasts, wondering deep down: 'What have we done?'

A dynamic that can happen at any time when the strength, courage and love of a persecuted person also affects his executioners. They too have wives and children and know the gestures of tenderness and goodness. Everything can then continue as before; yet, a sense of unease remains.

### 7.3.4 Mark and the Son (Mk 15:33–39)

Different again is the gaze in *Mark*. It is both challenging – in that it does not offer immediate footholds for understanding the events – and raw – because it does not assume that the viewer is *already* a believer. Although in many respects it is the most enigmatic account, it is also the most significant for grasping the concrete dynamics involving the characters.

> When it was noon, darkness came over the whole land until three in the afternoon. At three o'clock Jesus cried out with a loud voice, "Eloi, Eloi, lema sabachthani?" which means, "My God, my God, why have you forsaken me?" When some of the bystanders heard it, they said, "Listen, he is calling for Elijah." And someone ran, filled a sponge with sour wine, put it on a stick, and gave it to him to drink, saying, "Wait, let us see whether Elijah will come to take him down." Then Jesus gave a loud cry and breathed his last. And the curtain of the temple was torn in two, from top to bottom. Now when the centurion, who stood facing him, saw that in this way he breathed his last, he said, "Truly this man was God's Son!" (Mk 15:33–39).

It is not possible here to adopt the gaze suggested by Matthew. It is true that "darkness came over the whole land"; yet, no one seems to take this very seriously. Indeed, time is found to set up the mockery of Elijah and the sour wine. No earthquake, no *zombies*. The curtain of the temple rending is too far away for anyone to see.

In his rawness, Mark does not even offer John's symbolic clues, even though they are so difficult to interpret. There is no tunic, no blood mixed with water or intact bones.

Luke's gaze cannot be used either. Jesus is silent the whole time: he does not forgive or teach anyone; he simply suffers it all. He dies badly, worse than in *Matthew*, if possible. An inarticulate cry, just like most tortured people of all times.

Even the gaze directed at the condemned man is different. It is not that of a crowd or a group of people but the gaze of one man – "the centurion, who stood facing him". He is not looking around, he is not rethinking the whole affair, which he may not even have seen; instead, he has his gaze fixed on the dying man – "saw that in this way he breathed his last".

*Mark's* centurion is the only one who is looking in the right place, at the death of Jesus. What, then, did he see to arrive at the point of exclaiming, "Truly this man was God's Son?" What dynamic is being presented here?

This question is decisive. This soldier's gaze is decisive. Not grasping it puts the whole revelation at risk. For if, at the crucial moment – the centre of salvation history – we do not know what to look at and how to look, or we look in the wrong way, we are precluded from recognising it elsewhere.

If the exclamation depended on the centurion, let us say on the fact that he was a saint, it would mean that only saints can see something. Those whose eyes are not *already* pure see nothing. This, however, would not be enough because, from time immemorial, the God of Israel was recognisable to those who knew how to look with pure eyes, while the others "have eyes to see but do not see, [...] have ears to hear but do not hear, for they are a rebellious house" (*Ezek* 12:2). But the power of the cross should lie precisely in the fact that here, in this definitive revelation, even the rebels finally see.

Even more dangerous would be the interpretation that an inner transformation took place in this man's heart that led him to faith. An ambiguity stands out here that will run through all of Christianity. Where does what is most important, most decisive, take place: in the interior or in history? Does God reveal himself in history and is he recognised in the heart or, *vice versa*, does he reveal himself in the heart and is he recognised in history? Certainly both steps are needed, for history to become *my* history. Yet, this ambiguity must be dissolved. If the essential event happens internally, the centurion could even have stayed at home, in his room, and been suddenly enlightened, perhaps in a more dignified way than being involved in this slaughter. Instead, the text suggests that it is the very fact of being there that is essential, of seeing something that anyone could have seen, "facing him".

There is a dynamic we know that can help us understand *Mark's* gaze. It underlies *the idea that, at certain moments, relationships become visible*. For it happens that – in the last moments of life – the concern of the person who dies goes to the loved one who remains, to the children, to the cats or money he leaves behind. Watching him die, one can see what he really cared about. No matter what judgement we make of these bonds (they can be beautiful, frivolous or petty), what matters is that they are real; they are in fact the most real thing of all. And you can see them.

*Mark's* Jesus dies in a poor way, without any major cosmic upheaval, and without seeming any better than many other condemned men. Yet the detached gaze of a Roman soldier records a bond he sees. This man dies referring to someone, a God he considers Father. The centurion does not say it is a good idea to behave this way; we do not even know what idea of God he might have had in his head. He records one fact: for the condemned man, at the final moment, what is important is the bond with a God-the-Father who does nothing for him. It is not distant friends, not accusers, not palace intrigues or the fate of his cause that is ultimately important. It may be puzzling that Pilate makes a reference to the Kingdom above the cross, but this does not appear in Jesus' words. His thought, his basic bond, his suffering, is to know where the Father is. Perhaps the statement "Truly this man was God's Son!" can be read this way, as the acknowledgement of a bond.

It is the same statement that has already appeared twice in *Mark*, spanning his Gospel. A first time, at the beginning of the mission, at the baptism: "And a voice came from the heavens: 'You are my Son, the Beloved; with you I am well pleased'" (*Mk* 1:11). A second time, God speaks on the mount of transfiguration: "Then a cloud overshadowed them, and from the cloud there came a voice: 'This is my Son, the Beloved; listen to him!'" (*Mk* 9:7).

However, God's voice is always too much – or too little – because it is too ambiguous. It is John himself who reminds us of this, just before the Last Supper. Jesus and the Father exchange words of recognition with each other: "'Father, glorify your name.' Then a voice came from heaven, 'I have glorified it, and I will glorify it again!'" (*Jn* 12:28). Yet no one understood much: "The crowd standing there heard it and said that it was thunder. Others said, 'An angel has spoken to him'" (*Jn* 12:29). The bond that unites Father and Son cannot be something they say to each other; it must be something simple and obvious that anyone can recognise. This is why Mark puts the third and final affirmation of the identity of "Jesus Christ, [Son of God]" (*Mk* 1:1) in the mouth of the most unsuspected of witnesses. The crucial affirmation of his Gospel is this bare recognition by a character who will play no other role, either before or afterwards.

The simplicity of this gaze allows us to reread the other Gospels too, recognising that, from this point of view, they all say the same thing. Jesus died concerned for the Father. Perhaps relying on him, as in the *Gospel of Luke*, perhaps crying out to him, as in the *Gospel of Matthew*, perhaps even crying out *against* him. In any case, the focus was on the bond with him, as *John's Gospel* expresses throughout. At the end of his life, his central inheritance becomes evident. Everything he did stands or falls by this relationship.

## 7.4   What We Have Seen

At this point, it is worth pausing for a moment and casting our gaze backwards, to the events of the passion, and forwards, to what is to come, to try to describe in a single action the event that constitutes the heart of Christianity. One could pause and examine the resurrection first, and yet a part of the New Testament – and in particular the *Gospel of Mark* – suggests the idea that what there was to see was actually manifested *already here*. Those who want to bet on this story must be able to do so even now, content with what they have seen. What there is to be seen later, in the resurrection, can only appear if one has understood the meaning of events already here.

A man, drawing on the tradition of an obscure, oriental people, lived his life announcing and realising the presence of God. He spoke of a God who was close, lovingly bound to every man and woman like a father to his sons and daughters. He did so in a way that provoked a violent reaction from those who heard him, the people from whom he came and from whom he drew the substance of his ideas. He was judged to be too much. And for this he was condemned.

Subjected to torture, humiliation – felt all the more acutely the stronger the bond he felt with those *brothers* – and, finally, to death, this man had to use all his freedom and strength to remain faithful to the bond that united him to the God he proclaimed. Faithful even to those who were rejecting and killing him.

Those who followed him, and those who saw, had to decide what they were looking at. A difficult choice, yesterday as today, the more one grasps the serious, real reasons why this man's perspective could be contested. A choice that has to tell how his bond is real. The continuation of the story will say that death did not overcome this bond; yet the decisive elements of the choice are all already on the table at the moment of death. In fact, this man had to decide for himself *before* the resurrection, not *after*.

What has been seen is the heart of the world. The bond out of which the universe took form, *from which, in which* and *for which* all things exist, has been fully manifested in this human story. Death itself, the ultimate enemy, has shown itself to be *included* in this bond. It too is at his service; it too can be taken up as a constitutive moment of this bond. That is how he experienced it, and that is why he feared it, but he was not defeated by it.

This bond defines forever – because it has always existed – what persons, power and freedom are. This bond, in fact, has shown itself to be welcoming, capable of being fully realised in a man and, at the same time, open to all those who, in their own identity, power and freedom, wish to take part in it.

This is true, but it is not *simply* true. It is, in fact, a truth exposed to the power and freedom of each individual. To the lives of those who, in this bond, have been desired, willed, created and freed to be children, heirs of the one who first lived fully, corresponding to the bond from which he came, and thus made it possible for human desire to participate in it fully. This bond is open because it is involving.

Whatever the nature of those involved – divine, human or other – unique is the Spirit, unique is the power, unique the space of this filial dynamic because the eternal movement from which it originates and towards which it sets out and is drawn is unique.

## 8    An Absolute Claim

This was seen, even if not everything was immediately understood. The great deed of a son who had everything in his hands while everything was against him. He did his part, he gave everything. A great proof of himself. If in all this the issue was, 'We shall see who you are', 'We shall see what you are made of', the answer of events is unequivocal.

Starting from the whirlwind of a mess, in which everything came together against him, Jesus made it the place for the manifestation of his own name as Son and the paternal name of God. He did it alone. Masterfully. He did it also by managing not to unload the fury of events, the sin contained within them and the randomness of things to the heads of his murderers. His greatness was not used to belittle his neighbour: on the contrary, the tragic chance was borne without it becoming a curse for others. In this, he upheld and defended the name and fraternal dignity of all, for all, against all.

He showed that there is no place so dark, so wounded, that cannot be experienced as children and siblings. In order to do this, he had to put his own spin on it; he had to expose himself since reality did not speak words of sonship and brotherhood at all. It was not an observation but a stance on reality. The free action and word of Jesus imposed itself on events, changing their perspective. The more events plummeted, the stronger the need became to *give* and *say* to events a meaning they did not immediately have and did not say.

In all this, Jesus made an absolute claim, one which became more and more absolute as events proceeded. It should be clear from everything we have said so far that Jesus' great claim, the great wager, is not *on himself*, but *on God*. This claim was evidently that the meaning he imposed on reality was the meaning of God himself. That his way of acting literally corresponded to God's way of acting. He was saying: 'God is like this'.

The theology of the following centuries clearly grasped this crucial point. Christians believe in a triune God because they have seen him revealed on the cross. The Trinity is the name for the God manifested by Jesus on the cross.

However, the affirmation in principle that the triune God is manifested in the cross is not enough; categories are also needed to make explicit the *how* of this revelation. This is Jesus' wager: that, in his way of acting, God is made visible.

However, it would be a mistake to think that this wager concerns God alone. For from the way God is, it is reality itself that is redefined.

Two passages from the New Testament are central to grasping this wager, and they also allow us to understand how delicate this connection is and how much it risks remaining invisible.

The passion according to John begins basically, as in all the Gospels, with a farewell meeting. The peculiarity is that, in *John* 13, instead of the supper, there is a gesture by Jesus that manifests his greatness. In this passage, he is indeed the heir, the one who, "knowing that the Father had given him all things into his hands, and that he had come from God and was going to God" (*Jn* 13:3), definitively manifests the name he has received and, thus also, manifests the cause and the name of the one who generated and sent him. To live up to this mission and this inheritance, "he got up from supper, took off his outer robe, and tied a towel around himself. Then he poured water into a basin and began to wash the disciples' feet and to wipe them with the towel that was tied around him" (*Jn* 13:4–5). Much more clearly than the Synoptics, John anticipates here the sense of the tragedy to come. In the gesture of Jesus washing the disciples' feet, as well as in his allowing himself to be nailed to the cross, God's care for those whom he considers children by virtue of his name of Father is manifested. The heir has everything in his hands and serves his brothers, thus passing on to his brothers what he has received: "Do you know what I have done to you? You call me Teacher and Lord – and you are right, for that is what I am. So if I, your Lord and Teacher, have washed your feet, you also ought to wash one another's feet" (*Jn* 13:12–14).

We must, however, be very clear on one point. What is at stake here is *not* the goodness of Jesus. It is not his obedience or his willingness but the identity of the Father. To understand this we may look at another text, which, in a more formal way, interprets the same events. It is the hymn in the *Letter to the Philippians*: "Who, [though] he existed in the form of God, did not regard equality with God as something to be grasped, but emptied himself, taking the form of a slave, assuming human likeness" (*Phil* 2:6–7).[49]

The dynamic is similar. Someone who is very great stoops to do something very humble. The gamble of Jesus' death is all in that 'though'. Or rather in the deletion of that 'though'. The two texts, in fact, seem to say the same thing, but, if not read carefully, they end up meaning the opposite of each other. Stooping down, washing feet, humbling himself, giving his life for others is certainly the action of the Son. But does he do this *despite* being divine or *precisely because* he is divine? Put another way, does this represent the exception, the waiver, the excess of the divine – which normally does not bow down and wash anyone's feet – or is it instead the ultimate revelation? If you want to be like God, what do you do? If you want to be the true heir, with full power, and you want to use it as God uses it, what do you do?

It seems to me that *Phil* 2:6–7 must be read in the light of *Jn* 13:3. Jesus, *precisely because* he is divine in nature, is able to stoop – *as* God is able to stoop. Jesus, *precisely because* he has "everything in his hands" (*Jn* 13:3), all power, uses it *as* God uses it. Because God is like that.

Jesus' wager is all here. He claims that the gesture of stooping to help, to give, to forgive, is the *most typical* gesture of God-the-Father.

## 9  Checkmate

This is Jesus' claim, his active claim, enacted in his own flesh. The more events rush on, however, the less the action can be sustained. At a certain point, with death, the action ends. The game comes to an end. He had it all, he played it all, he lost. The game is over.

Giving such a radical centrality to the action of the Son, as I have tried to do, does not allow us to avoid this impasse. If Jesus was alone in speaking, silence remains at his death.

His words might please and fascinate, but they were, in fact, *his* words, *his* ideas. And reality is superior to the idea.[50] True, even when the idea is the love of God and the reality is a dead man. I believe that the disillusionment of the disciples on the road to Emmaus must be taken very seriously – precisely in order to understand what is to come later – "But we had hoped that he was the one to redeem Israel" (*Lk* 24:21). His word seemed to be effective, seemed

---

49  Cf. B. MAGGIONI – F. MANZI, *Lettere di Paolo*, Cittadella, Assisi 2005, 901–905.
50  Cf. FRANCIS, *Evangelii gaudium*, § 222–225.

to have an authority that could overcome reality, but, apparently, reality had prevailed. There is no anger at having been deceived, only disappointment, as at something that was expected after all. It was a beautiful dream, but we had to wake up.

Paul also invites us to stand in this dark place, before the resurrection, or rather, *as if* the resurrection were not. However, there is no disappointment in him but, rather, aggression. This place is decisive and merciless: if everything ends here, it is useless and false.

> And if Christ has not been raised, then our proclamation is in vain and your faith is in vain. We are even found to be misrepresenting God, because we testified of God that he raised Christ – whom he did not raise if it is true that the dead are not raised. For if the dead are not raised, then Christ has not been raised. If Christ has not been raised, your faith is futile and you are still in your sins. Then those also who have died in Christ have perished (*1 Cor* 15:14–18).

Jesus' wager was never about a dream. It was about reality. The reality of people who can change, of sin that can be forgiven, of sickness that can be healed. But if the final word is that of the cross, it would better to avoid sin, because there is no way to change sin, just as there is no way to heal death. If there is no transformation possible and the final word is *this* reality, it must be clearly stated. Otherwise, Paul argues, one ends up deceiving one's neighbour by virtue of ideas, perhaps very charming, but false, incapable of overcoming reality.

### Bibliographical Guidelines

For the theme of **handing over**, see: J. MOLTMANN, *The Way Jesus Christ. Christology in Messianic Dimensions*, HarperCollins Publisher, New York 1990, 172–178; ID., *The Crucified God. The Cross of Christ as the Foundation and Criticism of Christian Theology*, Fortress Press, Minneapolis 1993, 241–249; H.U. VON BALTHASAR, *Mysterium Paschale. The Mystery of Easter*, Ignatius Press, San Francisco 2000, 84–88. I refer to these authors to show how the first and most obvious meaning of the term – that is, the one that sees men, and Judas in particular, as the subjects of the handover – is not sufficient to render the theological drama that takes place here, and the active role that the Son plays in the whole affair. The Son cannot be represented merely as an object that passively undergoes the actions of the hands of men who pass him on, trying to shift the responsibility for his death on to each other.

The theme of handing over refers back to that of atonement and **Satan's rights** (R. SCHWAGER, *Der Sieg Christi über den Teufel*, in *Zeitschrift für katholische Theologie*, 103 [1981] 156–177). As St Anselm would later note (ANSELM OF CANTERBURY, *Why*

*God Became Man*, I.VII, in Id., *The Major Works*, Oxford University Press, Oxford 1998, 2007, 272–274), Gregory of Nazianzus had already ruled out the possibility that Satan could claim rights over man that he could assert at God's tribunal, but also that the ransom price could be paid to an implacable Father: "But if the ransom is not given to anyone except the one holding us in bondage, I ask to whom this was paid, and for what cause? If to the Evil One, what an outrage! For the robber would receive not only a ransom from God, but God himself as a ransom, and a reward so greatly surpassing his own tyranny that for its sake he would rightly have spared us altogether. But if it was given to the Father, in the first place how? For we were not conquered by him. And secondly, on what principle would the blood of the Only-begotten delight the Father, who would not receive Isaac when he was offered by his father but switched the sacrifice, giving a ram in place of the reason-endowed victim?" (Gregory of Nazianzus, *Festal Orations*, St Vladimir's Seminary Press, Yonkers (NY) 2008; XLV.22).

Very interesting is the track that suggests looking at the **Father as saved**, and not only saviour of the Son. The issue of thinking of Jesus' salvation (objective genitive) in a reciprocal manner with respect to the Father is both risky and necessary once the reciprocal character of subjective relations as such is allowed to emerge. Lacanian reflection itself offers insights and words that are sometimes disturbing or inconclusive (cf. I. Guanzini, *Lo spirito è un osso. Postmodernità, materialismo e teologia in Slavoi Žižek*, Cittadella, Assisi 2010, 177–241); they nevertheless invoke a Christian thought that is equal to them. "It is true that the storyette of Christ is presented, not as the enterprise of saving men, but as that of saving God. We must recognize that he who took on this enterprise, namely Christ, paid the price – that's the least we can say about it. We should be surprised that the result seems to satisfy people. [...] Whence it becomes conceivable that God's salvation is precarious and ultimately dependent upon the goodwill of Christians" (J. Lacan, *On Feminine Sexuality. The Limits of Love and Knowledge. Book XX. Encore 1972–1973*, W.W. Norton & Company, New York 1999, 108). See also Moltmann, *The Crucified God*, 200–290.

For references to **Idealism**, I indicate only a few classics for its reception in theology: H. Küng, *The Incarnation of God. An Introduction to Hegel's Theological Thought as Prolegomena to a Future Christology*, T&T Clark, Edinburgh 1987; W. Kasper, *Das Absolute in der Geschichte*, Matthias Gruenewald Verlag, Mainz 1965; X. Tilliette, *La christolgie idéaliste*, Desclée, Paris 1986. Interesting points can be found in L. Pareyson, *Essere libertà ambiguità*, Mursia, Milano 1998; F. Tomatis, *Kenosis del logos. Ragione e rivelazione nell'ultimo Schelling*, Città Nuova, Roma 1994; V. Limone, *Inizio e Trinità. Il neoplatonismo giovanneo nell'ultimo Schelling*, Edizioni ETS, Pisa 2013; I. Guanzini, *L'origine e l'inizio. Hans Urs von Balthasar e Massimo Cacciari*, Edizioni ETS, Pisa 2012.

For the theme of **recognition** in Hegel: A. Honneth, *The Struggle for Recognition: The Moral Grammar of Social Conflicts*, Polity Press, Cambridge 1995; Id., *Von der Begierde zu Anerkennung. Hegels Begründung von Slbstbewusstsein*, in

K. Vieweg – W. Welsch (Edd.), *Hegels Phänomenologiedes Geistes. Ein kooperativer Kommentar zu einem Schlüsselwerk der Moderne*, Suhrkamp, Frankfurt a.M. 2000, 15–32; L. Siep, *Anerkennung als Prinzip der praktischen Philosophie. Untersuchungen zur Hegels Jenaer Philosophie des Geistes*, Meiner Verlag, Hamburg 2014; P. Ricœur, *The Course of Recognition*, Harvard University Press, Cambridge – London 2005; Id., *Oneself as Another*, The University of Chicago Press, Chicago – London 1992, 298–356; F. Ceragioli, *«Il cielo aperto» (Gv 1,51). Analitica del riconoscimento e struttura della fede nell'intreccio di desiderio e dono*, Effatà, Cantalupa 2012, 25–104.

For the **psychological-psychoanalytical** root of the theme of desire and inheritance, the most consequence-laden interpretation is the one provided in the 1930s by A. Kojève, *Introduction to the Lecture of Hegel. Lectures on the Phenomenology of Spirit*, Cornell University Press, Ithaca – London 1980. For a reading: J. Lacan, *Écrits. The first Complete Edition in English*, W.W. Norton & Company, New York – London 2005; J. Butler, *Subjects of Desire. Hegelian Reflections in twentieth-century France*, Columbia University Press, New York 1987; C. Dumoulié, *Le désir*, Armand Colin – HER Éditeur, Paris 1999; P. Ricœur, *The Conflict of Interpretations. Essays in Hermeneutics*, The Athlone Press, London 1989, 99–210 and 468–497; A. Honneth, *Appropriating Freedom: Freud's Conception of Individual Self-Relation*, in Id., *Pathologies of Reason. On the Legacy of Critical Theory*, Columbia University Press, New York 2009, 126–145. For an approach to the subject: M. Recalcati, *Ritratti del desiderio*, Raffaello Cortina, Milano 2012; Id., *The Telemachus Complex. Parents and Children after the Decline of the Father*, Polity Press, Cambridge 2019. In this essay – which oscillates between analysis and hope – the profile of the rightful heir, Telemachus, who awaits/saves his father, is outlined. The interest lies in the focus placed on the son's expectations and actions; it is quite another matter to see whether, as would be desirable, these expectations really correspond to a detectable social and individual condition. Of particular interest in this sense is Recalcati's analysis of historical figures who had to reinvent their own provenance such as Leonardo (Id., *The Telemachus Complex*, 93), Flaubert (Id., *Jacques Lacan. I. Desiderio, godimento e soggettivazione*, Raffaello Cortina, Milano 2012, 424–466) and Joyce (Id., *Jacques Lacan. II. La clinica psicoanalitica: struttura e soggetto*, Raffaello Cortina, Milano 2016, 115–129).

The interweaving of the **cross and the Trinity**, i.e. the idea that the first and fundamental *vestigium trinitatis* is the cross, is one of the leading ideas of the Latin theological tradition from St Francis to Bonaventure to Hegel – albeit in very different ways. Cf. Moltmann, *The Crucified God*, 200–290; E. Jüngel, *God as the Mystery of the World. On the Foundation of the Theology of the Crucified One in the Dispute Between Theism and Atheism*, Bloomsbury T&T Clark, London – New York 2014, 343–367; H.U. von Balthasar, *Theo-drama. Theological dramatic Theory. IV. The Action*, Ignatius Press, San Francisco 1994, 319–388; Id., *Theo-logic. II. Truth of God*, Ignatius Press, San Francisco 2004, 109–146; A. Toniolo, *La theologia crucis nel contesto della* *modernità. Il rapporto tra croce e modernità nel pensiero di E. Jüngel, H.U. von Balthasar e G.W.F. Hegel*, Glossa, Roma – Milano 1995; N. HOFFMANN, *Kreuz und Trinität. Zur Theologie der Sühne*, Johannes Verlag, Einsiedeln 1982; E. PRENGA, *Il Crocifisso via alla Trinità. L'esperienza di Francesco d'Assisi nella teologia di Bonaventura*, Città Nuova, Roma 2009; É. VETÖ, *Da Cristo alla Trinità. Un confronto tra Tommaso D'Aquino e Hans Urs von Balthasar*, EDB, Bologna 2015; A. COUTINHO LOPES DE BRITO PALMA, *L'esperienza della Trinità e la Trinità nell'esperienza. Modelli di una loro configurazione*, Pontificia Università Gregoriana, Roma 2013. For an up-to-date overview: E. DURAND – V. HOLZER (edd.), *Les sources du renouveau de la théologie trinitaire au XX$^e$ siècle*, Cerf, Paris 2008; IDD. (edd.), *Les réalisations du renouveau de la théologie trinitaire au XX$^e$ siècle*, Cerf, Paris 2010.

CHAPTER 9

# The Heir's Father

The disaster of the cross is the defeat of all. A cruel and stupid reality and a series of reasonable objections drag things down to a point from which there is no turning back. The Son said yes to all this, made it his own and accepted it as the tragic place where he would bear witness to the names of all until his last breath. For his part, he wants to, must and can say: "It is finished" (*Jn* 19:30).

The Father says no.

## 1 No!

The word that must be perceived first at the scene of the murdered heir, a word that is dry, immediate: *no*. The Father's word on this event, his judgement, is one of condemnation. What has happened is not right; it is not according to his heart; it is not according to his will.

*Different* words resound at the same time, with the same force, about the same event. It is right that he who has given all and witnessed everything, accepts defeat at a certain point. "Master, now you are dismissing your servant in peace, according to your word" (*Lk* 2:29). However, it is important that there is no ambiguity about the Father's first word. It is a different word. 'No, I will not let you go. I will never say that it is OK. What I see is a scandal that will remain forever, a disgrace, a defeat'.

The word to be heard in this silence of death is, therefore, a no. However, and herein lies what is extraordinary, this no does not have the effect we would expect. In fact, even according to the parable of the wicked tenants, the word of the Father is a no. There is no approval but reprobation of the tragedy involving the tenants and his son. In the parable, this no of reprobation falling on the events causes the death of the tenants.

> "Now when the owner of the vineyard comes, what will he do to those tenants?" They said to him, "He will put those wretches to a miserable death and lease the vineyard to other tenants who will give him the produce at the harvest time" (*Mt* 21:40–41).

It is still a word modulated in the style of our words and our no's. Many times, in fact, when faced with evil that takes the reins of events, we try to oppose our no to what is happening. Our word, however, can *prevent* evil; it cannot change it. One can sometimes prevent the beloved from dying, but nothing can be done *after* he has died. "You in particular, will never die"[1] is the word our love seeks to oppose to death *before* it comes. That is why it is important to say no to sin *before it* happens;[2] afterwards, it is too late. What one can do afterwards, if at all, is to kill the murderers or condemn the sin and the sinner. Sometimes, one can only weep. Each of us is clear about this order of events. That is why Mary's words to Jesus, who shows up when Lazarus is already dead, describe a reality: "Lord, if you had been here, my brother would not have died" (*Jn* 11:21). You should have arrived *earlier*.

What happens after Jesus' death, however, does not correspond to the parable. One of the two outcomes is realised – the restoration of the Son: "The stone that the builders rejected has become the cornerstone" (*Mk* 12:10). And one is not realised – the death of the tenants: "He will come and destroy the tenants" (*Mk* 12:9).[3] Something new of the Father's way of acting is thus revealed. This *no* does not kill. Just as for Jesus affirming that God is Father entailed *at the same time* affirming the name of the children, in the same way, now, for the Father saving the name of the Son entails *at the same time* a definitive yes to all the children, even the murderous ones. If God had been overwhelmed by his own no, and had ended the affair with the slaughter of the parable, it would have meant that, indeed, all was lost.

Thus, the word of God proves to be *different*. It is able not only to stop reality but also to transform it in the same way that it is able to form it. It is a word

---

1 G. MARCEL, *Homo viator. Introduction to the Metaphysic of Hope*, St. Augustine's Press, South Bend (IN) 2010, 140.
2 It is the spiritual struggle directed not against bad actions but against bad thoughts from which actions originate (*cf.* T. ŠPIDLÍK, *La spiritualité de l'Orient chrétien. Manuel systématique*, Ed. Orientalia Christiana, Roma 1978, 225–237; ID., "Sentire e gustare le cose internamente". *Letture per gli Esercizi*, Lipa, Roma 2006, 99–114).
3 There is the possibility of interpreting the outcomes of the parable differently, and identifying three outcomes instead of two: 1) the resurrection of the Son; 2) the death of the tenants; and 3) the handing over of the vineyard to others. These three outcomes would all be realised: 1) the resurrection of Jesus; 2) the destruction of Jerusalem; and 3) the passing of the 'vineyard' from Israel to the church. This interpretation assumes that God has rejected the Jewish people in favour of a new people, and that the destruction of Jerusalem is God's reaction to the Son's murder. These are relevant assumptions. Yesterday – because they justified attitudes towards the Jewish people of which we feel ashamed today –, and today – because the covid-19 pandemic puts the hypothesis of divine punishment back at the centre of public discussion. It is precisely today's theological sensibility that, at the very moment when it proposes a more balanced relationship between the church and the Jewish people ("the Jews should not be presented as rejected or accursed by God, as if this followed from the Holy Scriptures ": SECOND VATICAN COUNCIL, *Nostra Aetate*, no. 4) and rejects vindictive interpretations, forces one to confront the fact that, if this is the case, only one of the outcomes of the parable is actually realized.

that, because of this, can be heard even by the dead, even by those who are no longer with us or not yet born.[4] Its justice does not merely judge, and thus sanction the existing, but can change it.

A word resonates here that is stronger than ideas and stronger than reality. It is a word capable of transforming, redefining reality itself. To understand its power, we can catch up with the *zombies* who, somewhat ironically, we left lost on the streets of Jerusalem in *Matthew's Gospel*. I would like to propose these unlikely characters as the first witnesses of the power of the Father's no. A no that is heard by the rocks, which do not bear it and break, and by the sky, which takes on the dark colour of negation. Yet, it is precisely these dead ones who, overwhelmed by an injunction, manifest its most disruptive content. A word resounds, saying no to death. Those who hear it are so affected by it that they do not resist and rise again. That injunction was not addressed to them, yet it is so clear, so absolute, that they cannot escape it, even if they do not know what to do with it – just as Matthew does not know what to do with it, abandoning them in Jerusalem without a follow-up. They hear a no addressed to their own death, a no that makes them live. The reality of their death is overcome by the word of God.

However, one should not be in a hurry and hope for a happy ending that simply cancels events. The word of God does not act like this; it does not erase but transforms, respecting events even at the moment of its clearest rejection. Were it otherwise, our reality – so often miserable compared with God's expectations – would simply be erased, and we with it. This life-giving no, on the other hand, respects the times and spaces of human tragedy. That is why a word spoken at the very moment of death will need to wait three days before bearing fruit.

Holy Saturday remains forever the testimony of a definitive word that has already been spoken, one which does not annul reality but knows how to take it on. The time when this word takes on and transforms the reality it has reached.

## 2  Yes!

If the word that resonates about *events* is a very clear and tragic no, it is because the word that resonates about the *person*, about the Son, is an equally clear yes. All this *not right* because he was *right*. In this death, there is no withdrawal of the word with which the Father had put all of himself into the Son's hands. He

---

4  *Cf.* H. KESSLER, *Sucht dem Lebenden nicht bei den Toten. Die Auferstehung Jesu Christi in biblischer, fundamentaltheologischer und sistematischer Sicht. Neuausgabe mit ausführlicher Erörterung der aktuellen Fragen*, Patmos Verlag, Düsseldorf 1987, 266–282.

is the Son, he is the heir, he is the one the Father wants. And not only because the Father says so, but because by his actions, by his ability to bear the name of all, he has assumed his own name.

If, during the passion, Jesus had remained alone to affirm the name of the Father, now it is the Father who remains alone to affirm the name of the Son, against the very reality of his death. There is an extraordinary force here, in both: that of affirming the other even in his absence. A force so one-sided that it almost resembles violence. Perhaps it is its deepest root. A capacity to speak and act even *apart from* the other. We usually see the dark side of this force, the one that acts against the other to humiliate him. Here, on the other hand, its extraordinarily bright side emerges. Violence, the ability to act against the other, is used to act against the reality that crushes him, and save him.

This *no and yes* insinuates itself, as Jesus had already proposed, between the person and reality. The yes to the person resonates in the no to reality. It had been so with the miracles, when Jesus had said no to the reality of illness and possession, thus freeing the person for his own future and his own freedom. In that case, saying yes to the person's life meant saying no to their concrete situation of evil. A no and a yes that were stronger than reality, and transformed it. In the same way – even more radically – this had been true of forgiveness. The no addressed to sin was always at the same time a yes addressed to the sinner, as much to his or her distorted freedom as to the possibility of a new future freedom.

One does not have to go far to encounter, in our experience, this ability to say no and yes at the same time. It is something we almost always find in parents' *no's*. They are never directed at the person, but always at the reality in which the child has ended up. They may appear one-sided and violent – and sometimes they really are – but at their root lies the desire to counteract a reality that does not correspond to the possibilities and life of the other.

## 3   I Am

The word of the Father thus rages against reality to confirm the Son. The word that had called him "beloved Son" is not withdrawn, not even when Jesus is dead. He is the rightful heir, the one who must be listened to.

At this point, however, one is in danger of feeling a sense of unease about the resurrection. A word is spoken over the Son and raises him. Someone who had stayed out of it suddenly appears with the full force of his weight and turns the tables. It seems a bit of a trick.

# THE HEIR'S FATHER

Three aspects seem important to me in order to avoid this sense of the artificial: 1) the core word is *not a word about Jesus*; 2) this word does *not come from outside*; 3) *the feeling remains that the accounts do not add up*.

## 3.1 For the Love of My Name

The no and the yes on the event and the person of Jesus derive from the fact that, at the core, what is at stake is not just the name of Jesus but the name of the Father. Similarly, it must be emphasised that the resurrection is an action of the Father that speaks of himself even more than of the Son. Powerfully summoned by this disaster, the Father must speak: speak of himself. Reveal at last who he is.

Even at first glance, this is why the Father's word does not come from outside as a trick. That is what it has always been about! Now, by acting and confirming the Son, the Father *talks about himself*. The yes pronounced upon the Son is also – and perhaps first and foremost – a yes pronounced upon himself.

For God the Father does not simply *accept* his own paternal name as an external definition, from others, but he *wants it*; he says yes to himself. That is why the 'no' pronounced at Christ's death is first and foremost a 'no' addressed to the desecration of his own name. Even more, it is a no addressed to the suffering of one's own bowels, to one's own death.

God is not uninterested in the Son, and he is not uninterested in himself. The philosophical insight that God loves himself does not stand in contrast with his gift-giving capacity but is its counterpoint. The reciprocal gift is not a reciprocal lack of interest, rather it is the *interest (inter-esse, inter-being) par excellence*. It does not deny self in the other, in a zero-sum game, but *wants* self in the other, where the sum is a mutual gain. The autonomy of self-interest is what allows one to hold the other's name even in its absence. When the other can no longer pronounce his or her own name, I can, in mutual inter-being, pronounce the name of both for both. Even more, when the other can no longer be for himself, he can survive in me – *inter-being* – because my name also holds his.

Therefore, God's word about his *own* name is the confirmation of the name Jesus had given him. The contestations addressed to Jesus are contested by God, for the sake of his name.

> My wrath is kindled against you and against your two friends, for you have not spoken of me what is right as my servant Job has. Now therefore take seven bulls and seven rams, and go to my servant Job, and offer up for yourselves a burnt offering, and my servant Job shall pray for you, for I will accept his prayer not to deal with you according to your folly, for you have not spoken of me what is right as my servant Job has done (*Job* 42:7–8).

The one who had appeared to be a blasphemer, and for this reason condemned, becomes the one to whom one can turn to hope to be saved from the wrath of God, jealous of his own name. A name blasphemed by those who wanted to defend it and defended by those who seemed to blaspheme it.

### 3.2  Resurrection, Mystery of Relationship

Is it perhaps a game of mirrors, in which each refers back to the other without being able to find a fixed point?

The attention I have tried to devote to the relationship that binds Father and Son, even at the cost of leaving the question of divine and human nature in the shade, serves precisely to avoid this risk. Namely, that, in the end, the divine nature is always safe, shunted from one to the other. Instead, what is at stake, what is seen and runs the risk of the concrete events of death and resurrection, is precisely the relationship between the two divine persons. It is this relationship that saves Jesus, not his super-powers. His person depends on another, and from him alone can hope for salvation. In the same way, the dignity of the Father had previously depended on his filial fidelity. Jesus is saved by another; he is not saved by himself. And the other saves because he alone maintains the interest in both.

That is why the Father was unreservedly involved in Jesus' death. His name was all there. That is why the Father is still involved with this dead man, and still says yes to this man and says no to his death. In his own life, speaking of the Father, Jesus spoke of himself. In his death, the Father, speaking of the Son, speaks of himself. In a relationship that defines them both dynamically, so that, as in a dance, the role of the one leading can change at any moment. This disproportionately increases the risk both of the conflict between the two and the insecurity of their own name, but, at the same time, also increases the richness of their lives disproportionately.

If words seem to be lacking here, it is because we are talking about the metaphysical heart of reality. It is an oscillation, an absolute gamble, involving every aspect of reality. It is a question of whether this mode of existence, so radically entrusted to relationship, is true or not. If it is not, the gamble is lost because, by relying on the other, one will end up losing oneself, and, perhaps, even the other. Otherwise, both will be saved. Something equally radical and dramatic had already appeared in Jesus' preaching. When he forbade divorce because "from the beginning it was not so" (*Mt* 19:8), he was claiming to be able to change the world in the name of an eschatological reality that was the truth from the beginning. A very dangerous gamble, as many had noted because, if it is not true, one ends up sacrificing the real on the altar of a dream.

I use the word 'metaphysics' to indicate such a gamble, knowing full well the ambiguity of the term. With this term I would like to indicate the intertwining of how *God is, how reality is* – from physics to biology – and *how the human is* – from psychology to economics to neuroscience. In the Christian vision, these realities are linked; every discovery or change in one has repercussions on the others. Scientific discoveries lead one to rethink God, but the opposite is also true: changing the idea of God cannot leave indifferent the way we look at what is around us, in everyday life. This interweaving is even more true within theology, in the web that binds the way we think about God, the human, church and morality. None of these thoughts is independent of the others. Christian morality depends on how we understand man and God, and at the same time it is morality that enables us to understand who God is: "By this everyone will know that you are my disciples, if you have love for one another" (*Jn* 13:35).

In the end, therefore, the gamble concerns *the whole*, the way in which that reality in which God makes himself present to the human is made. A metaphysical gamble. There are three aspects of reality in particular that I will attempt to reread later (*cf.* § 4 below) in the light of the radical rethinking of God proposed by Jesus, namely, what *identity, power* and *freedom* are, concepts that, albeit with differences, are to be found as much in the natural sciences as in the human sciences, as in theology.

### 3.3   *The Unprecedented Word of Correspondence*

With the resurrection, God himself takes a stand in this clash of realities. He does not do so by defining things from the outside, by uttering an extraneous word that falls upon the real and judges it. Instead, he does it by taking a position in this same reality. And his position is the position of the Son. His paternal name is in the name and person of his dead son.

Jesus lived and died for the Father and was right, because the Father lives for him.

Jesus did not want to live without the Father and was right, because the Father does not want to live without him.

Jesus died for the Father and was right, because the Father is with him in death.[5]

---

5  "Now it is our task to think through this identification of God and love in such a way that the subject and predicate in the statement 'God is love' interpret each other. We are to read the statement 'God is love' as an exposition of the self-identification of God with the crucified man Jesus" (JÜNGEL, *God as the Mystery of the World*, 425).

Jesus was right to make the Father the centre of himself, because the Father made Jesus the centre of himself. It is not an external word that saves him but a concrete stance, a choice of God's identity. There is a clash here between the reality of the living, of those who save their lives for themselves, and the reality of those who give their lives for one another. And God is not the judge sitting on a throne outside the game. He is aligned and involved with one of these two realities facing each other.

What seemed excessive, what sounded unheard of, namely, that God would accept such familiarity with a man, turned out to be true. What was frightening, namely, the risk of God being so over-exposed to the awkward gestures of a human being, turned out to be God's unreserved stance. The Father shows that he does not fear this exposure at all; on the contrary, he exposes himself even more.

This word is stronger than reality because it is not just a word. It is the very life of God. In this word God does not say, he *says himself*. He puts his own reality at stake in his relationship with another, and for this he exposes himself.

### 3.4  *Resurrection, Suspended Mystery*

At this point, we should be able to understand why, from the outset, it seemed that the accounts did not quite add up. Indeed, they do not add up. If the name game were only about the Father and the Son, the game would be over at this point. Jesus and the Father have won; the others have lost. They are lost. Instead, the game was much wider, and more serious. It concerned everyone's name. Or rather, it was about the Father's name as Father of all. One hand was won, the one concerning Jesus, but, in this very act, the game was extended to the names of all, one by one. And the fate of these names – and with it the fate of the Father's eternal name – remains open to the "revealing of the children of God" (*Rom* 8:19).

Even if marked by this first definitive victory, the full meaning of this story remains open, on the way. How dangerous was it for the Father to expose himself to the events of the Son? Very much. But there, in that man, he won. Neither of the two has retreated. How dangerous is it for God to have linked his name to the fragility of so many children's faces? Very much, and we still do not know how much.

This is why the fundamental image of the resurrection is an empty tomb. It indicates both the victory of one – or rather of two – and the uncertainty of the final outcome. That place remains open for each one, waiting to know whether, for each one, the Father's name can be the custodian of his own name.

This is why the word of resurrection is both joyful and disquieting. That is why the Christian condition still remains suspended, waiting. It would obviously be blasphemous to call it a defeated condition. But, more subtly, it would be equally blasphemous to call it a resolved condition. That would be to have failed to grasp what was really at stake. Not a game in which a powerful man, who was basically risking nothing, had already secured victory before even starting, but the restlessness of a paternal heart that must wait for the other's word before knowing the boundaries of its own name.

## 4 Rethinking God

Christianity and Christian theology come from here. They hope – or claim – to live and think from the complexity of these events. Like any starting point, there is something arbitrary in this; one starts because one is struck by something that seems to contain the possibility of giving meaning to the real. And one tries to think about it.

There are many obstacles that such an undertaking must face. The difficulty of understanding the message of an obscure eschatological prophet from Galilee in the first century A.D. and, at the same time, the difficulty of understanding and integrating the contestations – not easy to set aside – that led to his death. And then the difficulties involved in interpreting the hottest core of this story, namely, the death and resurrection of this prophet.

These difficulties are not just useless theological complications. They reflect a real difficulty that this man introduced into the history of thought, a challenge to think *differently* about God. There is a disturbing component in the way he spoke, in the way he acted and in the whole story of Jesus, which is part of the meaning of his life. It is in line with a characteristic trait of the God of Israel, namely, that of not presenting himself as the mere guarantor of reality but of inserting himself into historical events, giving them a direction, of demanding *conversion*, a change of direction. This applies to individual and social behaviour, and it applies to thought. Christian conversion, therefore, is not just a call to be less 'bad', but something more radical. It is the – destabilising – perception that God is not what one expected, and requires one to rethink every aspect of reality afresh. For those who want to grapple with this event theologically and try to think about it, it is a real hand-to-hand combat, involving every aspect of life and thought. This is what I have tried to enact so far. It starts with an apparent simplicity, an altogether 'cute' message about forgiveness, closeness and brotherhood. However, the cute aspects soon give way to bewilderment when one notices that they claim to apply to every aspect of life and reality – deeply disturbing it. At this point, thought can withdraw, either because it decides to devote itself to something else or because it decides to leave the field to pure action. These are not hyperbolic, but everlooming realities in Christian history. At all times, atheism or the temptation to cling to traditional forms of thought are part of the Christian DNA. Likewise, part of it is the suspicion that thought is not up to this theological development, and that it would be better to opt for less intellectual ways, be they mysticism, moral action or war.

However, those who decide to persevere in the claim of thinking all this will have to prepare themselves for radical theological turns in metaphysics, from anthropology to theology. This is something Christianity has always perceived and tried to do. Each epoch has obviously been challenged in its context and with its tools to identify the rethinking necessary to be up to the task.

There are three changes of mind I would like to propose as they seem to me decisive for the times we are living in. They have the characteristic of being both cultural and counter-cultural. On the one hand, they challenge Christianity and contemporary culture to take a position with respect to the idea of God, with the practical consequences that this entails. And this disturbs both society and the churches. On the other hand, however, they allow people to find their place and their peace. This, too, is a feature that seems to me to be constant in the work of Christianity: it allows people – the conformists, the poor and the murderers – to return home, but to return changed forever (*cf. Lk* 8:39).

### 4.1   *Paternity Rethought, or Mutual Identities*

During the life of Jesus, God, the Father of the heir, revealed himself as the one who binds his own identity and entrusts it to another, the Son. Not just a God who is not jealous of his own identity, but one who *desires to* possess himself only in relationship with another. In the passion, Jesus revealed this identity in his own flesh, exposing himself to the reciprocity of his relationship with God. He showed that he wants to be radically Son, who *desires* himself only in the relationship with the one he considers Father. In the resurrection, this reciprocity received its definitive confirmation and victory by extending itself to all sons, even the murderous sons. At this point, everyone's identity is changed forever. Even the last of the sinners will no longer wait for forgiveness as the unexpected and arbitrary gift of a 'grace', but rather as a challenge to the very name of God. For the Father does not forgive as an exception to his own imperturbability but, rather, out of fidelity to his name, to his paternal identity.

To imagine that God is able to expose himself to this extent, and to see in this the traits of his omnipotence, is still something that is easier said than experienced. Such reciprocity is such a heavy theological challenge that it cannot be believed simply as a truth of thought. Rather, it demands to be verified in reality, as it provokes a reality that largely fails to live up to this divine claim.

Perhaps the most scandalous trait lies in the fact that God does not rely only on relationship but on relationships. That is, he entrusts himself to relationships that are not his alone. In the events of the passion, the Father's name was linked not only to the relationship that Jesus had with him but also to the different relationships that involved the Son. One should not be afraid to observe this. On the cross, Jesus was able to endure in faithfulness to an absent Father because *other* relationships nourished him. Following *John's Gospel*, we can see the relationship with the Spirit – of which I am well aware that I have devoted insufficient attention – but also the relationships with his mother and the beloved disciple. The fact that God is not jealous of relationships, and allows and desires the Son to have other relationships than the one that binds him, is what allows the Spirit to be a true interlocutor, a true consoler of Jesus in his time of trial. But it also enables the woman of Nazareth, that autonomous and adult woman who had known how to stand by her son during his life, to remain at his side, to help and support him in disaster. These relationships are not concessions but the confirmation that God's identity is *reciprocal* and generates reciprocal identities.

Contemporary aspirations for an ascending soteriology – that is, for a proposal of salvation and life that does not simply fall from above but involves people in the play of their own freedom – has its theological foundation here. This is not a claim of contemporary people: instead, it is structural to the Christian vision. There is no abstract God, who can give life from outside with a gesture that does not touch him. And, therefore, there is no man or woman who can receive life without being involved with the giver, and with life itself. Instead, there is a paternal God who puts himself at stake in the relationship with his children: he truly risks, and, for this reason, the children are truly involved. What they are and will be is not indifferent to God's identity.

On the other hand, the Christian choice has always been to call God 'Father'. Not 'Lord', not 'King', not 'Head'. He is all these things also, but, in the first place, he is 'Father', which is a name of relationship.

It is precisely from this involving reciprocity that the temptation may arise for children to disown their origin and go off on their own. A gesture that can be condemned, but this is not the point. As in the parable of *Lk* 15:11–32, the argument is neither moral (the fact that the son is 'prodigal') nor theological (the fact that the father is 'forgiving'). That men make mistakes and that God is good is no great novelty. Instead, the reason why this parable has extraordinary metaphysical value lies in the fact that it describes this reciprocity. The identity of the Father is linked to the actions of the sons, even when they go astray or rebel; they are in fact sons, not servants. And of the two sons, the one who behaves most according to the Father's heart is the one who has gone astray.

Every reciprocity, in fact, envisages a real autonomy. It may entail risks, yet it is willed by God himself in that it avoids the greatest risk, namely, that the relationship becomes non-reciprocal, like the relationship with a servant ("For all these years, I have been working like a slave for you", *Lk* 15:29). Those who leave can return; those who are autonomous can choose; those who insult you can apologise. What you will have in the end is a rich relationship, one worth having. But those who stay still in fear and envy end up having no relationship at all. The face of God is at stake in this absence of relationship.

I would like to try to focus on two particular aspects that change if the metaphysical challenge of this reciprocity is taken seriously: the interplay that takes place between the active and passive dimensions and the dynamics of forgiveness.

### 4.1.1 Active or Passive?

What is greater, to be active or passive? What is more divine? The very moment it defines God as 'pure act' or 'almighty', the classical metaphysical tradition gives its answer. God acts; he does not suffer. Needless to say, this creates problems in recognising the divinity of Christ in his passion. One understands that the challenge of Christianity is to hold these two aspects together *in God himself*. One possible solution lies in giving an order, internal to the Trinity, which sees the Father – source and origin – as the one who is active and the Son as the one who is passive – begotten, sent, killed, raised.[6] This is not the track I would like to propose. The risk is that being active still maintains a rightful superiority over being passive which ends up having harmful consequences on relationships: the one who is active is superior and has the right to act at will over the inferior. This was the case with men over women, the rich over the poor, adults over children, priests over the laity, the strong over the weak, whether they were individuals, peoples, families.

> You know that among the Gentiles those whom they recognise as their rulers lord it over them, and their great ones are tyrants over them. But it is not so among you; instead, whoever wishes to become great among you must be your servant, and whoever wishes to be first among you must be slave of all. For the Son of Man came not to be served, but to serve, and to give his life a ransom for many (*Mk* 10:42–45).

---

6  J.P. Lieggi, *La sintassi trinitaria. Al cuore della grammatica della fede*, Aracne, Roma 2016.

At this point, it might seem that a simple reversal is taking place. In classical metaphysics, God is active and man passive, God the Father more active and God the Son more passive, whereas in Christianity it is God's property to serve and suffer. The concept of inheritance itself could lead in this direction: the Father-testator-dead is passive while the Son-heir-alive is active. Things are more complex than that. Or, perhaps, even simpler in that activity and passivity are not the criteria of value or supremacy but only the playing field of relationship. It is not 'better' or 'more divine' to be active than passive, or *vice versa*. Acting and withdrawing, touching and being touched, willing and obeying, carrying and being carried, receiving life and giving life, cannot be divided between Father and Son once and for all, or between God and man. Each is the one and the other, in the interplay of relationship.

Something similar happens in any successful love relationship. The relationship involves an exchange in which there is not simply one who gives and one who receives. I can save you today and you will save me tomorrow; I make you laugh now and you do the same for me later; I oblige and bind you on one thing and you me on another. No one wins if we do not win together because the point is not to establish who is greater but to allow identities to flourish. In fact, there can be unbalanced situations, where one is predominantly active and the other predominantly passive. This is not a problem, precisely because it is not a question of deciding who 'wins'.

This role play is evident in sex. It never works well if one does everything and the other does nothing. Be it ideas, initiative, verve, strength, but also rest, limits, patience – if the game is to decide *who is in charge*, it is a losing game. Whereas, precisely in sex – one of the realities in which our identity is exposed in the most radical, dangerous and beautiful way – it emerges how autonomy and availability, activity and passivity, carrying and being carried, are intertwined. This erotic comparison should not shock Christians. From the re-reading of the *Canticle of Canticles* by the church Fathers to St Teresa of Avila, there has always been a clear perception that in the passion, death and resurrection of Christ, something of the erotic relationship that binds the human being to God and God to Himself is shown. The Father is no less divine when he delivers everything into the hands of the Son and is no more divine when he raises him. The Son is no more Son in obeying the Father than he is in upholding his name in his place. They are a pair of lovers, at the most dramatic moment in the history of love, and *together*, in an absolute dance, in which each knows how to entrust himself to the other beyond all limits, they say who they are and make space for each of us. Passivity and activity are at the service of the dance, not *vice versa*.

The Christian vision of strength, power, wealth and even violence[7] has its roots here. These are good realities when put at the service of relationship.

### 4.1.2 Do You Forgive Me?

Perhaps the most radical form of passivity and activity is that which involves the dynamic of sin and forgiveness. The sinner not only does nothing, he even hurts, he destroys. And the one who forgives not only has to do, but has to fill the void and the wound left by the other. At the same time, the sinner is active in evil, and the one who forgives is passive, in the sense that he bears the burden of another's sinful action on himself. From this ambiguity derives the often uncertain attitude one can have towards sin: on the one hand we recognise it as a sign of weakness, but, at the same time, we can admire it for the strength, the power it is capable of exerting on reality. The same uncertainty is reflected in forgiveness: we recognise it as an act proper to the strong, yet it is difficult to escape the feeling that the one who forgives is always a little weak, humiliated.

Christian metaphysics resolves this ambiguity once and for all, precisely when it recognises that the Father brings his own identity into play in his relationship with the Son and his children.

If this were not so, God, the one who can forgive *par excellence*, would, in fact, do so with the detached gesture of one who decides the fate of others with a wave of his powerful hand.[8] It would be the arbitrariness of a Lord who decides life or death according to his own whim. So much so, there is nothing to disturb his identity. This is precisely why those who contested the paternal image of God proposed by Jesus had their reasons. Jesus, in fact, suggested the idea that God treats everyone as a sinner:[9] the powerful Lord is so arbitrary that he can consider everyone insufficient, everyone wretched. Precisely

---

7 This word may be perplexing, but it is used with good reason. Indeed, I do not believe that it is possible to simply expunge it from Christianity without finding oneself in difficulty when faced with a whole series of relationships in which, at a disenchanted glance, some role of violence clearly appears: from the education of children to the inquisition, from sex to self-defence. Not to mention the hierarchy of church relationships that can sometimes be perceived as objectively violent by those who suffer them. I do not believe it is possible to opt unilaterally for 'violence yes' or 'violence no', or even to refer simply to good or bad intentions. Rather, it is a question of understanding what role this dimension of human action plays in the dynamics of relationships.
8 A gesture masterfully rendered by Ralph Fiennes in S. Spielberg, *Schindler's List*, USA 1993. The Nazi in front of the mirror tries to realise the synthesis of power, forgiveness and arbitrariness in one touch. It will not work.
9 "For God has imprisoned all in disobedience, so that he may be merciful to all!" (*Rom* 11:32).

because he is *also* Father – they thought – he must take into account his children's efforts, however small and fragile.

Jesus' proposal, however, is more radical: God is not *also* Father, he *does not play* the Father. God is *only* and *always* Father. His gesture is not that of a benevolent Lord who grants grace to whomever he pleases, but reflects the identity of a Father forever bound to that of his children, even sinners. He shows mercy to all because he is bound to all, he cares for all as he cares for himself, he is involved with all. Their failure is first and foremost his failure as a Father. None of the children, however great, could claim so much, that is, to be involved in God's identity – and in this sense, and only in this sense, all are sinners. However, God's paternal choice of *himself*, of his *own name*, means that if he did not forgive, it would be his own name – even more than the fate of creatures – that would be offended. In this sense, all are wrapped up in the mercy of his bowels. A father who does not know how to forgive, who does not know how to find ways to live with his difficult children, only demonstrates the poverty of his fatherhood.

This risky involvement of God with his children was already felt clearly in the Old Testament.

> And the Lord said to Moses, "How long will this people despise me? And how long will they refuse to believe in me, in spite of all the signs I have done among them? I will strike them with pestilence and disinherit them, and I will make you a nation greater and mightier than they." But Moses said to the Lord, "Then the Egyptians will hear of it, for in your might you brought out this people from among them, and they will tell the inhabitants of this land. They have heard that you, O Lord, are in the midst of this people; for you, O Lord, are seen face to face, and your cloud stands over them and you go in front of them, in a pillar of cloud by day, and in a pillar of fire by night. Now if you kill this people all at one time, then the nations who have heard about you will say, "It was because the Lord was not able to bring this people into the land which he swore to give them that he slaughtered them in the wilderness." And now, therefore, let the power of the Lord be great in the way you promised when you spoke saying, 'The Lord is slow to anger and abounding in steadfast love, forgiving iniquity and transgressions, but by no means clearing the guilty, visiting the iniquity of the parents upon the children to the third and fourth generation.' Forgive the iniquity of this people, according to the greatness of your steadfast love, just as you have pardoned this people, from Egypt even until now" (*Num* 14:11–19).

Moses does not try to exploit his relationship with God or even his own love for the people. He knows that no one loves Israel more than God himself. It would be absurd to think of teaching God to do his job as Father. Moses simply reminds God of his own name, his own face. If he is ally and lover, and does not forgive, he looks bad himself. He has no other way but to remain faithful to the involvement he has chosen for himself.

### 4.1.3 Involved!

The sinners, therefore, are also involved and active in their sin. Firstly, because they have the real possibility and responsibility to humiliate the Father's face. A responsibility that is not taken away from them even when it leads to the murder of the Son, delivered into their hands. But, above all, they always remain active in the possibility of good. For the Father's heart never withdraws the possibility of a new, open, forgiven future, not even after the murder of the Son. This is what was seen in the passion: there is no sin that can exceed the salvation offered on the cross. One cannot go further than this; one cannot sin more than the Father is willing to forgive. Here, the metaphysical space of human action is simultaneously vastly expanded and reconfigured in blessing and relationship.

The poor are also involved and active with respect to the Father's identity. The Son announces to them an unprecedented possibility, that is, to be, even in their poverty, always and nevertheless children, sharers in the Father's identity. At the same time, the reciprocity of the Father's identity says a clear word about sin as well as poverty, and this word is the echo of the *no* that resounds in Jesus' resurrection and miracles. The Father entrusted himself to them out of love for their lives, against all sin and against all poverty. He did not do this as a masochist, to humiliate himself, but in the confidence that he could give glory to his name through his children, just as he did with his Son.

This is why Jesus, the Son, presents himself as the heir and the provocateur of the poor and sinners. He is the heir because he makes their filial identity his own; he is the provocateur because he unambiguously resonates the Father's desire for life that rages against all sin and misery.

### 4.2 *Sonship Rethought, or Shared Power*

If the Son inherits and the Father has not died, it means that power has been shared. But what does it mean to share something? This is not very clear even in the common usage of the term. A cake, properly speaking, is not shared. Either I eat it or you eat it; if anything, we can divide it, half for each. A car cannot be divided, because half a car is of no use to anyone. Perhaps it can be shared, if, together, we go the same way. Even more complicated is the case when it is power that is shared. Today, few would be willing to recognise their rulers as possessing power, as was the case in the time of absolute monarchies. Rather, we recognise that power belongs to citizens – it is therefore shared by all – but is exercised by rulers in a representative form. However, the many calls for more direct forms of democracy tell us much about the dissatisfaction with this form of power-sharing.

The story of Jesus calls into question the very nature of power. That is why the resurrection risks being so ambiguous: after describing the Father leaving everything in the hands of the Son, one might discover that he had left or shared nothing. The power had always been his, untouchable and incommunicable. Good for Jesus, who could thus be raised, but bad for the Son. For to be a Son of God, if God never dies and does not share power, is simply never to inherit, to remain without power forever.

It is precisely the death and resurrection, on the other hand, that show that power was truly shared, truly all of the Son, all of the Father, and at the same time able to involve humans as well. How could such a thing happen?

### 4.2.1 The Power of the Son

Jesus' life and death speak to us of a free man, master of his life and actions. Not a slave and not a child. He developed this freedom, this power, in dialogue with the people in his life and in dialogue with his God. He used his freedom to witness to the Father in himself. 'The Father wants such as these children'. He does not seek fearful worshippers but sons and daughters, because he expects much from them. He wants them to be involved in the heart of his definition of himself.

At this point, we understand what it means that Jesus was 'autonomous', and that in his autonomy there is also room for ours.

It means that the Father really knows how to give, and his gifts have no reserve, no limits. The Father does not lend, he gives, and he does not ask for return. Shared power never goes back to being undivided, because it never was. From here comes the power and autonomy of both the Son and the sons. Not from a rebellion and not from the desire of the sons to leave, but from the desire of the Father to have sons who know how to stand *before him* as true interlocutors and who know how to stand *by him* in the love that takes charge of their brothers. Adult and autonomous sons are needed for this.

The choice of the category of inheritance was intended to focus on this real sharing of power that puts the children at the centre. If to speak of inheritance is to speak of a power handed over, the cross and the resurrection redefine these concepts because they speak of a gift without return, and, thus, redefine forever both power and inheritance.

I would therefore like to try to return to the three contributions that made it possible to enrich the category of inheritance and use it beyond its legal limits, namely idealism, psychoanalysis and reflection on childhood (*cf.* above, ch. 8, § 3.1), in order to continue the discussion in the light of this filial power.

Compared with *Idealism*, which made the story of Christ one of the pivots of its reflection, the theoretical challenge remains to succeed in placing the subject at the centre in a truly relational form. The proposal of Christianity moves between two stumbling blocks. On the one hand, it must be a relational dimension that is not destined to pass, as a concluded moment in a story, or as a journey, a visit to otherness. In this case, the relationship would be bent to the subject, as a mere stage in its realisation. On the other hand, it must allow the autonomous subject not to be devoured by the relation. In this second case it would be the subject that would be bent to the relationship, as one of its components. If the story of Jesus does not offer a possibility of balance, one will end up, from time to time, neglecting the relationship or the individual, with totalitarian or individualistic outcomes.

Perhaps somewhat unexpectedly, my greatest concern today is directed to the individual. I often hear unnerving and resentful accusations against the individualism, the narcissism and the selfishness of the 'people of today'. As if people have fallen into a moral abyss. Sure, there are typically contemporary difficulties in managing relationships. However, an objective look at the 'good old days' might invite more caution. "Do not say, 'Why were the former days better than these?' For it is not from wisdom that you ask this" (*Eccl* 7:10). Few of us, I believe, would be comfortable with the family, parental, social and political relationships of the early 1900s, let alone the 15th century. However, I do not believe that these difficulties will be overcome with moralistic appeals to relationships. Instead, I believe that Christian thought can honour the modern and contemporary desire to give space to the autonomy of the subject and help him recognise it as grounded in the very desire of the Father. Perhaps this will unlock many relational potentials, much more than guilt can. Our contemporaries, or rather all of us, have not fallen into a moral abyss; we are simply facing crises and challenges typical of the Age of the Son, typical of children becoming adults. What I have wanted to show is how Jesus himself faced this decisive passage.

Also, with respect to *psychoanalysis* and various neuroscientific currents, the challenge involves the possibilities of the child. For there is no doubt about dependence, about the bond, about our being the fruit of histories and connections that precede and determine us. The question, if at all, is about the possibility of an adult and free assumption of dependence that does not simply seek to deny its roots but to use them for a life of its own.[10] Without this possibility,

---

10   *Cf.* A. HONNETH, *Appropriating Freedom: Freud's Conception of Individual Self-Relation*, in ID., *Pathologies of Reason. On the Legacy of Critical Theory*, Columbia University Press, New York 2009, 126–145.

relationships simply become an eternal return of the repressed, something that can never be assumed and that ultimately results in the mark of an insuperable unhappy consciousness. Instead, the whole story of Jesus, as I have tried to narrate it, is an assumption of bonds – personal, religious, theological, social – creatively recovered, as an adult. These bonds were to lead Jesus to death. Being simultaneously faithful to the Father, to friends, to Israel, to sinners, was to crush him as if in a vice. Yet, here, Jesus does not show himself defeated. He manages to manifest his identity as Son and respect his origin, his inheritance, leaving a unique, indelible mark on it. Within a perspective such as psychoanalysis, which gives so much weight to relationships, the Son's testimony remains as an open hope, of being able to speak one's name even in the midst of disaster.

Finally, with respect to the *Age of the son-child*, one should recognise the distinctiveness of childhood without turning it into a fetish. Both from an educational and a religious point of view, there can be risks. The absolute passivity of children, besides being false, cannot be mythologised as an ideal condition before God. The Father does not desire infant and sleeper children. He seeks gritty teenagers and adults. The free and creative activity, the carefree play of children – which is as unreal as passivity was previously – must not be mythologised as the religious or moral ideal of absolute spontaneity. Passivity and activity are not ends in themselves but serve to build identity and relationships. This is true in adults, but even more so in children, who, in their constructive relationship with adults, are on their way to their own adult identity, capable of taking charge and generating other identities.

### 4.2.2 The Power of the Father

If what has been described so far is filial power, what will be the fate of paternal power? It can only be transformed.

The affirmation that God is 'Father Almighty' is meant to resonate with what happened in the death and resurrection of Jesus. Otherwise it ends up being loaded with an insoluble ambiguity. During the Son's life, *power* and *paternity* explained each other, like the power that enabled the blind to see and the mute to speak, whereas, during the passion, these two names enter into a tension that demands a decision, in which the very name of God depends on it. Is he Father or is he Almighty? What is being sought to affirm? The power of a father or the power of fatherhood? The variation seems minimal, but it changes everything. On the one hand, there is a Father who seizes all power for himself. If understood in this way, one then has all the difficulties of finding a place for the Son and the Spirit alongside this absolute power. On the other hand, there is someone who understands his power only in a paternal and generative way, that is, by sharing it.

In Christianity, the God who is the origin of everything is generative and shares power. This forces one to rethink power itself, when it wants to be true power.

Shared power is not divided. The Father does not give half of his power to the Son and keep half. The power of God remains undivided, all in the Father, all in the Son. As if to say that power is not a cake. If that were the case, at Jesus' death half (or rather a third) of God's power would have died – would have been lost. Instead, on the cross all of God dies in the Son and all of God lives in the Father.

In a family or a well-knit team, something similar happens. The fact of sharing power, that is, the fact that the leader decides to be joined by someone to whom he really gives all his power, means that the power in circulation is not halved. When one of them is absent, the other acts for him too, with all the power; when it is the other who is absent, the former takes over. A good idea of one is a good idea of all. In this way, each has the power of both. Thus, he who shares power has power even while he sleeps.

There is a particular aspect of the parable of the two sons in *Lk* 15 that speaks of this sharing and often reappears precisely in the cruxes of metaphysics. One might ask: what does the father do with his patrimony? We see two different stages.

When the younger son leaves, the father "divided his assets between them" (*Lk* 15:12). Logically, the real problem with the return of the younger son lies in the fact that the father should no longer have anything to give him. Instead: "Quickly, out a robe – the best one – and put it on him; put a ring on his finger and sandals on his feet. And get the fatted calf and kill it, and let us eat and celebrate" (*Lk* 15:22–23). But where does the father get all this stuff from? From the elder son's share? Or had he kept a fund and not given the younger his due, i.e. half?

Even more subtle and tragic is what the father says to his elder son: "All that is mine is yours" (*Lk* 15:31). This does not ring true. At most, the elder son may be entitled to half of the patrimony, not all of it. If it is all the elder's, the father should have given nothing to the younger, either on departure or return. If, on the other hand, it is all of each of the sons, the father should have given everything to the younger immediately.

The father in the parable seems to understand patrimony in a strange way. In practice, he believes that he owns it all and, at the same time, that he can give it all to each of his sons, even several times, in case they lose it or squander it. Yet, this seems exactly the correct way to understand the power marked by fatherhood.

### 4.2.3 A Host of Involved

The Father shares his power. With everyone. And he configures all power as shared. Whoever wants to exercise power – and everyone exercises power because God gives power to everyone – is brought to the edge of this recognition. Its origin is shared because each, as a son, has received his power from others. Its exercise is shared because power configures the mutual faces of brothers.

Whoever exercises power, therefore, does so before God, before the origin of all power. Whoever does not know, or does not want, to experience power as shared, will find himself exercising it against its origin. Against a God who is the enemy of life, when life is considered a solitary booty, without generation and without delivery. Against a God who is the enemy of the world, when the world signifies a selfishness that recognises nothing to anyone but oneself. Against a God who is the enemy of God, when God is not Father, when he is only a monarch *legibus solutus*, who demands justice and love but is careful not to get involved in this.

The relationship with others, therefore, is the real metaphysical gamble on how and who God is. The judgement on this gamble is not postponed until after death but involves the possibility of life itself. The one who does not recognise the shared nature of power condemns himself to become the one who destroys his own face, the face of others and the face of God. He condemns himself to be truly powerless eventually, to deprive himself of the only true power, that of generation. He condemns himself to waste the true power he has been given, in an attempt to generate himself.

Jesus' statement: "Those who want to save their life will lose it" (*Mk* 8:35) is thus not a moral appeal, but a theological-metaphysical statement on the reality of God and the world.

The consequences of this involvement invade every aspect of relationships and reality, and everyone, inside and outside the church, is challenged by it. The true power we have been given dictates that it is we who must find ways to realise this call to live power as "the revealing of the children of God" (*Rom* 8:19). Everyone is called upon. I am convinced that all the major challenges facing our world pass through this hub. Today in particular – precisely because science, technology and social development have given us such great power – uncertainty or pretence are no longer possible. It will not be possible to find a decent way of living together politically without recognising the shared nature of power and finding concrete ways of exercising it. This is particularly evident within the church. It is no longer possible to quote Paul – "There is no longer Jew or Greek; there is no longer slave or free; there is no longer male and female; for all of you are one in Christ Jesus" (*Gal* 3:28) – and appeal to synodality without recognising that this means finding concrete historical forms so that each one is recognised as having the power that the Father has willed to entrust to him.

In fact, to speak of synodality, even when it is the pope who does so, cannot be the granting of absolute power. This is not a humanistic principle but a theological one. The differences between clergy and laity, men and women, young and old, even between Christians and non-Christians, are always subject to the fact that we are all children of a Father who wanted to share his power with each one.

I will not even try to go into the details of how this brotherhood is to be realised.[11] This is a task that involves everyone, in every aspect of life. I need only note that it is here, in the eschatological call to fraternity, that the ultimate challenge of our time is at stake, as Christians, but also as men and women.

For Christians, this challenge has a Christological root. In fact, it passes from the recognition that Jesus himself was capable of putting his own inheritance, his own power, his own history on the line in the concrete encounters – disciples, parents, the poor, teachers, and sinners – in which he moulded his life. Precisely for this reason, a Christology that does not know how to start from the bottom and prefers to leave Jesus in the untouchable and unique solitude of his divine nature, risks not helping us today to live the challenge of our time.

### 4.3   *Fraternity Rethought, or Freedom in Relation*

Talking about the story of Jesus leads to talking about us. Talking about *his* freedom and *his* bonds leads *to* talking about *our* freedom and *our* bonds. After all, this was always the point, right from the beginning. The Father exposed himself to the Son's action and even more to the relationships the Son would establish with his brothers. And he won. In doing so, however, he decided to expose himself also to the actions of all the children and especially to the relationships they would decide to establish with one another. This game, however, is still open and risky. From the time he has wanted to be Father and not to be envious of others and the relationships that others establish but has decided to expose himself and his own glory to the bond and bonds, the Father has been the Living One, the one who lives in the becoming of relationships.[12] And God has never been anything other than this.

---

11   Pope Francis' encyclical *Fratelli tutti* is an attempt to put this perspective into practice.
12   *Cf.* E. JÜNGEL, *God's Being is in Becoming. The Trinitarian Being of God in the Theology of Karl Barth*, T&T Clark Ltd, Edinburg 2001.

It is not easy to be the creature of such a God. The risk is very high on both sides. In the first place, it is risky for God himself. If he fails the challenge of fraternity, his face cannot emerge unscathed. The nail holes that remain in the Son's hands *after* the resurrection (*cf. Jn* 20:24–29) are the unmistakable sign that the tragedy of our relationships does not leave God indifferent. It will not be possible to forget human defeats, to simply erase them like a dream ending badly. For us, however, there is an even greater risk. If we are not capable of living the Son's inheritance in brotherhood, what awaits us will be fratricidal warfare, aggravated – not mitigated – by the Son's proclamation. There is, indeed, an immense risk in telling men that they are children of God. It exposes them to the fear and envy that every announcement of a great inheritance unleashes. As long as there is nothing or almost nothing to inherit, no inheritance to fight for, it will only be a matter of sharing the 'daily bread'. But where people know that they are children of kings, the wildest desires and passions are unleashed, and with them the most terrible wars.

If we are not capable of living as brothers, it would have been better if none of this had happened. It would have been better to have been and be children of a servant, or rather children of no one, with nothing to share and nothing to risk. What men and women decide to do is uncertain; what is certain is what God has decided to do and be.

The place where one can see how this challenge can be overcome is in the life of the Son: "For there is no other name under heaven given among mortals by which we must be saved" (*Acts* 4:12).

### 4.3.1    The Bonds of a Lifetime

Jesus was the one who knew how to live his life in the fullness of his bonds, honouring the best of what he had received. He did not simply copy them; he took them up creatively by inserting his own name and the name of the Father into the simplicity of what he lived. Where these bonds proved to be inadequate and resisted the greatness and dignity to which he wanted to elevate them, he was able to carry them for others, taking them on and showing the unprecedented strength of the relationship. His most characteristic trait was precisely this: although he was the Son, he did not keep this relationship for himself, but brought it into play, with his identity, in his relationships with those he met. For he knew that the Father is not jealous of relationships; rather, he desires them. The Father, who is the first, the foundation of every possible relationality, wants the Son to expose himself again in his relationship with his brothers and sisters.

Jesus, therefore, knows how to live up to a double movement. He lives his relationship with his brothers and sisters, and in this he respects his provenance from the Father. He lives the relationship with the Father, and in this he takes up and redefines all fraternal relationships.

More radically, it is freedom itself that is being redesigned. It does not begin where others' ends. Rather it begins where others' begins.[13] One cannot be children if not in the creative resumption of the relationship with the Father. One cannot be brothers if not by placing oneself in relationships with others in an exposed and risky way. Even more so, it is the very name of each one, one's own name, that needs relationships to define itself and move from being an empty and interchangeable symbol to a unique and personal identifier.

All this is part of everyone's experience. Yet, Jesus makes a theological fact of it. Even God defines himself before another; even God lives from his own relationships. This is why, according to Jesus, our dependence is not the sign of creaturely fragility but the echo of Trinitarian relationships. Man is the image of God insofar as he can consciously live his own freedom in the relationships that constitute him. To the extent that it lives in relationships, the whole of creation bears traces, in its own way, of the relationship, the generation from which everything comes.

At this point, one grasps what it means to affirm creation *in Christ*. When it is affirmed that "all things came into being through him" (*Jn* 1:3; *cf.* 1:10), that "all things have been created through him and for him" (*Col* 1:16) and that it pleased God that "through him God was pleased to reconcile to himself all things" (*Col* 1:20) or, again, that "from him and through him and to him are all things" (*Rom* 11:36), it is not a matter of affirming primarily something of the Son, but of the Father. If God had not, from the beginning, had room for another, there would be no room for anything else. These affirmations are not intended to present Jesus as some kind of demiurge but to show the original generativity of God in whose space every other presence is placed. The story of Jesus fills these statements with content because it shows to what extent the Father is involved with the fruit of his generation. In him we discover not only that what exists comes from his love but also that "his steadfast love endures forever" (*Ps* 136), that is, that the choice to bind his name to the fragility of the name of his creatures knows no revocation.

---

13   This is the reversal of the liberal principle that reciprocal selfishness is altruism, i.e. that public virtues derive from private vice. Here it is the opposite: reciprocal altruism is selfishness, i.e. the strength of the relationship guards everyone's possibility of existence. One lives only in relationship with the other. That this can give rise to even worse forms of perversion and exploitation of the relationship is certainly true and part of God's own risk. It is probably why its liberal reverse may seem to many a safer path.

### 4.3.2 Co-Heirs

The statement that all are sons, with true autonomy and true power in their hands, because all are co-heirs of the patrimony, is not something self-evident in itself.

> [I pray] that the God of our Lord Jesus Christ, the Father of glory, may give you a spirit of wisdom and revelation as you come to know him, so that, with the eyes of your heart enlightened, you may know what is the hope to which he has called you, what are the riches of his glorious inheritance among the saints, and what is the immeasurable greatness of his power for us who believe, according to the working of his great power (*Eph* 1:17–19).

And yet, it is not something that is simply impossible. It is something that can be seen.

> God put this power to work in Christ when he raised him from the dead and seated him at his right hand in the heavenly places, far above all rule and authority and power and dominion, and above every name that is named, not only in this age but also in the age to come (*Eph* 1:20–21).

The challenge to believe in this inheritance in order to live it in brotherhood is the ultimate theological challenge. Precisely because it is not self-evident, and precisely because it is not simply already done, it involves people as brothers and sisters in the eschatological construction of the Kingdom. It is not an eschatology that refers to a time beyond time but it has *social* traits. It involves the freedom of the children as it involved the freedom of the Son. It involves the freedom of the Father who brings his own free identity into play in his relationship with his children and in the relationships the children establish with each other.

Since its manifestation, this eschatological-social dream has exhibited the features of risk and challenge. In some ways, this danger was evident even before its appeal. That is why the one who first glimpsed and announced it, John the Baptist, described it as an axe already resting at the base of the tree (*cf. Mt* 3:10–12). Such an involvement of God, who becomes 'near', does not allow anyone to hide. Such shared power will either lead to the Kingdom or to the slaughter of brothers, unleashing a hatred that is all the greater the stronger the bond that unites them. God himself cannot avoid taking responsibility for having put his children in such a position.

I would like to think that there is a perception of this in the statement of the *Our Father* asking, "do not bring us to the time of trial [lead us not into temptation]" (*Mt* 6:13 and *Lk* 11:4). It may be objected that God does not lead anyone into temptation – which is why the Italian translation has been changed to 'do not abandon us to temptation' – but this is not entirely accurate. Sure, if the temptation is 'killing' or 'coveting another man's wife', God obviously does not lead one to do these things. However, he is no stranger to our greatest temptation. He shared his power, his freedom, his identity with us. He has put his desire on the line with us. But desire is not to be played with. He could not have been unaware that this would trigger delusional desires. That is why, at the very moment we pray to God, calling him Father, we ask that this privilege, this right, not be transformed into the temptation to consider ourselves the only children, into the temptation to use the power and freedom God has given us to oppress and humiliate. Or simply to be comfortable while our brothers and sisters suffer. I believe that Jesus was well aware of this risk, if only because it was the temptation he had to confront in the last hours of his life.

### Bibliographical Guidelines

For an introduction to the immense subject of the **resurrection** – a subject which rarely manages to produce a truly convincing discussion – see: H. KESSLER, *Sucht dem Lebenden nicht bei den Toten. Die Auferstehung Jesu Christi in biblischer, fundamental-theologischer und sistematischer Sicht. Neuausgabe mit ausführlicher Erörterung der aktuellen Fragen*, Patmos Verlag, Düsseldorf 1987; E. CASTELLUCCI, *Davvero il Signore è risorto. Indagine teologico-fondamentale sugli avvenimenti e le origini della fede pasquale*, Cittadella, Assisi 2005; F.G. BRAMBILLA, *Il Crocifisso risorto. Risurezione di Gesù e fede dei discepoli*, Queriniana, Brescia 2011; G. FERRETTI (ed.), *La risurrezione mistero del desiderio. Un dialogo interdisciplinare*, eum, Macerata 2006; F. SCANZIANI (ed.), *Ripensare la risurrezione*, Glossa, Milano 2009; E. FALQUE, *The Metamorphosis of Finitude. An Essay on Birth and Resurrection*, Fordham University Press, New York 2012; A. GESCHÉ, *Dieu pour penser. VI. Le Christ*, Les Éditions du Cerf, Paris 2001, 129–194.

For an approach to a theology that focuses on the **Father**: F.X. DURRWELL, *Le Père. Dieu en son mystère*, Les Éditions du Cerf, Paris 1993; K. RAHNER, *Theos in the New Testament*, in ID., *Theological Investigations. Volume I*, Helicon Press, Baltimore 1961, 79–148; J. GALOT, *Le coeur du Père*, Éditions Desclée de Brouwen, Paris – Louvain 1957; M. BRACCI, *Paterologia. Per una teologia del Padre*, San Paolo, Cinisello Balsamo 2017; X. LACROIX, *Passeurs de vie. Essai sur la paternité*, Bayard, Paris 2004. For the theme of paternity in Lacan, see also: J. LACAN, *Les complexes familiaux dans la formation de l'individu*, in ID., *Autre écrits*, Éditions du Seuil, Paris 2001, 23–84; ID., *Noms-du-Pére*, Éditions du Seuil, Paris 2005; ID., *On Feminine Sexuality. The Limits of Love and Knowledge. Book XX. Encore 1972–1973*, W.W. Norton & Company,

New York – London 1999. See also M. RECALCATI, *Cosa resta del padre? La paternità nell'epoca ipermoderna*, Raffaello Cortina, Milano 2011; L. ZOJA, *The Father. Historical, Psychological and Cultural Perspectives*, Brunner-Routledge, Hove 2001. To support the reasons for a real **reciprocity** between Father and Son: W. PANNENBERG, *Systematic Theology. Vol. I*, T&T Clark International, London – New York, 2004, 259–336.

The nexus linking theology, power and **violence is** crucial and can be variously analysed and denounced as in: P. WALTER (ed.), *Das Gewaltpotential des Monotheismus und der dreieine Gott*, Herder, Freiburg i. Br. 2005; P. TILLICH, *Die Philosophie der Macht*, Coloquium Verlag Otto H. Hess, Berlin – Dahlem 1956; J. BUTLER, *The Psychic Life of Power: Theories in Subjection*, Stanford University Press, Stanford (CA) 1997. For the theme of violence, particularly in relation to love: J.L. MARION, *The erotic Phenomenon*, The University of Chicago Press, Chicago – London 2007; G.C. PAGAZZI, *Tua è la potenza. Fidarsi della forza di Cristo*, San Paolo, Cinisello Balsamo 2019; CH. YANNARÁS, *Person and Eros*, Holy Cross Orthodox Press, Brookline/MA 2007; ID., *On the Absence and Unknowability of God. Heidegger and the Areopagite*, T&T Clark International, London – New York 2005, 99–110; E. SALMANN, *Amore e violenza*, in ID., *Presenza di Spirito. Il cristianesimo come gesto e pensiero*, Messaggero, Padova 2000, 461–471; BENEDICT XVI, *Deus caritas est* (2015), nn. 2–18; RICHARD OF SAINT VICTOR, *The Four Degrees of Violent Charity*, in H. FEISS (ed.), *On Love: A Selection of Works of Hugh*, Adam, Achard, Richard, and Godfrey of St. Victor, Brepols Publishers, Turnhout 2012, 261–300. Perhaps, however, it is in literature that one can find traces of the luminous traits of this nexus. An unsurpassed reflection can be found in F. O'CONNOR, *The Violent Bear It Away*, Farrar, Straus and Giroux, New York 1960; EAD., *Wise Blood*, Harcourt, San Diego (CA) 1952, as well as many of his short stories (EAD., *The Complete Stories*, Farrar, Straus and Giroux, New York 1971). The power of this reflection on violence is not given by its pervasive presence (in other authors one can find much higher levels of it), but by its being an integral – and in many respects decisive – part of the relationship between God and man – a lucid commentary on the fact that "it is a fearful thing to fall into the hands of the living God" (*Heb* 10:31). This is even more evident in the poetic-mystical vein where I would like to mention the work of David Maria Turoldo: here, the violence with which God makes himself present to man – alongside the violence of man on man, man on God, man on nature and reality on man – is transformed into poetry. Among the many possible quotations I would choose D.M. TUROLDO, *Udii una voce*, in ID., *O sensi miei ... Poesie 1948–1988*, Rizzoli, Milano 1990, 59–173.

I deliberately chose not to make the theme of **generation** the pivot of my discussion, as would have been possible (G. ANGELINI et al., *Di generazione in generazione. La trasmissione dell'umano nell'orizzonte della fede*, Glossa, Milano 2012). Having chosen to use the category of inheritance made me want to avoid giving too much space to other concepts (generation, desire, recognition, freedom, etc.) that could have legitimately stolen the show. In any case, I would like to quote a text from Thomas that honours this possible lead: "This generation is the beginning of every other generation, since it alone perfectly accepts the generating nature, while all the others – in which what is generated receives only part of the substance of what is generating, or a similarity to it – are imperfect. Hence it is necessary that from this same generation, by some form of imitation, every other generation should derive: 'From this is called all fatherhood in heaven and on earth' (Eph 3:15). And this is why the Son is called 'first-born of creation' (Col 1:15), to designate the origin and imitation of generation, but not the essential reason itself. [...] And this generation is not only the origin of creatures, but also of the Holy Spirit, who proceeds from the begetter and the begotten" (THOMAS AQUINAS, *Super Boetium de trinitate. Prologus*). Cf. the commentary on this text in P. SEQUERI, *L'amore della ragione. Variazioni sinfoniche su un tema di Benedetto XVI*, EDB, Bologna 2012, 93–101. For approaches to this perspective: M. CACCIARI, *Generare Dio*, il Mulino, Bologna 2017; M. MAGATTI – C. GIACCARDI, *Generativi di tutto il mondo, unitevi! Manifesto per la società dei liberi*, Feltrinelli, Milano 2014; J.-P. SONNET, *Generare è narrare*, Vita e pensiero, Milano 2015; M. GAUCHET, *Il figlio del desiderio. Una rivoluzione antropologica*, Vita e pensiero, Milano 2010; V. ROSITO, *Lo spirito e la polis. Prospettive per una pneumatologia politica*, Cittadella, Assisi 2016, 45–72 and 103–112. For a different perspective: N. BERDYAEV, *The Meaning of the Creative Act*, Semantron Press, 2009.

CHAPTER 10

# The Space of the Heirs

In this last chapter, what remains is to try to draw out the metaphysical and anthropological consequences of what happened in Christ's death and resurrection. The space of our being and acting is reconfigured by these events. It is a filial space that involves everyone. Strictly speaking, it does not involve only human beings but every aspect of reality, physical and spiritual, personal and relational, human and animal. It involves men and women no less than mountains and rivers, stars and galaxies. It is, in short, a change in metaphysics.

Theologically speaking, what should be produced here is a Christian metaphysics, i.e. a treatise on the Holy Spirit. In fact, space and time as configured in Christianity, as well as a doctrine of being and becoming, find their most correct location in the Spirit, i.e. in that person, that movement, that open space of God that is traversed by his desire to be Father and to have before him a reality that corresponds in a filial way.

All this is beyond the scope of this book; rather, it would require another one. I will, therefore, limit myself to hinting at a few paths that might be intriguing in the direction of a metaphysics of the Holy Spirit, postponing their development to a more appropriate space. An attempt to give a name to the nameless Spirit.

## 1 The Son and the Sons

### 1.1 *The Space of the Spirit*

To speak of inheritance is to identify a *space*. The tones can be different. Sometimes they are those of the emptiness left by death or of absence and abandonment. One can only inherit if someone has made space, left. When one is abandoned, one has to inherit; one is forced quickly to pick up the heritage of the other – whether positive or negative – and come to terms with it. Somehow, one must suddenly become one's own parent.

However – especially when the inheritance is left by someone who is still alive, not constrained by death – the tones can also be those of autonomy, of trust, of encouragement to inhabit a space left open for everyone.

One can understand here the importance of not separating Jesus' death from his life. While it is true that it is through death that, in the dark tones of God's abandonment and distance, we see the extent to which God is able to hand over the inheritance, it is in Jesus' life that we can find its meaning. The space left by the Father is a free life which Jesus can inhabit by defining his own name and identity in his relationships with others, complex but fascinating.

In Christianity, this space is called the Holy Spirit. It is in the space of the Spirit that children learn to say *Abba*, that they learn to become brothers or sister and to become themselves. Not on a track that allows only progress or derailment but in a context that is habitable, rich, plural and relaxed. It is in this vast space that there is room for the positive and plural differences in which the face of each is defined. Differences of gender, of culture, of possibilities, of charisms, of abilities.

It is in the space of the Spirit that the Son is eternally begotten, and in the same space that he lives his own human sonship. The space of the Spirit is therefore both the space that Jesus inhabits and the space that Jesus offers so that it can be inhabited by his brothers and sisters.

This space is the very generativity of the Father. That is why it can be called "Spirit of your Father" (*Mt* 10:20), because it is the space that the Father has had for his own Son from the beginning. But it can also be called "Spirit of his Son" (*Gal* 4:6), because it is in the Son that we can see it filled in its proper form. Finally, it is so wide that it can also be called "Spirit of adoption [sonship] (υἰοθεσία, *hyiothesía*)" (*Rom* 8:15), indicating that there is room for all of us in the plural difference of the forms of our sonship.

It should come as no surprise that this can take on an ambiguous form. It resembles the dismay that many of us felt – I certainly did – when the training-wheels were taken off our bicycles as children. On the one hand, it was pure abandonment: weeping and unaided, we had to set off far away, betrayed by nature (the wheels and gravity) and by those we loved (the mother who encouraged us). On the other hand, it was the beginning of a new autonomy, of open spaces and unexplored roads. It is important to find these ambiguities in the Christian space and discover the hidden reason for them.

There is *the Father's departure/absence* that can take on the tones of abandonment and betrayal (on God's part), or of rebellion and sin (on man's part). Its profound reason, however, lies in the real space that the Father offers to the autonomy of those he wants in front of him. It is the autonomy of the person, that is, the possibility of developing a relationship with oneself, the ability to stand, or ride a bike, without having to depend on others like infants. The possibility of perverting this space, turning in on oneself, must not obscure its good origin, the dream of having adult children. It is also the autonomy of relationships with each other, that is, the possibility of becoming oneself in the midst of a network of intriguing and dangerous, everyday and beautiful relationships, with respect to which God is not only not jealous, but which he desired first. Again, the possibility of the perversion of these relationships, of abuse and violence, must not make us forget their origin: the Father's desire to see children living as siblings, capable of becoming generative fathers and mothers in their turn. No love, of lovers, of parents, of friends, but also no love for the things and beauty of the world is, in the first instance, negative. God himself wanted our identity to be generated in this space, in the desire for and confrontation with people and things.

Believing that God is not envious is perhaps the sharpest challenge for anyone who wants to proclaim the name of the Christian God. Ambiguity is always lurking, and with it the fear that can drive one to a prudence unworthy of God's trust. I happened to experience a similar moment and I remember it very well, as if it had happened yesterday. I was twenty-five years old and had fallen in love. The matter was rather complicated and so I confided in an old Jesuit, quite sure that he would advise me to follow a prudent path, and leave that relationship. My heart was breaking at the thought. So I presented the matter precisely, without hiding, but also determined to defend my position. This old man with a good face and jovial manner listened to me very carefully and then told me that love is from God, and that, if I was going to live this before God, I should be careful, but not afraid, and not back down. This man was teaching me who God is. It is easy to talk about love and trust in the abstract; it is more difficult to do so in the dangerous complexity of our biographies. Even more difficult when what is at stake is not one's own autonomy, but that of others. In giving me that advice, he was not speculating on the strength of my feelings or the future of that love, but on the very identity of God. Many years later, I have not forgotten that.

Then there is *the departure/absence of the Son*. The presence of Jesus in Scripture, in the sacraments, in the poor, cannot conceal the fact that Jesus is simply not present, not as he was when he walked the roads of Galilee. The Firstborn is gone. He will return, but in the meantime he is gone.

> When he had said this, as they were watching, he was lifted up, and a cloud took him out of their sight. While he was going and they were gazing up toward heaven, suddenly two men in white robes stood by them. They said, "Men of Galilee, why do you stand looking up toward heaven? This Jesus, who has been taken up from you into heaven, will come in the same way as you saw him go into heaven" (*Acts* 1:9–11).

This departure of his has dramatic aspects. It imposes a strain on those who want to believe in him because he does not simply offer himself to the eye, to direct, everyday experience. Perhaps even then it would not be easy – as it was not for those who actually were in touch with him – but it would certainly seem *easier*. The New Testament – and more modestly every book about Jesus, including this one – was written to try to cope with this absence. And yet the ultimate reason for this departure is not abandonment. The Son left so that all might become sons. "It is to your advantage that I go away, for if I do not go away, the Advocate will not come to you, but if I go, I will send him to you" (*Jn* 16:7).

The Firstborn leaves room for his brothers, room to live out their own autonomous relationship with the Father. In this way, his sonship does not become useless but, on the contrary, shows the greatness of his own liberality. Our sonship does not *depend* on his, as if, in order to speak to the Father, we always had to ask permission, as second-class sons. Rather, our sonship is *freed* from his; it finds in his the space of its own possibility and realisation. If it is true that we are 'sons in the Son', it is also true that we are 'sons in the Spirit', the same Spirit that guided Jesus' filial freedom.

The absence of the Firstborn also opens up the space of brotherhood. He too, like the Father, is not jealous of the relationships that constitute us. He is so little as to identify himself with his brother, especially the one that is least. To those who would like to see him, who would consider the relationship with him indispensable in order to be worthy of their name as sons, as "blessed by the Father", called to "inherit the Kingdom" (*Mt* 25:34), he proposes to play their sonship simply in the fraternal relationship, without any attention-seeking or any envy: "Just as you did it to one of the least of these brothers and sisters of mine, you did it to me" (*Mt* 25:40).

### 1.2 *The Space of Co-Heirs*

In inheriting the Kingdom, we inherit a space characterised by blessing, autonomy in relationships, generativity. Christian metaphysics draws this space open because this is the place where sons and brothers can give themselves, the place of the possible realisation of paternal desire. Here, in the real space of filial possibility, there are forces that can be assumed, dynamics that allow sonship and configure the form of sons.

The history of theology recordts the struggle to come up with a concept of God, the human and reality that can live up to this space, that can describe it as it is and the possibilities of life it offers us. It is not easy to form and use a conceptual arsenal that can try to describe all this. The form of its revelation, in fact, is a historical event, with all the richness – but also with all the limitations – that this entails, for those who want to try to account for it in a more abstract language.

Two traits in particular stand out and make a Christian metaphysics complex. Its *dynamic* character and its *singular* character. These are clearly aspects that can be problematic if the philosophical endeavour is to grasp *universal forms* instead.

When describing something, one may be interested in grasping its form or rather its dynamics. The two can never be completely separated, yet there can be different emphases, depending also on the descriptive tool that is used. A photograph, a statue or a police report tend to describe the form, to say 'that's how it is', whereas a novel, a film or a psychoanalyst's notebook try to report a movement, a direction, a set of forces that meet and collide, generating an action.

Excessive attention to forms does not help Christian theology precisely because, in the plural space of the Father, there is no such thing as *one* form of sonship; there may be traits, styles – as if to say that in some respects sons resemble one another –, but above all there will be movements, dynamics and forces that generate and grow sons. Or that prevent this.

When applied to Christianity, therefore, metaphysics concerned with describing forms is likely to have problematic consequences. For if we ask ourselves about the relationship between the form of Jesus' sonship and ours, what will emerge is above all the difference. We *are not* the Son; we were not "in the beginning with God" (*Jn* 1:2); we are created, not begotten. This helps us to understand who we are, but leaves us without help in knowing what we are called to and who we can be. If we focus on the form, we cannot properly desire Jesus' inheritance to be ours. Hence, by calling ourselves *adopted children*, the emphasis will inevitably fall on the difference of adoption. This way of proceeding might be more apt if we were stones. The effort to describe the *state* of a thing, its composition, can be of use when the thing to be described is inert. It is this and, within certain limits, it cannot be anything else.

If, however, after looking at the story of Jesus, we affirm that God is Father, or that God is love, what we need is a conceptual toolkit that is less static, one that allows us to describe the relationships that bind people together and the way in which these relationships generate or change them. We sense that Jesus' effort was not to make us 'know our place', to contain *hubris*, but rather to invite us as adult children into a relationship.

This is why the aim of a Christian metaphysics will not be to establish forms but rather to describe relational dynamics, movements, forces, which account for the *arising* (creation), *manifestation* (redemption) and *fulfilment* (eschatology) of the possibility of God's children. The name Christianity gives to all this, as to a single force, is Holy Spirit. In fact, the space we have described above is not a fixed space but is traversed by a movement so impelling that Paul will describe it as a "groaning" that involves us, all creatures and, first of all, God himself (*Rom* 8:26). Two typically hereditary movements are expressed in this groaning: the push for the sons to take on the inheritance, not to hold themselves back, and the counter-push for this inheritance not to be held back as a jealous possession. The filial position is actually threatened on both sides: both by the fear that leads one not to take on the inheritance and by a different fear that prevents one from sharing it.

From this perspective, the similarities and identities that bind us to Jesus emerge more clearly. The emphasis here rests on the *children*, rather than on their being *adopted*. Identical is the Father from whom everything comes and towards whom everything goes. The origin is common (*cf. Heb* 2:11) and so is the fatherhood to which everything is subject (*cf. 1 Cor* 15:20–28). Identical is the Spirit that sustains this filial movement. Different, however, are the faces of the sons. However, this difference does not contradict the identity of the Spirit since the power of the Spirit *desires* the diversity of the sons. The unity of this force generates plurality of forms because it is a force of relationship.

The second character of Christian metaphysics emerges here, namely, its having to deal with the *singular*. It is, at the same time, the problem of the singularity of Jesus and the singularity of each person. At the origin of a possible Christian metaphysical reflection is the historical-singular event of Jesus' life. At the end of such a reflection is the historical sonship of individuals, not of an indistinct mass, but of sons and daughters who each have their own filial right, their own relationships, their own singularity and uniqueness.

One finds this idea in the account of a Jewish tradition reported by Martin Buber: "Before his end, Rabbi Sussja said: In the world to come I will not be asked, 'Why were you not Moses?' I will be asked, 'Why were you not Sussja?'".[1]

The force of the Spirit, therefore, is a force that knows only proper names because it is the force of the One who is only Father and who knows only children. He knows and encourages each individual ("He calls his own sheep by name and leads them out", *Jn* 10:3) and each individual thing in its uniqueness, in its proper name ("He determines the number of the stars; he gives to all of them their names", *Ps* 147:4).

A perplexity may arise at this point. What happens to the centrality of Jesus for Christian metaphysics? To what extent is his role indispensable? Is he perhaps destined to pass away? Can one perhaps be a child *apart from* him? The perplexity is legitimate and is rooted in the particularity of Christian mediation.

---

[1] M. BUBER, *The Way Of Man According To The Teachings Of Hasidism*, Pendle Hill, Wallingford (PA) 1960, 21.

## 1.3 *Mediation Beyond Mediation*

Similarly to what we have seen for the activity/passivity pair, so also for the mediation/immediacy binomial it is not possible, from a Christian perspective, simply to opt for one of the two terms to the detriment of the other. Both combine to form an original polarity. Both are redefined from the perspective of the relationship.

### 1.3.1 Relationship and Mediation

Common experience and psychological research converge in the idea that relationships involve mediation. Each of our relationships makes use of some form of medium (such as skin, sound, light) or instrument (such as language, images or concepts), which allows us to make contact with the other. Even with respect to ourselves, we do not have the possibility of direct contact but are forced to know ourselves in a mediated way by the gaze of others, by the words and concepts that others provide us with. This is our condition. We can live it satisfactorily when these mediations take on successful or artistic forms; yet, in this, there seems to be the trace of a condemnation, of an imposed limitation. Can we not overcome these mediations and really meet each other? Are we condemned to conclude that an immediate relationship is not possible?

The Christian experience is led to review this sense of dissatisfaction with the pervasiveness of mediation in the light of the story of Jesus. In him, we have seen a relationship with self that is radically mediated by the relationship with another, the Father. We have also been able to see in this, not the mark of a condemnation but the open space of the possibility of a real relationship with self and with the Father. We have sensed that, for Jesus, an immediate relationship with self, which would be independent of the Father and the others, would not be the realisation of a dream but the plunging into a nightmare. The hope of being able to generate oneself in the immediacy of self is a wicked hope. It cannot even be called a mirage because a mirage represents something good, albeit illusory. Here, however, we are faced with something worse: it is the very object of hope that is wrong. In the immediacy of self, one is not free, one is alone. One does not really love by aiming at immediacy with the other but devours him or herself.

The mystery of Jesus' death and resurrection unmasked the falsity of this hope forever in that it showed that God himself, in the person of the Father, does not have an immediate relationship with himself but passes through the Son. The Father does not think of himself; he thinks of the Son. He does not love himself; he loves the Son and loves himself in the Son. The Father has no other name than that which expresses the relationship that binds him to another. Mediation, therefore, is not something God discovers in the relationship with his creation but something that has always been part of his identity, his nature. Nor is the relationship with the Son simply immediate – hence the insight that even the generation of the Son takes place in the dynamic space mediated by the Spirit. This emerges most strongly when one sees the Son able, in the Spirit, to stand *before* the absence of the Father, and, at the same time, one sees the Father able, in the Spirit, to stand *before* the death of the Son. If the relationship were one of simple immediacy, neither would be possible, and each would be overwhelmed by the absence of the other.

### 1.3.2 Relation and Immediacy

However, this original, structural and theological character of mediation does not speak of the impossibility *of the* relationship, but rather of its free possibility *in* mediation. The Father does not know the Son by hearsay and, conversely, the Son does not know the Father indirectly. The relationship that binds them is a real relationship, the most real that can be thought of.

In the life of Jesus, this immediacy took on a disconcerting tone:

> Philip said to him, "Lord, show us the Father, and we will be satisfied". Jesus said to him, "Have I been with you all this time, Philip, and you still do not know me? Whoever has seen me has seen the Father. How can you say, 'Show us the Father'? Do you not believe that I am in the Father and the Father is in me? The words that I say to you, I do not speak on my own; but the Father who dwells in me does his works. Believe me that I am in the Father and the Father is in me" (*Jn* 14:8–11).

Philip's request shows exactly the trace of that dream of immediacy we saw above. It is something that expresses a genuine desire, that of a mystical, direct relationship, and tries to realise it, thinking it can do without mediation. Instead, *in mediation*, the relationship is direct. Equally wrong, therefore, would be to imagine Jesus as the one who commandeers the Father and makes him visible only to those whom he wants. A kind of Franz Kafka's *Castle* clerk. When Jesus is asked to teach how to pray, he teaches a prayer – which later becomes *the* prayer of Christians – in which he himself does not appear at all. It is his prayer to the Father, the one with which Jesus addresses him directly, and with which he invites everyone into a direct relationship. Jesus' mediation does not take a fee but addresses the Father. The gaze directed on him is diverted to the object of the theological relationship, namely, the Father. This is the function of his mediation, namely, to go beyond mediation to the real and constitutive relationship with the Father.

This gesture of the Son does not apply only with respect to the Father. With respect to the *singularity of every relationship*, Jesus invites us to experience his mediation as an appeal to immediacy. He is the force that generates relationships, not the intermediary that controls them. Relationships with brothers and sisters, relationships with one another, are also direct, real relationships. One can certainly be invited to relate to the poor or the enemy – that is, to whom we would *not* wish to relate – by the fraternal power of the Son and the paternal power of the Father. Yet, immediately, these give way to a love that must simply be for the other, for the individual. One cannot love by proxy, and it is not this to which the Trinity invites us.

Thus, the eschatological horizon of Christian fraternity is not represented by a mass of individuals who love only the Son but by a choral ensemble of real relationships in which the identity and freedom of each are brought into play in singular relationships. Still less can it be represented by the idea that "God may be all in all" (*1 Cor* 15:28) if this means that, in the end, there is only God. This is not God's desire. There would be no point in the eternal generation of the Son or the historical creation of the world, if ultimately, everything was simply to be restored to the absolute silence of one alone. If this were the case, we would be the living and God the dead, whereas God is the living *par excellence* in that he generates life in himself and in others. "He is God not of the dead, but of the living, for to him all of them are alive" (*Lk* 20:38).

### 1.3.3 The Mediation of the Son

Jesus is not the one who does not allow any freedom to be exercised unless it passes through him. Rather, he is the one who frees each person's responsibility and identity in true singular relationships. In this, he fulfils the Father's will to extend his own inheritance. In doing so, he brings himself, his own identity, into play again and again, exposing it to the action of those he has involved. In this, too, he reflects the Father's will not to be except in relationship with the other.

It is thus a mediation that, on the one hand, aims to disappear, so that the Father's life with his children may shine forth, but, on the other hand, is destined never to pass away. In the first place for him himself. His involvement with his brothers and sisters is not functional; it is structural. He can be the Only-Begotten of the Father even alone, but, if the Father wants many sons, and he himself wants to be the First-Born of many, this cannot be without a true involvement of human freedoms. He who saved the name of all has his own name *exposed to* the actions of all. The saviour wants to be saved because he wants others to take on an inheritance that is truly theirs, while always remaining his own. The responsibility that Jesus offered to all involves him forever. It does not pass, because his openness to let himself be touched by the lives of those he is not afraid to call brothers does not pass, and it does not pass because this space of filial possibility remains wide open forever.

### 1.3.4 Inheritance Passed On

There is a, perhaps unexpected, effect of this filial co-responsibility which is noticeable only when it is looked at in all its seriousness. It is not a matter of a teenage responsibility, which is necessarily a bit fake since it is covered by the responsibility of a parent who is always around the corner. Instead, it is a true adult responsibility, whose boundaries are open. We can see this especially in evil, when we notice that there is no limit to what God allows one man to do to another. God does not revoke the freedom and responsibility of his children, even when they set up death camps.

However, it is another aspect that I would like to emphasise. This adult responsibility implies that the inheritance received is in turn passed on. The forms and forces of this process are entrusted to us, to our freedom. What we have before us is an open space, as much for our own sonship as for the possibility of the children of tomorrow. A theology of inheritance is a theology of transmission, *a theology of tradition*. Something that has been life for us must become life for others. And the 'traditional' forms that guarantee the transmission of the force that makes children must be preserved. Only the adolescent thinks he can invent the future from today – and he is excusable because after all, he only arrived yesterday. The adult feels the weight of having received forms that have enabled him to live as a son and the responsibility to transmit them in a vital way.

Herein lies the unexpected aspect. Precisely in order to correspond to the gesture of freedom with which the Son relativised all religious forms – temple, law, worship, Sabbath, priesthood – many of these things will have to be resumed and preserved, without thinking that we can simply declare in the abstract rights that may be valid at most for those who affirm them. Precisely out of respect for the many freedoms that have made history for this proclamation of dignity and sonship, the forms they have given us will have to be rethought and handed on. That is, it is a question of respecting tradition because, to all intents and purposes, inherited sonship is a work of tradition, a heritage that passes from one hand to another and, in these transfers, risks being lost. Tradition must always be relived, revised and rethought so that it can be a true transmission of that same original patrimony.

From this perspective, I believe we can look at the particular work of the cloistered Augustinian nuns, in their monastery in the middle of the Apennines, from where this book started. They guard an ancient form – which to many may seem original to say the least – capable of guaranteeing the transmission of a Spirit that can be perceived quite clearly by anyone willing to listen. They too, like anyone who cares about the future of Christianity today, find themselves having to rethink their tradition to make it capable of offering to those who will come tomorrow what it offered to them. Such a form of life could be abandoned because it is judged obsolete, or transformed to such an extent that it is no longer what it was. But perhaps a greater risk would lie in wanting to keep it simply identical to itself. This would turn it into a relic, something to be displayed in a museum. Instead, it is fascinating to observe the ability to bring tradition to life in the effort to keep it what it is: a living force. As long one acts like this, one can act in the filial certainty of being in the midst of a living tradition that has never ceased to renew and generate.

Something similar, I believe, can apply to the challenges that the forms of the Catholic Church face in our time of rapid change. Other churches – more or less inclined to innovation or preservation of their forms – also face similar challenges. It would be a shame if the sentiments guiding these transitions were the arrogance of those who believe they are the first to receive this inheritance or the fear of those who prefer to hide their treasure in a hole rather than play it out in the complexity of the moment.

## 2      Challenges Token Up

In conclusion, I would like to try to return to the challenges that emerged at the beginning of this journey, both on the theological-christological front (*cf.* above, ch. 1, § 1), as well as on that of dialogue with contemporary sensibilities (*cf.* above, ch. 3, § 1) in order to show how a Christology of the *heir* tries to meet them, and what further paths it points to.

### 2.1     *Theological Challenges*

The perspective of inheritance focuses on the freedom of the Son. It seeks to provide categories so that we can see at work and narrate the freedom of a man realised in his relationships, with men and women, and with God.

It presents itself as a *Christology from below*, for two reasons at least. Firstly, because the bond with the Father does not exclude other bonds. On the contrary. In many ways, the bond with the Father appears only later, after one has witnessed the human inheritances of Jesus – the mother, the relatives, the teacher, etc. The freedom to realise oneself before God does not relieve one of the freedom to realise oneself in the fullness of human relationships. Secondly, it is a Christology from below because it pays attention to what can be seen. Relationships, dynamics, bonds, are charged with theological significance only because they can be seen. The way in which the Son assumes his task, lives in faithfulness, makes another the centre of his own identity: all this is something that can be *seen*. What is so daily visible – like the dynamics that characterise the relationships of each of us – has the potential to question, challenge and invite us.

The perspective of inheritance demands an *ascending soteriology*. The fundamental dynamic of freedom is that of Christ. In him we see a humanity involved, in its choices, in its relationships, in its freedom. At the same time, this 'ascent' of freedom of his invites the freedom of each person to get involved in the same space. What avoids the risk of *self-salvation* is that, in inheritance, freedom is always understood as relationship. It is my freedom at stake, but it is only so because the other offers and opens up concrete possibilities for me.

Finally, inheritance is a Christological perspective that seeks to highlight aspects of so-called *elevating grace*. On the one hand, Jesus' action liberates from sin. It holds wide open a possibility of forgiveness, a permanent access to the fullness of the paternal inheritance, even in the face of the greatest sin. No fault, no offence can change the name of God. On the other hand, the most important aspect of Jesus' action is not this; it does not have to do with sin but with the possibilities of a filial life. The desire of the father is not simply for the prodigal son to return; rather, he wants him to return so that he can give him "the robe – the best one [...], ring on his finger and sandals on his feet" (*Lk* 15:22), so that he can live as a prince. God forgives so that the forgiven may live as sons, the lost may be found and the dead may come back to life (*cf. Lk* 15:32).

### 2.2  *Contemporary Challenges*

The story of Jesus and the way he lived, if read with theological categories that know how to bring out his relationships and freedom, can establish a fruitful dialogue with contemporary sensibilities, in which recognition, opoosition and encounter are possible.

The contemporary focus on the *conditional* character of freedom is not challenged by Jesus in the name of an abstract and absolute creativity. The heir does not create from nothing; he starts from the condition of the gift he has received. This allows us to understand that it is not a condemnation to discover oneself conditioned. Instead, it offers concrete paths so that the interweaving of bonds – which in Jesus has nothing like the pastel tones of a fairy tale – can become the real space of a free identity. God himself lives from this interweaving.

The story of Jesus takes place in a time and under conditions that are in many ways different from our own, not comparable to the tide of options that overwhelm us today, leaving us *drunk*, or seasick, or more often both. Yet, Jesus clearly shows a path, the possibility of charting a course that can turn the jumble of options into opportunities. His path is traced by the Father's desire for the face of a son and the spacious liberality that is manifested in this desire. The Father desires us to be children and is fully involved in this. However, his involvement does not translate into an obsessive presence, a ruthless control, but rather a space of trust in which to execute this desire. It is the same space that God has always granted himself, the space of the Spirit. Faced with the contemporary risk of losing the call of life in the sea of possibilities, Christ shows how a road can be traced even in objectively dramatic conditions. This road does not originate from the genius of the person who has traced it but from the curious and involved availability of the Father, who has found, in the Son, a perfect match.

Lastly, we have seen how contemporary freedom seems to be shot through with suspicion, a *dark background* that seems to question the meaningfulness of the world. Does existence really make sense, or is it not rather a blind mechanism? Does what has happened to me really make sense, or is it not, rather, the result of mere chance?

One must not be hasty on this point. There is no doubt that, following the example of Jesus, Christianity fights despair and the pain of non-meaning wherever it is found. However, it does and can only do so by involving freedom. It cannot be a prior assurance, a definitive reassurance. If it were, it would gain a meaning to which our lives would be indifferent. The meaningfulness of the world, on the other hand, is given and won day by day in the freedom of the children.[2] It is not simply given. If our world grasps a vertigo of uncertainty in the face of the abyss of possible non-sense, Christianity points to a path that skirts the abyss, but does not eliminate it: the path traced by Jesus. Its risk speaks not only of something dark, but also something sublime. It says to what extent God accepted the risk of freedom, for himself and for us, in the desire to have someone stand before him as a son. The sense of bewilderment cannot be eliminated, only experienced in the confidence of sons.

### Bibliographical Guidelines

As I have tried to outline it in its dynamic and singular dimension, the space of the children is **pneumatological and Trinitarian.** Among the many possible references: H.U. von Balthasar, *Theo-logic. III. The Spirit of Truth,* Ignatius Press, San Francisco 2005; G. Marchesi, *La Cristologia trinitaria di Hans Urs von Balthasar. Gesù Cristo pienezza della rivelazione e della salvezza,* Queriniana, Brescia 1997; P. Martinelli, *La morte di Cristo come rivelazione dell'amore trinitario nella teologia*

---

2   *Cf.* G. Auzou, *Le don d'une conquête. Étude du livre de Josué,* Édition de l'orante, Paris 1964.

*di H.U. von Balthasar*, Jaca Book, Milano 1995; M. Bordoni, *La cristologia nell'orizzonte dello Spirito*, Queriniana, Brescia 1995; R. Penna, *Lo Spirito di Cristo. Cristologia e pneumatologia secondo un'originale formulazione paolina*, Paideia, Brescia 1976; J. Moltmann, *The Trinity and the Kingdom. The doctrine of God*, Fortress Press, Minneapolis 1993; Id., *History and the Triune God: Contributions to Trinitarian Theology*, SCM Press, London 1991; Id., *God in Creation. An Ecological Doctrine of Creation. The Gifford Lectures 1984–1985*, SCM Press, London 1985; Id., *The Spirit of Life. A Universal Affirmation*, Fortress Press, Minneapolis 1992; C.M. Lacugna, *God for Us. The Trinity and Christian Life*, Harper San Francisco, San Francisco (CA) 1991; E. Salmann, *Neuzeit und Offenbarung. Studien zur trinitarischen Analogik des Christentums*, Studia Anselmiana, Roma 1986; Id., *Der geteilte Logos. Zum offenen Prozeß von neuzeitlichem Denken und Theologie*, Studia Anselmiana, Roma 1992; the appeal made by Salmann in his Id., *La natura scordata. Un futile elogio dell'ablativo*, in Id., *Presenza di Spirito. Il cristianesimo come gesto e pensiero*, Messaggero, Padova 2000, 306–323 is something I would like to develop in pneumatological form in a forthcoming book.

**Recent proposals** include: P. Coda, *Dalla Trinità. L'avvento di Dio tra storia e profezia*, Città Nuova, Roma 2011; Id., *Il logos e il nulla. Trinità religioni mistica*, Città Nuova, Roma 2003; G. Greshake, *Der dreieine Gott. Eine trinitarische Theologie*, Herder, Freiburg im Br. 1997; P. Coda – A. Clemenzia, *Il terzo persona. Per una teologia dello Spirito Santo*, EDB, Bologna 2020; A. Bertuletti, *Dio mistero dell'unico*, Queriniana, Brescia 2014; J.P. Lieggi, *La sintassi trinitaria. Al cuore della grammatica della fede*, Aracne, Roma 2016; L. Sandonà, *Dialogica. Per un pensare teologico tra sintassi trinitaria e questione del pratico*, Città Nuova, Roma 2019.

Cues for such thinking can come **from Eastern theology** (S. Bulgakov, *The Comforter*, Wm.B. Eerdmans Publishing, Grand Rapids (MI) 2004; P. Florenski, *The Pillar and Ground of the Truth*, Princeton University Press, Princeton – Oxford 1997, 39–105; I. Zizioulas, *Communion and Otherness: Further Studies in Personhood and the Church*, T&T Clark, London – New York 2006; Ch. Yannarás, *Relational Ontology*, Holy Cross Orthodox Press, Brookline/MA 2011; Id., *On the Absence and Unknowability of God. Heidegger and the Areopagite*, T&T Clark International, London – New York 2005), with special recognition for the Jesuit who appears in this chapter (T. Špidlík, *L'idée russe. Une autre vision de l'homme*, Éditions Fates, Arsonval 1994; Id., *Il professor Ulipispirus e altre storie*, Lipa, Roma 1997), and from psychology, where I particularly direct attention to the **Russian cultural-historical psychology** (L.S. Vygotskij, *Pensiero e linguaggio*, Laterza, Roma – Bari 1992; L. Mecacci, *Psicologia moderna e postmoderna*, Laterza, Roma – Bari 1999; O. Liverta Sempio [ed.], *Vygotskij, Piaget, Bruner. Concezioni dello sviluppo*, Raffaello Cortina, Milano 1998).

One can also follow the track of **Rombach's ontology of structure**, with the understanding that this is in many ways an isolated track (H. Rombach, *Strukturontologie. Eine Phänomenologie der Freiheit*, Karl Alber Verlag, Freiburg – München 1971;

A. DE SANTIS, *Dalla dialettica al kairós. L'ontologia dell'evidenza in Heinrich Rombach*, Studia Anselmiana, Roma, 2002) with very different theological takes: K. HEMMERLE, *Theses Towards A Trinitarian Ontology*, Angelico Press, New York 2000 (cf. V. GAUDIANO, Introduzione, in K. HEMMERLE, *Un pensare ri-conoscente. Scritti sulla relazione fra filosofia e teologia*, Città Nuova, Roma 2018, 25–27; E. PRENGA, *Il darsi trinitario. Ontologia e fenomenologia trinitaria*, in P. CODA – A. CLEMENZIA – J. TREMBLAY [edd.], *Un pensiero per abitare la frontiera. Sulle tracce dell'ontologia trinitaria di Klaus Hemmerle*, Città Nuova – Sophia University Institute, Roma 2016, 44–48); A. GANOCZY, *Der dreieinige Schöpfer. Trinitätstheologie und Synergie*, Wissenschaftliche Buchgesellschft, Darmstadt 2001 (cf. L. VANTINI, *Il sé esposto. Teologia e neuroscienze in chiave fenomenologica*, Cittadella, Assisi 2017, 189–238); E. SALMANN, *Neuzeit und Offenbarung. Studien zur trinitarischen Analogik des Christentums*, Studia Anselmiana, Roma 1986, 29–33 and 105–162.

For the relationship between **mediated and immediate**, I refer to A. GRILLO, *Teologia fondamentale e liturgia. Il rapporto fra immediazza e mediazione nella riflessione teologica*, Messaggero, Padova 1995, of which I would like to quote the second of the concluding theses: "Since all mediation presupposes the 'obviousness' of an immediacy to be mediated, mediation – if understood in an absolute way, i.e. separate from immediacy – turns into a dangerous immediacy, because the more it is misunderstood as immediacy, the more illusory it is as mediation. This one-sidedness of thinking and acting – which believes it has already come to terms once and for all with the mediated and the immediate – is the most decisive part of the theological blindness of the (post)modern age" ID., *Teologia fondamentale e liturgia*, 262). See also: J. FEINER, *Offenbarung und Kirche – Kirche und Offenbarung*, in FEINER J. – LÖHRER M., *Mysterium Salutis. Grundriss Heilsgeschichtlicher Dogmatik. Band I. Die Grundlagen heisgeschichtlicher Dogmatik*, Benziger Verlag, Einsiedeln 1965, 497–544 for the ecclesiological aspects (which most of the volume deals with); H.U. VON BALTHASAR, *Explorations in Theology. I. The Word Made Flesh*, Ignatius Press, San Francisco 1989, 11–148, for the aspects relating to Scripture; K. RAHNER, *Foundations of Christian Faith. An Introduction to the Idea of Christianity*, Darton Longman & Todd, London 1978, 138–175 for the theological-fundamental aspects; F.D.E. SCHLEIERMACHER, *Brief Outline for the Study of Theology*, Wipf and Stock, Eugene (OR) 2007 for a general and long-standing background.

For reflection **on forms and forces**, see P. SEQUERI, *Il sensibile e l'inatteso. Lezioni di estetica teologica*, Queriniana, Brescia 2016, 98–104; D. CORNATI, *«Ma più grande è l'amore». Verità e giustizia di agápe*, Queriniana, Brescia 2019. Several insights can be found in D. CORNATI – E. PRATO (edd.), *Fratello Dio. Invenzioni a più voci. Studi in onore di Pierangelo Sequeri nel suo LXXV compleanno*, Glossa, Milano 2020 (CORNATI – PRATO (edd.), Fratello Dio, especially: G.C. PAGAZZI, *La forma delle forze*, 273–290; R. OTTONE, *La polifonia delle voci*, 231–240). Other paths are those that dialogue variously with Spinoza's work (G. DELEUZE, *Cosa può un corpo. Lezioni su Spinoza*, Ombre corte, Verona 2007; F. ZOURABICHVILI, *Deluze. Une philosophie de l'événement*, Presses Universitaires de France, Paris 1994) or with psychoanalysis (R. BERNET, *Force, Drive, Desire. A Philosophy of Psychoanalysis*, Northwestern University Press, Evaston/IL 2020) or with the intertwining of pneumatology and contemporary science (W. PANNENBERG, *Systematic Theology. Vol. I*, T&T Clark International, London – New York, 2004, 370–384; ID., *Systematic Theology. Vol. II*, T&T Clark International, London – New York, 2004, 59–135).

# Bibliography

For the Bible, the *New Revised Standard Version Updated Edition* (NRSVUE), Copyright © 2021 National Council of Churches of Christ in the United States of America, is used.

ALLISON D.C. JR., *The Historical Christ and the Theological Jesus*, Wm. B. Eerdmans Publishing Company, Grand Rapids (MI) 2009.
AMMANITI M. – GALLESE V., *La nascita della intersoggettività. Lo sviluppo del sé tra psicodinamica e neurobiologia*, Raffaello Cortina, Milano 2014.
ANGELINI G. ET AL., *Di generazione in generazione. La trasmissione dell'umano nell'orizzonte della fede*, Glossa, Milano 2012.
ANSELM OF CANTERBURY, *Why God Became Man*, in ID., *The Major Works*, Oxford University Press, Oxford 1998.
ARENDT H., *The Human Condition*, The University of Chicago Press, Chicago 1998.
ID., *Eichmann in Jerusalem. A Report on the Banality of Evil*, Penguin Classics, London 2006.
AUZOU G., *Le don d'une conquête. Étude du livre de Josué*, Édition de l'orante, Paris 1964.
BADANO C., *Il possibile fra l'essere e il nulla. Il ritorno della questione ontologica fondamentale nella filosofia del Novecento*, Edizioni Unicopoli, Milano 2009.
BAGGIO A.M. (ed.), *Il principio dimenticato. La fraternità nella riflessione politologica contemporanea*, Città Nuova, Roma 2007.
BAKER L.R., *Persons and Bodies. A Constitution View*, Cambridge University Press, Cambridge – New York 2000.
BALOCCO D., *Dal cristocentrismo al cristomorfismo. In Dialogo con David Tracy*, Glossa, Milano 2012.
BALTHASAR H.U. VON, *Explorations in Theology. I. The Word Made Flesh*, Ignatius Press, San Francisco 1989 (ed. orig. *Verbum caro. Skizzen zur Theologie I*, Johannes Verlag, Einsiedeln 1960).
ID., *The Glory of the Lord. A Theological Aesthetics. I. Seeing the Form*, Ignatius Press, San Francisco 2009 (ed. orig. *Herrlichkeit. Schau der Gestalt*, Johannes Verlag Einsiedeln, Freiburg 1961).
ID., *The Glory of the Lord. A Theological Aesthetics. V. The Realm of Metaphysics in the Modern Age*, Ignatius Press, San Francisco 1991 (ed. orig. *Herrlichkeit. Im Raum der Metaphysik*, Johannes Verlag, Einsiedeln 1965).
ID., *Mysterium Paschale. The Mystery of Easter*, Ignatius Press, San Francisco 2000 (ed. orig. *Theologie der drei Tage*, Benziger Verlag, Zürich 1969).
ID., *Theo-drama. Theological dramatic Theory. III. Dramatis Personae: Person in Christ*, Ignatius Press, San Francisco 1992 (ed. orig., *Theodramatik. Die Personen des Spiels. II. Die Personen in Christus*, Johannes Verlag, Einsiedeln 1978).

Id., *Theo-drama. Theological dramatic Theory. IV. The Action*, Ignatius Press, San Francisco 1994 (ed. orig., *Theodramatik. Die Handlung*, Johannes Verlag, Einsiedeln 1980).

Id., *Theo-logic. II. Truth of God*, Ignatius Press, San Francisco 2004 (ed. orig. *Theologik. Wahrheit Gottes*, Johannes Verlag, Einsiedeln 1985).

Id., *Theo-logic. III. The Spirit of Truth*, Ignatius Press, San Francisco 2005 (ed. orig. *Theologik. Der Geist der Wahrheit*, Johannes Verlag Einsiedeln, Freiburg 1987).

Barbaglio G., *I racconti della Passione. Indagine storica sul processo e la morte di Gesù di Nazaret*, EDB, Bologna 2015.

Baricco A., *The Game. A Digital Turning Point*, McSweeney's, San Francisco 2020 (ed. it. *The game*, Einaudi, Torino 2018).

Beauchamp P., *L'un et l'autre Testament. Essai de lecture*, Éditions du Seuil, Paris 1976.

Id., *L'un et l'autre Testament. Accomplir les Écritures*, Éditions du Seuil, Paris 1990.

Becchi E. – Julia D. (edd.), *Storia dell'infanzia. II. Dal Settecento ad oggi*, Laterza, Roma – Bari 1996.

Beck U., *I rischi della libertà*, Il Mulino, Bologna 2000.

Id. *World at Risk*, Polity Press, Cambridge 2009 (ed. orig. *Weltrisikogesellschaft, Auf der Suche nach der verlorenen Sicherheit*, Suhrkamp Verlag, Frankfurt am Main 2007).

Berdyaev N., *The Meaning of the Creative Act*, Semantron Press, 2009.

Berlin I., *Two Concepts of Liberty*, in Id., *Liberty*, Oxford University Press, Oxford 1995, 166–217 (ed. orig., *Two Concepts of Liberty*, Clarendon Press, Oxford 1958).

Id., *Russian Thinkers*, Penguin Books, London 1978.

Bernet R., *Force, Drive, Desire. A Philosophy of Psychoanalysis*, Northwestern University Press, Evaston/IL, 2020.

Bertuglia C.S. – Vaio S., *Complessità e modelli. Un nuovo quadro interpretativo per una modellizzazione nelle scienze della natura e della società*, Bollati Boringhieri, Torino 2011.

Bertuletti A., *Dio mistero dell'unico*, Queriniana, Brescia 2014.

Biblia, *Vademecum per il lettore della bibbia*, Morcelliana, Brescia 2017.

Bloch M., *The Historian's Craft*, Manchester University Press, Manchester – New York, 1992 (ed orig. *Apologie pour l'histoire ou Métier d'historien*, Armand Colin Éditeur, Paris 1993).

Bocchi G. – Ceruti M., *Caso/necessità*, in Telfener U. – Casadio L. (edd.), *Sistemica. Voci e percorsi nella complessità*, Bollati Boringhieri, Torino 2003, 150–153.

Bonhoeffer D., *Prisoner for God. Letters and Papers from Prison*, The Macmillan Company, New York 1959 (ed. orig., *Wiederstand und Ergebung. Briefe und Aufzeichnungen aus der Haft*, Chr. Kaiser – Gütersloher Verlagshaus, Gütersloh 1998).

Bordoni M., *La cristologia nell'orizzonte dello Spirito*, Queriniana, Brescia 1995.

Id., *Gesù di Nazaret. Presenza, memoria, attesa*, Queriniana, Brescia 2000$^4$.

# BIBLIOGRAPHY

Id., *Gesù di Nazaret Signore e Cristo. Saggio di cristologia sistematica. 1. Problemi di metodo*, EDB, Bologna 2016.

Id., *Gesù di Nazaret Signore e Cristo. Saggio di cristologia sistematica. 2. Gesù fondamento della cristologia*, EDB, Bologna 2017.

Id., *Gesù di Nazaret Signore e Cristo. Saggio di cristologia sistematica. 3. Il Cristo annunciato dalla Chiesa. Tomo 1*, EDB, Bologna 2018.

Id., *Gesù di Nazaret Signore e Cristo. Saggio di cristologia sistematica. 3. Il Cristo annunciato dalla Chiesa. Tomo 2*, EDB, Bologna 2019.

Bowlby J., *Attachment and Loss. 2. Separation: Anxiety and Anger*, Hogarth Press, London 1982.

Bracci M., *Paterologia. Per una teologia del Padre*, San Paolo, Cinisello Balsamo 2017.

Brambilla F.G., *La soteriologia in prospettiva drammatica*, in *La Scuola Cattolica* 128 (2000) 209–269.

Id., *Redenti nella sua croce. Soddisfazione vicaria o rappresentanza solidale?* in Manca G., *La redenzione nella morte di Gesù. In Dialogo con Franco Giulio Brambilla*, San Paolo, Cinisello Balsamo 2001, 15–83.

Id., *Il Crocifisso risorto. Risurrezione di Gesù e fede dei discepoli*, Queriniana, Brescia 2011.

Brown R.E., *The Death of the Messiah. From Gethsemane to the Grave. A Commentary on the Passion Narratives in the Four Gospels. Vol. I–II*, Doubleday, New York 1994.

Buber M., *The Way Of Man According To The Teachings Of Hasidism*, Pendle Hill, Wallingford (PA) 1960.

Bulgakov S., *The Comforter*, Wm.B. Eerdmans Publishing, Grand Rapids (MI) 2004.

Butler J., *Subjects of Desire. Hegelian Reflections in twentieth-century France*, Columbia University Press, New York 1987.

Id., *The Psychic Life of Power: Theories in Subjection*, Stanford University Press, Stanford (CA) 1997.

Cacciari M., *Labirinto filosofico*, Adelphi, Milano 2014.

Id., *Re Lear. Padri, figli, eredi*, Saletta dell'uva, Caserta 2016.

Id., *Generare Dio*, il Mulino, Bologna 2017.

Canobbio G. (ed.), *La fede di Gesù*, EDB, Bologna 2000.

Canobbio G. – Coda P. (edd.), *La teologia del XX secolo. Un bilancio. 2. Prospettive sistematiche*, Città Nuova, Roma 2003.

Carr D.M., *Holy Resilience. The Bible's Traumatic Origins*, Yale University Press, New Haven/CT – London 2014.

Carrère E., *The Kingdom*, Penguin Books, London 2018 (ed. orig. *Le Royaume*, P.O.L. Éditeur, Paris 2014).

Casaldáliga P. – Vigil J.M., *Spirituality of Liberation*, Orbis Books, Maryknoll (NY) 1994 (ed. orig. *Espiritualidade da libertação*, Vozes, Petrópolis 1993).

Castellucci E., *Davvero il Signore è risorto. Indagine teologico-fondamentale sugli avvenimenti e le origini della fede pasquale*, Cittadella, Assisi 2005.

Castellucci E., *Una «carovana solidale». La fraternità come stile dell'annuncio in Evangelii gaudium*, San Paolo, Cinisello Balsamo 2018.

Casula G. – Ancona G. (edd.), *L'identità e i suoi luoghi. L'esperienza cristiana nel farsi dell'umano*, Glossa, Milano 2008.

Ceragioli F., *«Il cielo aperto» (Gv 1,51). Analitica del riconoscimento e struttura della fede nell'intreccio di desiderio e dono*, Effatà Editrice, Cantalupa 2012.

Ciancio C., *Libertà e dono dell'essere*, Marietti, Genova – Milano 2009.

Ciola N., *Gesù Cristo Figlio di Dio. I. Vicenda storica e sviluppo ecclesiale*, Borla, Roma 2012.

Ciola N. – Pitta A. – Pulcinelli G. (edd.), *Ricerca storica su Gesù. Ricerche e prospettive*, EDB, Bologna 2017.

Coda P., *Il logos e il nulla. Trinità religioni mistica*, Città Nuova, Roma 2003.

Id., *Dalla Trinità. L'avvento di Dio tra storia e profezia*, Città Nuova, Roma 2011.

Coda P. – Clemenzia A., *Il terzo persona. Per una teologia dello Spirito Santo*, Città Nuova, Roma 2020.

Coda P. – Clemenzia A. – Tremblay J., *Un pensiero per abitare la frontiera. Sulle tracce dell'ontologia trinitaria di Klaus Hemmerle*, Città Nuova, 2016.

Commissione Teologica Internazionale, *La coscienza che Gesù aveva di sé stesso e della sua missione* (1985), in Id., *Documenti 1969–2004*, Edizioni Studio Domenicano, Bologna 2006, 333–352.

Cornati D., *«Ma più grande è l'amore». Verità e giustizia di agápe*, Queriniana, Brescia 2019.

Cornati D. – Prato E., *Fratello Dio. Invenzioni a più voci. Studi in onore di Pierangelo Sequeri nel suo LXXV compleanno*, Glossa, Milano 2020.

Costa P., *The Post-Secular City. The New Secularization Debate*, Brill Schöningh, Paderborn 2022 (ed. orig. *La città post-secolare. Il nuovo dibattito sulla secolarizzazione*, Queriniana, Brescia 2019).

Costa V., *Alterità*, il Mulino, Bologna 2011.

Coutinho Lopes De Brito Palma A., *L'esperienza della Trinità e la Trinità nell'esperienza. Modelli di una loro configurazione*, Pontificia Università Gregoriana, Roma 2013.

Cozolino L., *The Neuroscience of Human Relationship. Attachment and the Developing Social Brain*, W.W. Norton & Company, New York – London 2014.

Cozzi A., *Conoscere Gesù Cristo nella fede. Una cristologia*, Cittadella, Assisi 2014.

D'Agostino S., *Esercizi spirituali e filosofia moderna. Bacon, Descartes, Spinoza*, Edizioni ETS, Pisa 2017.

D'Alessio D., *Nello specchio dell'altro. Riflessioni sulla fede nate dal confronto con Jacques Lacan*, in *La Scuola Cattolica* 131 (2003), 181–267.

De Caro M. – Lavazza A. – Sartori G. (edd.), *Siamo davvero liberi? Le neuroscienze il mistero del libero arbitrio*, Codice Edizioni, Torino 2010.

DE CARO M. – MORI M. – SPINELLI E. (edd.), *Libero arbitrio. Storia di una controversia filosofica*, Carocci, Roma 2014.

DEHAENE S., *Consciousness and the Brain. Deciphering How the Brain Codes Our Thoughts*, Viking Penguin, New York 2014.

DELEUZE G., *Cosa può un corpo? Lezioni su Spinoza*, Ombre corte, Verona 2007.

DELEUZE G. – GUATTARI F., *Anti-Oedipus. Capitalism and Schizophrenia*, Penguin Books, London 2009 (ed. orig. *L'Anti-Oedipe*, Les Éditions de Minuit, Paris 1972).

DE MARCHI S., *Gesù. I primi trent'anni. Un'indagine biblico-narrativa*, Cittadella Editrice, Assisi 2015.

DE MONTICELLI R., *La novità di ognuno. Persona e libertà*, Garzanti, Milano 2012.

DEPEDER G., *La singolarità di Gesù Cristo. Indagine nella cristologia italiana contemporanea*, Messaggero, Padova 2013.

DE SANTIS A., *Dalla dialettica al kairós. L'ontologia dell'evidenza in Heinrich Rombach*, Studia Anselmiana, Roma, 2002.

DIANICH S. – TORCIVIA C., *Forme del popolo di Dio fra comunità e fraternità*, San Paolo, Cinisello Balsamo 2012.

DOWNING F.G., *Feasible Researches in Historical Jesus Tradition: A Critical response to Chris Keith*, in *Journal for the Study of the New Testament* 40 (2017) 51–61.

DUMOULIÉ C., *Le désir*, Armand Colin – HER Éditeur, Paris 1999.

DUNN J.D.G., *Christianity in the Making. I. Jesus remembered*, Wm. B. Eerdmans Publishing Company, Grand Rapids (MI) 2003.

ID., *A New Perspective on Jesus. What the Quest for the Historical Jesus Missed*, Backer Academic, Grand Rapids (MI) 2005.

DURAND E., *Évangile et Providence. Une théologie de l'action de Dieu*, Les Éditions du Cerf, Paris 2014.

DURAND E. – HOLZER V. (edd.), *Les sources du renouveau de la théologie trinitaire au XX$^e$ siècle*, Les Éditions du Cerf, Paris 2008.

IDD. (edd.), *Les réalisations du renouveau de la théologie trinitaire au XX$^e$ siècle*, Les Éditions du Cerf, Paris 2010.

DÜRRENMATT F., *The Pledge*, Signet Book, New York 1960 (ed. orig. *Das Versprechen. Requiem auf den Kriminalroman*, Arche, Zürich 1958).

DURRWELL F.X., *Le Père. Dieu en son mystère*, Les Éditions du Cerf, Paris 1993.

EDELMAN G.M., *Bright Air, Brilliant Fire. On the Matter of the Mind*, Basic Books, New York 1992.

ID., *Wider than the sky. The Phenomenal Gift of Consciousness*, Yale University Press, New Haven – London 2004.

ID., *Second Nature. Brain Science and Human Knowledge*, Yale University Press, New Haven – London 2006.

ELLIOT J.K., *The Apocryphal New Testament. A Collection of Apocryphal Christian Literature in an English Translation*, Clarendon Press, Oxford 1993.

Eörsi A., *Haec scala significat ascensum virtutum. Remarks on the Iconography of Christ Mounting the Cross on a Ladder*, in *Arte cristiana* 85 (1977) 151–166.

Essen G., *Die Freiheit Jesu. Der neuchalkedonische Enhypostasiebegriff im Horizont neuzeitlicher Subjekt- und Personphilosophie*, Pustet Verlag, Regensburg 2001.

Falchini C. (ed.), *Abitare come fratelli insieme. Regole monastiche d'Occidente*, Qiqaion, Magnano 2016.

Falque E., *The Metamorphosis of Finitude. An Essay on Birth and Resurrection*, Fordham University Press, New York 2012 (ed. orig. *Métamorphose de la finitude. Essai philosophique sur la naissance et la résurrection*, Les Éditions du Cerf, Paris 2004).

Feiner J., *Offenbarung und Kirche – Kirche und Offenbarung*, in Feiner J. – Löhrer M., *Mysterium Salutis. Grundriss Heilsgeschichtlicher Dogmatik. Band I. Die Grundlagen heilsgeschichtlicher Dogmatik*, Benziger Verlag, Einsiedeln 1965, 497–544.

Ferrara A., *The force of the Example. Explorations in the Paradigm of Judgment*, Columbia University Press, New York 2008 (ed. it. *La forza dell'esempio. Il paradigma del giudizio*, Feltrinelli, Milano 2008).

Ferretti G. (ed.), *La resurrezione mistero del desiderio. Un dialogo interdisciplinare*, eum, Macerata 2006.

Feuerbach L., *Über Materialismus und Spiritualismus, besonders in Beziehung au die Willensfreiheit*, in Id., *Gesammelte Werke. Teil 11. Kleinere Schriften 4 (1851–1866)*, De Gruyter Akademie Forschung, Berlin 1990, 53–186.

Florenski P., *The Pillar and Ground of the Truth*, Princeton University Press, Princeton – Oxford 1997.

Foucauld Ch. de, *Oeuvres spirituelles. Antologie*, Éditions du Seuil, Paris 1959.

Franco G. (ed.), *Alla ricerca della verità. Discussioni sul Gesù di Nazaret di Joseph Ratzinger – Benedetto XVI*, Lupo editore, Copertino 2009.

Gaboardi R., *«Un Dio a parte». Che altro? Jacques Lacan e la teologia*, Glossa, Milano 2016.

Gadda C.E., *That Awful Mess of Via Merulana*, New York Review Books, New York 2000 (ed. it. *Quer pasticciaccio brutto de via Merulana*, Adelphi, Milano 2018).

Galot J., *Le coeur du Père*, Éditions Desclée de Brouwen, Paris – Louvain 1957.

Gamberini P., *Questo Gesù (At 2,32). Pensare la singolarità di Gesù*, EDB, Bologna 2005.

Ganoczy A., *Der dreieinige Schöpfer. Trinitätstheologie und Synergie*, Wissenschaftliche Buchgesellschft, Darmstadt 2001.

Gauchet M., *Il figlio del desiderio. Una rivoluzione antropologica*, Vita e Pensiero, Milano 2010.

Gaudiano V., *Introduzione*, in Hemmerle K., *Un pensare riconoscente. Scritti sulla relazione fra filosofia e teologia*, Città Nuova, Roma 2018, 25–27.

Gesché A., *Dieu pour penser. VI. Le Christ*, Les Éditions du Cerf, Paris 2001.

Green J.B., *The death of Jesus*, in Holmén T. – Porter S.E., *Handbook for the Study of the Historical Jesus. I–IV*, Brill, Leiden–Boston 2011, 2383–2409.

GREGORY OF NAZIANZUS, *Festal Orations*, St Vladimir's Seminary Press, Yonkers (NY) 2008.
GRELOT P., *L'espérance juive à l'heure de Jésus*, Desclée, Paris 1979.
GRESHAKE G., *Der dreieine Gott. Eine trinitarische Theologie*, Herder, Freiburg im Br. 1997.
GRILLMEIER A., *Christ in Christian Tradition. Vol. I. From the Apostolic Age to Chalcedon (451)*, Mowbray & Co. Limited, London 1965.
ID., *Christ in Christian Tradition. Vol. II. From the Council of Chalcedon (451) to Gregory the Great (590-604). Part Two. The Church of Constantinople in the Sixth Century*, Mowbray & Co. Limited, London 1989. (ed. orig. *Jesus der Christus im Glauben der Kirche. Band II/2. Die Kirche von Konstantinopel im 6. Jahrhundert*, Herder, Freiburg im Br. 1989).
ID., *Christ in Christian Tradition. Vol. II. From the Council of Chalcedon (451) to Gregory the Great (590-604). Part Four. The Church of Alexandria with Nubia and Ethiopia after 451*, Mowbray & Co. Limited, London 1996. (ed. orig. *Jesus der Christus im Glauben der Kirche. Band II/4. Die Kirchen von Alexandrien Nubien und Äthiopien nach 451*, Herder, Freiburg im Br. 1990).
ID., *Christ in Christian Tradition. Vol. II. From the Council of Chalcedon (451) to Gregory the Great (590-604). Part One. Reception and Contradiction. The Development of the Discussion about Chalcedon from 451 to the Beginning of the Reign of Justinian*, Mowbray & Co. Limited, London 1987. (ed. orig. *Jesus der Christus im Glauben der Kirche. Band II/1. Das Konzil von Chalcedon (451). Rezeption und Widerspruch (451-518)*, Herder, Freiburg im Br. 1991).
ID., *Christ in Christian Tradition. Vol. II. From the Council of Chalcedon (451) to Gregory the Great (590-604). Part Three. The Churches of Jerusalem and Antioch from 451 to 600*, Oxford University Press, Oxford 2013. (ed. orig. *Jesus der Christus im Glauben der Kirche. Band II/3. Die Kirchen von Jerusalem und Antiochien von 451 bis 600*, Herder, Freiburg im Br. 2002).
GRILLO A., *Teologia fondamentale e liturgia. Il rapporto fra immediatezza e mediazione nella riflessione teologica*, EMP, Padova 1995.
ID., *Genealogia della libertà. Un itinerario tra filosofia e teologia*, San Paolo, Cinisello Balsamo 2013.
GRONCHI M., *Trattato di Gesù Cristo figlio di Dio salvatore*, Queriniana, Brescia 2008.
GUANZINI I., *Lo spirito è un osso. Postmodernità, materialismo e teologia in Slavoj Žižek*, Cittadella Editrice, Assisi 2010.
ID., *L'origine e l'inizio. Hans Urs von Balthasar e Massimo Cacciari*, Edizioni ETS, Pisa 2012.
GUANZINI I. – APPEL K., *Il neognosticismo*, San Paolo, Cinisello Balsamo 2019.
GUARDINI R., *Der Gegensatz. Versuche zu einer Philosophie des Lebendigkonkreten (1925)*, Matthias Gruenewald Verlag, Mainz 1985.

ID., *Freiheit Gnade Schicksal. Drei Kapitel zur Deutung des Daseins* (1948), Kösel Verlag, München 1956.

ID., *The Lord*, Gateway Editions, Washington DC 1996 (ed. orig. *Der Herr. Betrachtungen über die Person und das Leben Jesu Christi* (1937), Werkbund Verlag, Wurzburg 1964).

GUASTELLO S.J. – KOOPMANS M. – PINKUS D., *Chaos and Complexity in Psychology*, Cambridge University Press, New York 2009.

GUTIERREZ G., *A Theology of Liberation. History, Politics, And Salvation*, Orbis Books, Maryknoll (NY) 1973 (ed. orig. *Teología de la liberación. Perspectivas*, CEP, Lima 1971).

HADOT P., *Philosophy as a Way of Life. Spiritual Exercises from Socrates to Foucault*, Blackwell Publishers, Oxford – Malden (MA) 1995 (ed. orig. *Exercices spirituels et philosophie antique*, Études Augustiniennes, Paris 1987).

HAWTHORNE G.F. – MARTIN R.P. – REID D.G., *Dictionary of Paul and His Letters*, InterVarsity Press, Downers Grove (IL) 1993.

HEGEL G.W.F., *Gessammelte Werke. Band 6. Jenaer Systementwürfe III*, Felix Meiner Verlag, Hamburg 1976.

ID., *The Phenomenology of Spirit*, Cambridge University Press, Cambridge 2018.

HEMMERLE K., *Theses Towards A Trinitarian Ontology*, Angelico Press, New York 2000 (ed. orig. *Thesen zu einer trinitarischen Ontologie*, Johannes Verlag Einsiedeln, Freiburg 1992).

ID., *Un pensare riconoscente. Scritti sulla relazione fra filosofia e teologia*, Città Nuova, Roma 2018.

HERZEN A., *From the Other Shore*, in ID., *Selected Philosophical Works*, Foreign Languages Publishing House, Moscow 1956.

HICKOK G., *The Myth of Mirror Neurons. The Real Neuroscience of Communication and Cognition*, W.W. Norton & Company, New York 2014.

HOFFMANN N., *Sühne. Zur Theologie der Stellvertretung*, Johannes Verlag, Einsiedeln 1981.

ID., *Kreuz und Trinität. Zur Theologie der Sühne*, Johannes Verlag, Einsiedeln 1982.

HOLMÉN T. – PORTER S.E., *Handbook for the Study of the Historical Jesus. I–IV*, Brill, Leiden – Boston/MA 2011.

HONNETH H., *The Struggle for Recognition: The Moral Grammar of Social Conflicts*, Polity Press, Cambridge 1995 (ed. orig. *Kampf um Anerkennung. Zur moralischen Grammatik sozialer Konflikte*, Suhrkamp, Frankfurt a.M. 1992).

ID., *Von der Begierde zu Anerkennung. Hegels Begründung von Selbstbewusstsein*, in K. VIEWEG – W. WELSCH (EDD.), *Hegels Phänomenologie des Geistes. Ein kooperativer Kommentar zu einem Schlüsselwerk der Moderne*, Suhrkamp, Frankfurt a.M. 2000, 15–3.

ID., *Appropriating Freedom: Freud's Conception of Individual Self-Relation*, in ID., *Pathologies of Reason. On the Legacy of Critical Theory*, Columbia University Press, New York 2009, 126–145.

Id., *Freedom's Right. The Social Foundation of Democratic Life*, Polity Press, Cambridge 2014 (ed. orig. *Das Recht der Freiheit. Grundriß einer demokratischen Sittlichkeit*, Suhrkamp Verlag, Berlin 2011).

Id., *Three, Not Two, Concepts of Liberty: A Proposal to Enlarge Our Moral Self-Understanding*, in Zuckert R., Kreines J. (edd.), *Hegel on Philosophy in History*, Cambridge University Press, Cambridge 2017, 177–192 (ed. orig. *Drei, niche zwei Begriffe der Freiheit. Ein Vorschlag zur Erweiterung unseres moralischen Selbstverständnisses*, in *Internationales Jahrbuch für philosophische Anthropologie* 5/1 (2015) 113–130.

Id., *La libertà negli altri. Saggi di filosofia sociale*, Il Mulino, Bologna 2017.

Ibba G., *La teologia di Qumran*, EDB, Bologna 2002.

Id., *Qumran. Correnti del pensiero giudaico (III a.C.–I d.C.)*, Carocci, Roma 2007.

Idel M., *Il figlio nel misticismo ebraico. I. Tarda antichità, medioevo aškenazita e qabbalah estatica*, Centro Studi Campostrini, Verona 2013.

Id., *Il figlio nel misticismo ebraico. II. Zohar, qabbalah cristiana e ḥassidismo*, Centro Studi Campostrini, Verona 2014.

Joas H., *Faith as an Option: Possible Futures for Christianity*, Stanford University Press, Redwood City (CA) 2014 (ed. orig., *Glaube als Option. Zukunftsmöglichkeiten des Christentums*, Herder, Freiburg im Br. 2012).

Jonas H., *The Imperative of Responsibility: In Search of Ethics for the Technological Age*, University of Chicago Press, Chicago 1984 (ed. orig. *Das Prinzip Verantwortung*, Insel Verlag, Frankfurt am Main 1979).

Id., *Gnosis und spätantiker Geist*, Vandenhoek & Ruprecht, Göttingen 1988.

Jossa G., *Gesù e i movimenti di liberazione della Palestina*, Paideia, Brescia 1980.

Id., *La condanna del Messia. Problemi storici della ricerca su Gesù*, Paideia, Brescia 2010.

Id., *Voi chi dite che io sia? Storia di un profeta ebreo di nome Gesù*, Paideia, Torino 2018.

Jüngel E., *God's Being is in Becoming. The Trinitarian Being of God in the Theology of Karl Barth*, T&T Clark Ltd, Edinburgh 2001 (ed. orig., *Gottes Sein ist im Werden*, J.C.B. Mohr (Paul Siebeck), Tübingen 1964).

Id., *The World as Possibility and Actuality. The Ontology of the Doctrine of Justification*, in Id., *Theological Essays*, Bloomsbury T&T Clark, London – New York 2014, 95–123 (ed. orig. *Die Welt als Möglichkeit und Wirklichkeit. Zum ontologischen Ansatz der Rechtfertigungslehre*, in *Evangelische Theologie* 29 (1969) 417–442).

Id., *God as the Mystery of the World. On the Foundation of the Theology of the Crucified One in the Dispute Between Theism and Atheism*, Bloomsbury T&T Clark, London – New York 2014 (ed. orig., *Gott als Geheimnis der Welt. Zur Begründung der Theologie der Gekreuzigten im Streit zwischen Theismus und Atheismus*, J.C.B. Mohr (Paul Siebeck), Tübingen 1977).

Kandel E.R., *Psychiatry, Psychoanalysis, and the New Biology of Mind*, Psychiatric Publishing Inc., Washinton D.C – London 2005.

KASPER W., *Das Absolute in der Geschichte*, Matthias Gruenewald Verlag, Mainz 1965.
ID., *Jesus the Christ*, Continuum Books, London 2011 (ed orig. *Jesus der Christus*, Matthias-Grünewald-Verlag, Mainz 1974).
KEITH C., *The Narratives of the Gospels and the Historical Jesus: Current Debates, Prior Debates and the Goal of Historical Jesus Research*, in *Journal for the Study of the New Testament* 38 (2016) 426–455.
KESSLER H., *Sucht dem Lebenden nicht bei den Toten. Die Auferstehung Jesu Christi in biblischer, fundamentaltheologischer und sistematischer Sicht. Neuausgabe mit ausführlicher Erörterung der aktuellen Fragen*, Patmos Verlag, Düsseldorf 1987.
ID., *Christologie*, in SCHNEIDER T., *Handbuch del Dogmatik. Band I*, Patmos Verlag, Düsseldorf 1992, 241–444.
KEY E., *The Century of the Child*, The Knickerbocker Press, New York 2020.
KLEIN M., *On Observing the Behaviour of Young Infants (1952)*, in ID., *Envy and Gratitude and Other Works: 1946–1963. The Writings of Melanie Klein. Vol. 3*, Hogarth Press, London 1987, 94–121.
KOJÈVE A., *Introduction to the Lecture of Hegel. Lectures on the Phenomenology of Spirit*, Cornell University Press, Ithaca – London 1980 (ed. orig., *Introduction à la lecture de Hegel*, Gallimard, Paris 1947).
KÜNG H., *The Incarnation of God. An Introduction to Hegel's Theological Thought as Prolegomena to a Future Christology*, T&T Clark, Edinburgh 1987 (ed. orig. *Menschwerdung Gottes. Eine Einführung in Hegels theologisches denken als Prolegomena zur eine künftige Christologie*, Verlag Herder K G, Freiburg im Br. 1970).
LACAN J., *Écrits. The first Complete Edition in English*, W.W. Norton & Company, New York – London 2005 (ed. orig., *Écrits*, Éditions du Seuil, Paris 1966).
ID., *On Feminine Sexuality. The Limits of Love and Knowledge. Book XX. Encore 1972–1973*, W.W. Norton & Company, New York – London 1999 (ed. orig. *Le séminaire de Jacque Lacan. Livre XX. Encore (1972–1973)*, Éditions du Seuil, Paris 1975).
ID., *Les complexes familiaux dans la formation de l'individu*, in ID., *Autre écrits*, Éditions du Seuil, Paris 2001, 23–84.
ID., *Autre écrits*, Éditions du Seuil, Paris 2001.
ID., *Noms-du-Pére*, Éditions du Seuil, Paris 2005.
LACOSTE J.-Y. (ed.), *Histoire de la théologie*, Éditions du Seuil, Paris 2009.
LACROIX X., *Passeurs de vie. Essai sur la paternité*, Bayard, Paris 2004.
LACUGNA C.M., *God for Us. The Trinity and Christian Life*, Harper San Francisco, San Francisco (CA) 1991.
LAFONT G., *Histoire théologique de l'Église catholique. Itinéraire et formes de la théologie*, Les Éditions du Cerf, Paris 1994.
LANDI A., *Figlio diletto o ultimo dei profeti? Identità e missione cristologica in Mc 12,1–12*, in *Rivista Biblica* 56 (2008) 199–219.
LEGRENZI P. – UMILTÀ C., *Neuro-mania. Il cervello non spiega chi siamo*, Il Mulino, Bologna 2009.

BIBLIOGRAPHY

LIEGGI J.P., *La sintassi trinitaria. Al cuore della grammatica della fede*, Aracne, Roma 2016.

LIMONE V., *Inizio e Trinità. Il neoplatonismo giovanneo nell'ultimo Schelling*, Edizioni ETS, Pisa 2013.

LIVERTA SEMPIO O. (ed.), *Vygotskij, Piaget, Bruner. Concezioni dello sviluppo*, Raffaello Cortina, Milano 1998.

LURIA A.R., *The Man with a Shattered World*, Harvard University Press, Cambridge 1972.

ID., *The Mind of a Mnemonist. A Little Book about a Vast Memory*, Harvard University Press, Cambridge – London 1987.

LUZ U., *Matthew 1–7. A Commentary*, Fortress Press, Minneapolis 2007 (ed. orig. *Das Evangelium nach Mathäus. I*, Neukirchener Verlag, Neukirchener – Vluyn 2005).

MAFFEIS A., *Dossier sulla giustificazione. La dichiarazione congiunta cattolico-luterana, commento e dibattito teologico*, Queriniana, Brescia 2000.

MAGATTI M. – GIACCARDI C., *Generativi di tutto il mondo, unitevi! Manifesto per la società dei liberi*, Feltrinelli, Milano 2014.

MAGGIONI B. – MANZI F., *Lettere di Paolo*, Cittadella, Assisi 2005.

MAGRIS A., *Destino, provvidenza, predestinazione. Dal mondo antico al cristianesimo*, Morcelliana, Brescia 2008.

MAIOLINI R., *Tra fiducia esistenziale e fede in Dio. L'originaria struttura affettivo-simbolica della coscienza credente*, Glossa, Milano 2005.

ID., *Il tema teologico-fondamentale del morire di Gesù come motivo di credibilità. Considerazioni a partire da un confronto con la soteriologia "drammatica" di Raymund Schwager (1935–2004)*, in Quaderni teologici del seminario di Brescia, *Di fronte alla morte*, Morcelliana, Brescia 2009, 49–105.

ID., *Libertà*, Cittadella Editrice, Assisi 2015.

MALABOU C., *Ontology of the Accident. An Essay on Destructive Plasticity*, Polity Press, Cambridge 2012 (ed. orig. *Ontologie de l'accident*, Éditions Léo Scheer, Paris 2009).

MANZI F. – PAGAZZI G.C., *Il pastore dell'essere. Fenomenologia dello sguardo del Figlio*, Cittadella, Assisi 2001.

MARCEL G., *Homo viator. Introduction to the Metaphysic of Hope*, St. Augustine's Press, South Bend (IN) 2010 (ed. orig. *Homo viator. Prolègomenes à une métaphysique de l'espérance*, Montaigne, Paris 1944).

MARCHESI G., *La Cristologia trinitaria di Hans Urs von Balthasar. Gesù Cristo pienezza della rivelazione e della salvezza*, Queriniana, Brescia 1997.

MARGUERAT D., *La ricerca del Gesù storico tra storia e teologia*, in Teologia 33 (2008) 37–54.

MARION J.L., *The Erotic Phenomenon*, The University of Chicago Press, Chicago – London 2007, Siena 2007 (ed. orig. *Le phénomène érotique. Six méditations*, Éditions Grasset & Fasquelle, 2003).

MARTIN J., *Jesus. A Pilgrimage*, HarperOne, San Francisco 2014.

Martinelli P., *La morte di Cristo come rivelazione dell'amore trinitario nella teologia di H.U. von Balthasar*, Jaca Book, Milano 1995.

Marx K., *Early Writings*, Penguin Books, London – New York 1992.

McKnight S., *Jesus and His Death. Historiography, the Historical Jesus, and Atonement Theory*, Baylor University Press, Waco (TX) 2005.

Mecacci L., *Cervello e storia. Ricerche sovietiche di neurofisiologia e psicologia*, Editori Riuniti, Roma 1977.

Id., *Psicologia moderna e postmoderna*, Laterza, Roma – Bari 1999.

Meiattini G., *Sentire cum Christo. La teologia dell'esperienza cristiana nell'opera di Hans Urs von Balthasar*, Pontificia Università Gregoriana, Roma 1998.

Meier J.P., *A Marginal Jew. Rethinking the Historical Jesus. 1. The Roots of the Problem and the Person*, Doubleday, New York 1991.

Id., *A Marginal Jew. Rethinking the Historical Jesus. 2. Mentor, Message and Miracles*, Doubleday, New York 1994.

Id., *A Marginal Jew. Rethinking the Historical Jesus. 3. Companions and Competitors*, Doubleday, New York 2001.

Id., *A Marginal Jew. Rethinking the Historical Jesus. 4. Law and Love*, Doubleday, New York 2009.

Id., *A Marginal Jew. Rethinking the Historical Jesus. 5. Probing the Authenticity of the Parables*, Doubleday, New York 2017.

Menke K.-H., *Stellvertretung. Schlüsselbegriff christlichen Lebens und theologische Grundkategorie*, Johannes Verlag Einsiedeln, Freiburg 1991.

Metz J.B., *Mystik der offenen Augen. Wenn Spiritualität aufbricht*, Verlag Herder GmbH, Freiburg im Br. 2011.

Moioli G., *L'esperienza spirituale. Lezioni introduttive*, Glossa, Milano 1992.

Moltmann J., *Theology of Play*, Harper & Row, New York 1972 (ed. orig., *Die ersten Freigelassenen der Schöpfung. Versuche über die Freude an der Freiheit und das Wohlgefallen am Spiel*, Chr. Kaiser Verlag, München 1971).

Id., *The Crucified God. The Cross of Christ as the Foundation and Criticism of Christian Theology*, Fortress Press, Minneapolis 1993 (ed. orig., *Der gekreuzigte Gott. Das Kreuz Christi als Grund und Kritik christlicher Theologie*, Chr. Kaiser Verlag, München 1972).

Id., *The Trinity and the Kingdom. The Doctrine of God*, Fortress Press, Minneapolis 1993 (ed. orig., *Trinität und Reich Gottes. Zur Gotteslehre*, Chr. Kaiser Verlag, München 1980).

Id., *The Way Jesus Christ. Christology in Messianic Dimensions*, HarperCollins Publisher, New York 1990 (ed. orig. *Der Weg Jesu Christi. Christologie in messianischen Dimensionen*, Chr. Kaiser Verlag, München 1989).

Id., *History and the Triune God: Contributions to Trinitarian Theology*, SCM Press, London 1991 (ed. orig. *In der Geschichte des dreieinigen Gottes. Beiträge zur trinitarische Theologie*, Chr. Kaiser Verlag, München 1991).

ID., *The Spirit of Life. A Universal Affirmation*, Fortress Press, Minneapolis 1992 (ed. orig. *Der Geist des Lebens. Eine ganzheitliche Pneumatologie*, Chr. Kaiser Verlag, München 1991).

ID., *God in Creation. An Ecological Doctrine of Creation. The Gifford Lectures 1984–1985*, SCM Press, London 1985 (ed. orig. *Gott in der Schöpfung. Ökologische Schöpfungslehre*, Chr. Kaiser Verlag, München 1985).

ID., *Ethics of Hope*, Fortress Press, Minneapolis 2012 (ed. orig. *Ethik der Hoffnung*, Güterslohrer Verlag, Güterloh 2010).

MONOD J., *Chance and Necessity. An Essay on the Natural Philosophy of Modern Biology*, Vintage Books, New York 1972 (ed. orig. *Le hasard et la nécessité. Essai sur la philosophie naturelle de la biologie moderne*, Éditions du Seuil, Paris 1970).

MORI M., *Gli spiriti e le macchine. Il determinismo moderno*, in DE CARO M. – MORI M. – SPINELLI E. (edd.), *Libero arbitrio. Storia di una controversia filosofica*, Carocci, Roma 2014, 261–284.

MORIN E., *Le Méthode. 1. La Nature de la Nature*, Éditions du Seuil, Paris 1977.

MUGNAI M., *Possibile necessario*, Il Mulino, Bologna 2013.

NARDIN R., *Cristologia: temi emergenti*, in CANOBBIO G. – CODA P. (edd.), *La teologia del XX secolo. Un bilancio. 2. Prospettive sistematiche*, Città Nuova, Roma 2003, 23–87.

NERI M., *Gesù affetti e corporeità di Dio. Il Cuore e la fede*, Cittadella, Assisi 2007.

ID., *Il corpo di Dio. Dire Gesù nella cultura contemporanea*, EDB, Bologna 2010.

NIETZSCHE F., *The Anti-Christ, Ecce Homo, Twilight of the Idols, and Other Writings*, Cambridge University Press, Cambridge New York 2005.

NOCETI S., *Diacone? Quale ministero per quale Chiesa*, Queriniana, Brescia 2017.

NOËL É. (ed.), *Le hasard aujourd'hui*, Éditions du Seuil, Paris 1991.

O'COLLINS G., *Christology. A Biblical, Historical, and Systematic Study of Jesus Christ*, Oxford University Press, Oxford 1995.

O'CONNOR F., *Wise Blood*, Harcourt, San Diego (CA) 1952.

EAD., *The Violent Bear It Away*, Farrar, Straus and Giroux, New York 1960.

EAD., *The Complete Stories*, Farrar, Straus and Giroux, New York 1971.

OSCULATI R., *La teologia cristiana nel suo sviluppo storico. I. Primo millennio*, Cinisello Balsamo 1996.

ID., *La teologia cristiana nel suo sviluppo storico. II. Secondo millennio*, Cinisello Balsamo 1997.

OSTO G., *Come olio profumato. Scorribande sulla fraternità*, Cittadella, Assisi 2018.

OTTONE R., *La chiave del castello. L'interesse teologico dell'empatia di Gesù*, EDB 2018.

ID., *La polifonia delle voci*, in CORNATI D. – PRATO E., *Fratello Dio. Invenzioni a più voci. Studi in onore di Pierangelo Sequeri nel suo LXXV compleanno*, Glossa, Milano 2020, 231–240.

Paganini S., *Cappuccetto rosso e la creazione del mondo. Come si interpreta un testo*, EDB Bologna 2018.

Pagazzi G.C., *La singolarità di Gesù come criterio di unità e differenza nella chiesa*, Glossa, Milano 1997.

Id., *In principio era il legame. Sensi e bisogni per dire Gesù*, Cittadella Editrice, Assisi 2004.

Id., *C'è posto per tutti. Legami fraterni, paura, fede*, Vita e Pensiero, Milano 2008.

Id., *L'identità custodita. Il Primogenito e i suoi fratelli*, in ATI, *L'identità e i suoi luoghi. L'esperienza cristiana nel farsi dell'umano*, Glossa, Milano 2008.

Id., *Fatte a mano. L'affetto di Cristo per le cose*, EDB, Bologna 2013.

Id., *Tua è la potenza. Fidarsi della forza di Cristo*, San Paolo, Cinisello Balsamo 2019.

Id., *La forma delle forze*, in Cornati D. – Prato E., *Fratello Dio. Invenzioni a più voci. Studi in onore di Pierangelo Sequeri nel suo LXXV compleanno*, Glossa, Milano 2020, 273–290.

Pannenberg W., *Jesus. God and Man*, SCM Press, Canterbury 1968 (ed. orig., *Grundzüge der Christologie*, Gütersloher Verlagshaus, Gütersloh 1964).

Id., *Systematic Theology. Vol. I*, T&T Clark International, London – New York, 2004.

Id., *Systematic Theology. Vol. II*, T&T Clark International, London – New York, 2004.

Pareyson L., *Ontologia della libertà. Il male e la sofferenza*, Einaudi, Torino 1995.

Id., *Essere libertà ambiguità*, Milano 1998.

Id., *Esistenza e persona*, Il Melangolo, Genova 2002.

Paris L., *Sulla libertà. Prospettive di teologia trinitaria tra neuroscienze e filosofia*, Città Nuova, Roma 2012.

Id., *Ereditare. La passione del Figlio*, in S. Zeni – C. Curzel (edd.), *La speranza della croce. Stile del cristiano*, EDB, Bologna 2017, 73–94.

Id., *Teologia e neuroscienze. Una sfida possibile*, Queriniana, Brescia 2017.

Id., *Neuroscienze e pastorale. Spunti per un confronto*, in *Rivista del clero italiano* 99 (2018), 429–441.

Id., *Il sogno di Adamo – Il sogno di Cristo*, in *Parole di vita* 2 (2019) 37–40.

Id., *La libertà di Gesù*, in *Presbyteri* 2 (2019) 97–108.

Id., *Tra vocazione e scelte, il senso della libertà*, in A. Steccanella (ed.), *Scelte di vita e vocazione. Tracce di cammino con i giovani*, Edizioni Messaggero – Facoltà Teologica del Triveneto, Padova 2019, 151–184.

Pecorara Maggi M.R., *Il processo a Calcedonia. Storia e interpretazione*, Glossa Milano 2006.

Penna R., *Lo Spirito di Cristo. Cristologia e pneumatologia secondo un'originale formulazione paolina*, Paideia, Brescia 1976.

Id., *I ritratti originali di Gesù il Cristo. Inizi e sviluppi della cristologia neotestamentaria. I. Gli inizi*, San Paolo, Cinisello Balsamo 1996.

Id., *I ritratti originali di Gesù il Cristo. Inizi e sviluppi della cristologia neotestamentaria. II. Gli sviluppi*, San Paolo, Cinisello Balsamo 1999.

Pesch O.H., *Warum hast du so große Ohren? Rotkäppchen – "theologisch" zu Gehör gebracht*, Herder, Freiburg im Br. 1993.

Pontifical Biblical Commission, *De sacra Scriptura et christologia*, Libreria Editrice Vaticana, Roma 1994.

Id., *What Is Man? A Journey Through Biblical Anthropology*, Darton, Longman & Todd Ltd, London 2021.

Prenga E., *Il Crocifisso via alla Trinità. L'esperienza di Francesco d'Assisi nella teologia di Bonaventura*, Città Nuova, Roma 2009.

Id., *Il darsi trinitario. Ontologia e fenomenologia trinitaria*, in Coda P. – Clemenzia A. – Tremblay J., *Un pensiero per abitare la frontiera. Sulle tracce dell'ontologia trinitaria di Klaus Hemmerle*, Città Nuova, 2016, 31–49.

Rahner K., *Theos in the New Testament*, in Id., *Theological Investigations. Volume I*, Helicon Press, Baltimore 1961, 79–148 (ed. orig. *Theos im Neuen Testament*, in *Schriften zur Theologie. I*, Benzinger, Einsiedeln 1960, 91–167).

Id., *Current Problems in Christology*, in Id., *Theological Investigations. Volume I*, Helicon Press, Baltimore 1961, 149–200. (ed. orig. *Probleme der Christologie von heute*, in *Schriften zur Theologie. I*, Benzinger, Einsiedeln 1960, 169–222).

Id., *Foundations of Chritian Faith. An Introduction to the Idea of Christianity*, Darton Longman & Todd, London 1978 (ed. orig. *Grundkurs des Glaubens. Einführung in den Begriff des Christentums*, Verlag Herder KG, Freiburg im Br. 1976).

Ratzinger J./Benedict XVI, *Jesus of Nazareth. From the Baptism in the Jordan to the Transfiguration*, Bloomsbury, London 2007.

Recalcati M., *L'uomo senza inconscio. Figure della nuova clinica psicoanalitica*, Raffaello Cortina, Milano 2010.

Id., *Cosa resta del padre? La paternità nell'epoca ipermoderna*, Raffaello Cortina, Milano 2011.

Id., *Ritratti del desiderio*, Raffaello Cortina, Milano 2011.

Id., *Jacques Lacan. Vol I. Desiderio, godimento e soggettivazione*, Raffaello Cortina, Milano 2012.

Id., *The Telemachus Complex. Parents and Children after the Decline of the Father*, Polity Press, Cambridge 2019 (ed. it. *Il complesso di Telemaco. Genitori e figli dopo il tramonto del padre*, Feltrinelli, Milano 2013.

Id., *Jacques Lacan. Vol. II. La clinica psicoanalitica: struttura e soggetto*, Raffaello Cortina, Milano 2016.

Id., *Le nuove melanconie. Destini del desiderio nel tempo ipermoderno*, Raffaello Cortina, Milano 2019.

Richard of Saint Victor, *The Four Degrees of Violent Charity*, in H. Feiss (ed.), *On Love: A Selection of Works of Hugh, Adam, Achard, Richard, and Godfrey of St. Victor*, Brepols Publishers, Turnhout 2012, 261–300.

Ricoeur P., *The Conflict of Interpretations. Essays in Hermeneutics*, The Athlone Press, London 1989 (ed. orig. *Le conflit des interprétations*, Éditions du Seuil, Paris 1969).

ID., *Oneself as Another*, The University of Chicago Press, Chicago – London 1992 (ed. orig. *Soi-même comme un autre*, Éditions du Seuil, Paris 1990).

ID., *The Course of Recognition*, Harvard University Press, Cambridge – London 2005 (ed. orig. *Percours de la reconnaissance*, Éditions Stock, Paris 2004).

RICOEUR P. – JÜNGEL E., *Metapher. Zur Hermeneutik religiöser Sprache*, Chr. Kaiser Verlag, München 1974.

RIONDATO M., *In un mondo non-necessario. Scienze della natura, filosofia, teologia a confronto sulla nozione di «contingenza»*, EMP, Padova 2021.

RIZZOLATTI G. – SINIGAGLIA C., *Mirrors in the Brain. How Our Minds Share Actions and Emotions*, Oxford University Press, New York 2008 (ed. it. *Specchi nel cervello. Come comprendiamo gli altri dall'interno*, Raffaello Cortina, Milano 2006).

ROMBACH H., *Strukturontologie. Eine Phänomenologie der Freiheit*, Karl Alber Verlag, Freiburg – München 1971.

ROSITO V., *Lo spirito e la polis. Prospettive per una pneumatologia politica*, Cittadella, Assisi 2016.

ROSSI G. – ALETTI M. (ed.), *Psicologia della religione e teoria dell'attaccamento*, Aracne, Roma 2009.

ROTH P., *Patrimony. A True Story*, Simon & Schuster, New York 1991.

SANDERS E.P., *Jesus and Judaism*, Fortress Press, Philadelphia 1985.

SALMANN E., *Neuzeit und Offenbarung. Studien zur trinitarischen Analogik des Christentums*, Studia Anselmiana, Roma 1986.

ID., *Der geteilte Logos. Zum offenen Prozeß von neuzeitlichem Denken und Theologie*, Studia Anselmiana, Roma 1992.

ID., *Contro Severino. Incanto e incubo del credere*, Piemme, Casale Monferrato 1999.

ID., *Presenza di spirito. Il cristianesimo come gesto e pensiero*, Edizioni Messaggero, Padova 2000.

ID., *Presenza di spirito. Cristianesimo come stile di pensiero e di vita*, Cittadella, Assisi 2011.

SALVADORI I., *L'autocoscienza di Gesù. "In tutto simile a noi eccetto il peccato"*, Città Nuova, Roma 2011.

SALVIOLI M., *La misericordia invisibile del Padre nella compassione visibile di Gesù, il Figlio. Per una fenomenologia di Gesù in chiave anagogica*, in Divus Thomas 2 (2008) 22–110.

SANDONÀ L., *Dialogica. Per un pensare teologico tra sintassi trinitaria e questione del pratico*, Città Nuova, Roma 2019.

SARAMAGO J., *The Gospel According to Jesus Christ*, Harcourt Brace & Company, San Diego (CA) 1994 (ed. orig. *O Evangelho segundo Jesus Cristo*, Caminho, Lisboa 1991).

SCANNONE J.C., *La teología del pueblo. Raíces teológicas del papa Francisco*, Éditions Lessius, Bruxelles 2017.

SCANZIANI F. (ed.), *Ripensare la risurrezione*, Glossa, Milano 2009.

## BIBLIOGRAPHY

SCHELLING F.W.J., *The Ages of the World (1811)*, State University New York Press, New York 2019.
SCHLEIERMACHER F.D.E., *Brief Outline for the Study of Theology*, Wipf and Stock, Eugene (OR) 2007.
SCHWAGER R., *Der Sieg Christi über den Teufel*, in Zeitschrift für katholische Theologie, 103 (1981) 156–177.
SEGALLA G., *Sulle tracce di Gesù. La "Terza ricerca"*, Cittadella Editrice, Assisi 2006.
SEMERARO MD., *Charles del Foucauld. Esploratore e profeta della fraternità universale*, San Paolo, Cinisello Balsamo 2016.
SENNETT R., *The Corrosion of Character: The Personal Consequences of Work in the New Capitalism*, W.W. Norton & Company, New York 1998.
SEQUERI P., *La «storia di Gesù»*, in G. COLOMBO (ed.), *L'evidenza della fede*, Glossa, Milano 1988, 235–275.
ID., *L'interesse teologico di una fenomenologia di Gesù: giustificazione e prospettive*, in Teologia 23 (1998) 289–329.
ID., *L'umano alla prova. Soggetto, identità, limite*, Vita e Pensiero, Milano 2002.
ID., *L'amore della ragione. Variazioni sinfoniche su un tema di Benedetto XVI*, EDB, Bologna 2012.
ID., *Il sensibile e l'inatteso. Lezioni di estetica teologica*, Queriniana, Brescia 2016.
SESBOÜÉ B., *Jésus-Christ dans la tradition de l'Eglise*, Descléè, Paris 1982.
ID., *Jésus-Christ l'unique médiateur. Essai sur la rédemption et la salut. 1. Problématique et relecture doctrinale*, Descleé, Paris 1988.
ID., *Jésus-Christ l'unique médiateur. Essai sur la rédemption et la salut. 2. Les récits du salut: Proposition de sotériologie narrative*, Descleé, Paris 1991.
SEUNG S.S., *Connectome. How the Brain's Wiring Makes Us Who We Are*, Houghton Mifflin Harcourt, Boston (MA) 2012.
SEVERINO E., *Legge e caso*, Adelphi, Milano 2020.
SIEGEL D.J., *The Developing Mind. Second Edition*, The Gilford Press, New York 2012.
SIEP L., *Anerkennung als Prinzip der praktischen Philosophie. Untersuchungen zur Hegels Jenaer Philosophie des Geistes*, Meiner Verlag, Hamburg 2014.
SIX J.-F., *Itinéraire spirituel de Charles de Foucauld*, Editions du Seuil, Paris 1958.
SOBRINO J., *Jesus the Liberator. A Historical-Theological Reading of Jesus of Nazareth*, Orbis Books, New York 1993 (ed. orig. *Jesucristo liberador. Lectura histórico teológica de Jesús de Nazaret*, Editora Vozes, Petropolis 1993).
SOLOVIOV V.S., *Philosophical Principles of Integral Knowledge*, Wm. B. Eerdmans Publishing Company, Grand Rapids (MI) 2008.
SONNET J.-P., *Generare è narrare*, Vita e Pensiero, Milano 2015.
ŠPIDLÍK T., *La spiritualité de l'Orient chrétien. Manuel systématique*, Ed. Orientalia Christiana, Roma 1978.

ID., *L'idée russe. Une autre vision de l'homme*, Éditions Fates, Arsonval 1994.

ID., *Il professor Ulipispirus e altre storie*, Lipa, Roma 1997.

ID., *"Sentire e gustare le cose internamente". Letture per gli Esercizi*, Lipa, Roma 2006.

STANDAERT B., *Évangile selon Marc. Commentaire, Troisième partie Marc 11,1 à 16,20*, J. Gabalda et Cie, Pendé 2010.

STUDER B., *Trinity and Incarnation. The Faith of the Early Church*, The Liturgical Press, Collegeville (MI) 1993 (ed. orig. *Gott und unsere Erlosung im Glauben der Alten Kirche*, Patmos Verlag, Düsseldorf 1985).

TAYLOR C., *A Secular Age*, Harvard University Press, Cambridge (MA) 2007.

TELFENER U. – CASADIO L. (edd.), *Sistemica. Voci e percorsi nella complessità*, Bollati Boringhieri, Torino 2003.

TESTAFERRI F., *Una "quarta ricerca" del Gesù storico?* in *Teologia* 38 (2013) 382–400.

THEISSEN G. – MERZ A., *The Historical Jesus: A Comprehensive Guide*, Fortress Press, Philadelphia 1998 (ed. orig. *Der historische Jesus. Ein Lehrbuch*, Vandenhoeck & Ruprecht, Göttingen 1996).

THEOBALD CH., *Le christianisme comme style. Une manière de faire de la théologie en postmodernité*, Les Éditions du Cerf, Paris 2007.

ID., *Selon l'Ésprit de sainteté: genèse d'une théologie systématique*, Les Éditions du Cerf, Paris 2015.

ID, *Fraternità. Il nuovo stile della Chiesa secondo papa Francesco*, Qiqaion, Magnano 2016.

TILLICH P., *Die Philosophie der Macht*, Coloquium Verlag Otto H. Hess, Berlin – Dahlem 1956.

TILLIETTE X., *La christolgie idéaliste*, Desclée, Paris 1986.

TOLKIEN J.R.R., *The Hobbit or There and Back Again*, HarperCollins Publishers, New York 1995. (ed. orig. George Allen & Unwin, London 1937).

TOMATIS F., *Kenosis del logos. Ragione e rivelazione nell'ultimo Schelling*, Città Nuova, Roma 1994.

TONIOLO A., *La theologia crucis nel contesto della modernità. Il rapporto tra croce e modernità nel pensiero di E. Jüngel, H.U. von Balthasar e G.W.F. Hegel*, Glossa, Roma – Milano, 1995.

TUROLDO D.M., *O sensi miei ... Poesie 1948–1988*, Rizzoli, Milano 1990.

VANTINI L., *Il sé esposto. Teologia e neuroscienze in chiave fenomenologica*, Cittadella, Assisi 2017.

VETÖ É., *Da Cristo alla Trinità. Un confronto tra Tommaso D'Aquino e Hans Urs von Balthasar*, EDB, Bologna 2015.

VYGOTSKIJ L.S., *Pensiero e linguaggio*, Laterza, Roma – Bari 1992.

WALTER P. (ed.), *Das Gewaltpotential des Monotheismus und der dreieine Gott*, Herder, Freiburg im Br. 2005.

YANNARÀS CH., *On the Absence and Unknowability of God. Heidegger and the Areopagite*, T&T Clark International, London – New York 2005.

ID., *Person and Eros*, Holy Cross Orthodox Press, Brookline/MA 2007.
ID., *Relational Ontology*, Holy Cross Orthodox Press, Brookline/MA 2011.
ZENI S., *La simbolica del grido nel Vangelo di Marco. Aspetti antropologici e teologici*, EDB, Bologna 2019.
ZIZIOULAS I., *Communion and Otherness: Further Studies in Personhood and the Church*, T&T Clark, London – New York 2006.
ZOJA L., *The Father. Historical, Psychological and Cultural Perspectives*, Brunner-Routledge, Hove 2001 (ed. it. *Il gesto di Ettore. Preistoria, storia, attualità e scomparsa del padre*, Bollati Boringhieri, Torino 2000).
ZOURABICHVILI F., *Deluze. Une philosophie de l'événement*, Presses Universitaires de France, Paris 1994.

# Videography

ABRAMS J.J. – LINDELOF D. – LIEBER J., *Lost* (television series), USA 2004–2010.
BENIOFF D. – WEISS D.B., *Game of Thones* (television series), USA 2011–2019.
JONES T., *Monty Python's Life of Brian*, United Kingdom 1979.
LAWRENCE F., *The Hunger Games: Chatching Fire*, USA 2013.
ID., *The Hunger Games: Mockingjay 1*, USA 2014.
ID., *The Hunger Games: Mockingjay 2*, USA 2015.
MORETTI N., *Palombella Rossa*, Italy, 1989.
ID., *Habemus papam*, Italy, 2011.
PARENTI N., *Superfantozzi*, Italy 1986.
REINER R., *A Few Good Men*, USA 1992.
ROSS G., *The Hunger Games*, USA 2012.
ROTHENBERG J., *The 100* (television series), USA 2014–2020.

# Index

Abrams J.J.   21
Augustine of Hippo   113
Aletti M.   47
Allison D.C. jr.   26
Ammaniti M.   45, 55
Ancona G.   137
Angelini G.   203
Anselm of Canterbury   10, 173
Antonello da Messina   91
Appel K.   25
Arendt H.   131
Auzou G.   217

Badano C.   131
Baggio A.M.   115
Baker L.R.   46, 55
Balocco D.   97
Balthasar H.U. von   22, 49, 55–56, 93, 132, 173–176, 217–219
Báñez D.   113
Barbaglio G.   38
Baricco A.   17
Beauchamp P.   76
Becchi E.   142
Beck U.   54
Benedict XIV   113
Benedict XVI   16, 24, 203 (cf. Ratzinger J.)
Benioff D.   20
Berdyaev N.   204
Berlin I.   25, 48, 56, 128
Bernet R.   220
Bertuglia C.S.   132
Bertuletti A.   24, 218
Bloch M.   1, 16
Bocchi G.   132
Bonaventure   176
Bonhoeffer D.   139
Bordoni M.   62–63, 76, 80, 218
Bowlby J.   93
Bracci M.   202
Brambilla F.G.   24–25, 202
Brown R.E.   34, 38, 156
Buber M.   210
Bulgakov S.   218
Butler J.   141, 175, 203

Cacciari M.   25, 137–138, 174, 204
Canobbio G.   27, 76
Carpenter A.M.   XV
Carr D.M.   38
Carrère E.   21
Casadio L.   132
Casaldáliga P.   97
Cassibba R.   47
Castellucci E.   115, 202
Casula L.   137
Ceragioli F.   56–57, 175
Ceruti M.   132
Ciancio C.   56
Ciola N.   38, 76, 102
Clemenzia A.   218–219
Coda P.   76, 218–219
Colombo G.   96
Cornati D.   219
Costa P.   45, 54
Costa V.   55
Coutinho Lopes De Brito Palma A.   176
Cozolino L.   56
Cozzi A.   27, 76
Curzel C.   5

D'Agostino S.   96
D'Alessio D.   55
De Caro M.   43, 47
De Marchi S.   96
De Monticelli R.   45, 56
De Santis A.   219
Descartes R.   47
Dehaene S.   119
Deleuze G.   143, 220
Depeder G.   55
Dianich S.   115
Dionysius the Areopagite   14
Downing F.G.   38
Dürrenmatt F.   123–124
Dumoulié C.   175
Dunn J.D.G.   36, 38
Durand E.   131, 176
Durrwell F.X.   202

Edelman G.M.   119–120

Eörsi A.   153
Essen G.   27

Faggioli M.   IX
Falchini C.   115
Falque E.   202
Feiner J.   219
Ferrara A.   46, 55
Ferretti G.   202
Feuerbach L.   25
Fiennes R.   190
Flavius Josephus   69
Florenski P.   218
Foucauld Ch. de   115
Francis of Assisi   9, 62, 74, 175
Francis (pope)   54, 115, 172, 198
Franco G.   27
Freud S.   26, 142

Gaboardi R.   55
Gadda C.E.   122
Gallese V.   45, 55
Galli C.M.   XI
Galot J.   202
Gamberini P.   41, 55
Ganoczy A.   219
Gauchet M.   204
Gaudiano V.   219
Gesché A.   26, 202
Giaccardi C.   204
Goethe J.W. von   136
Granqvist P.   47
Green J.B.   38
Gregory of Nazianzus   174
Grelot P.   76
Greshake G.   218
Grillmeier A.   8, 27
Grillo A.   56, 219
Gronchi M.   24
Guanzini I.   25, 174
Guardini R.   7, 121, 124, 153
Guastello S.J.   132
Guattari F.   143
Guido da Siena   153
Gutiérrez G.   97

Hadot P.   96
Haslinger H.   XI

Hawthorne G.F.   148
Hegel G.W.F.   25, 56, 115, 141, 174–176
Hemmerle K.   219
Herzen A.   128
Hickok G.   55
Hoffmann N.   25, 176
Holmén T.   38
Holzer V.   176
Honneth A.   56, 174–175, 194
Hulsbosch A.   27

Ibba G.   61
Idel M.   76

Jefferson, Th.   104
Joachim of Fiore   141
Joas H.   54
Jonas H.   54, 96
Jones T.   22
Jossa G.   31–32, 35–36, 38, 126
Jüngel E.   1, 131, 175–176, 183, 198
Julia D.   142

Kafka F.   212
Kandel E.R.   56
Kant I.   122
Kasper W.   76, 174
Keith C.   38
Kessler H.   76, 179, 202
Key E.   142
Klein M.   93
Kojève A.   56, 175
Koopmans M.   132
Küng H.   174

Lacan J.   46, 54–56, 174–175, 202
Lacoste J.-Y.   113
Lacroix X.   202
Lacugna C.M.   218
Lafont G.   114
Landi A.   149
Lavazza A.   43
Lawrence F.   144
Legrenzi P.   43
Lieber J.   21
Lieggi J.P.   188–218
Limone V.   174
Lindelof D.   21

# INDEX

Liverta Sempio O.   218
Löhrer M.   218
Luciani R.   X
Luria A.R.   26
Luz U.   72

Maffeis A.   10
Magatti M.   204
Maggioni B.   172
Magris A.   131
Maiolini R.   25, 55
Malabou C.   131
Manca G.   24
Manzi F.   96, 151, 172
Marcel G.   178
Marchesi G.   217
Marguerat D.   26
Marion J.L.   203
Martin J.   38
Martin R.P.   148
Martinelli P.   217
Marx J.H. (Groucho)   75
Marx, K.   25, 115
Mcevoy J.G.   X, XIV
McKnight S.   3, 38
Mecacci L.   26, 219
Meiattini G.   56
Meier J.P.   3, 14, 26, 29, 33, 37, 50–51, 63, 66–70, 72, 76, 82–83, 86, 104, 106, 149–150
Menke K.-H.   25
Merz A.   38
Metz J.B.   97
Moioli G.   96
Molina L. de   113
Moltmann J.   12, 54, 76–77, 132, 173–175, 218
Monod J.   120, 132
Moretti G. (Nanni)   144
Mori M.   47
Morin E.   132
Mugnai M.   131

Nardin R.   76
Neri M.   96
Nicholson J.   160
Nietzsche F.   111, 115
Noceti S.   XI, 140
Noël É.   132

O'Collins G.   76
O'Connor F.   203
Osculati R.   27, 113–114
Osto G.   115
Ottone R.   96, 220

Pacino di Buonaguida   153
Paganini S.   19
Pagazzi G.C.   52, 55, 96, 115, 137, 151, 156, 203, 219
Pannenberg W.   27, 203, 220
Parenti N.   22
Pareyson L.   25, 56, 174
Paris L.   IX–XIV, 5, 44–45, 56, 158
Paul V   113
Pecorara Maggi M.R.   27
Pelagius   113
Penna R.   61, 76, 80, 132, 151, 218
Pesch O.H.   19
Pinkus D.   132
Pitta A.   38
Porter S.E.   38
Prato E.   219
Prenga E.   176, 219
Pulcinelli G.   38

Rahner K.   X, 27, 202, 219
Ratzinger J.   16, 27 (cf. Benedict XVI)
Recalcati M.   54, 134, 143, 175, 203
Reid D.G.   166
Reiner R.   160
Richard of Saint Victor   203
Ricoeur P.   1, 140–141, 175
Riondato M.   131
Rizzolatti G.   45, 55
Rombach H.   218–219
Rooney S.   X
Rosito V.   204
Ross G.   144
Rossi G.   47
Roth Ph.   134
Rothenberg J.   144
Rousseau J.-J.   62

Salmann E.   22, 25, 96, 131, 203, 218–219
Salvadori I.   27
Salvioli M.   96
Sanders E.P.   19, 31, 34–35, 37, 64, 76

Sandonà L.   218
Saramago J.   21
Sartori G.   43
Sartre J.P.   56
Scannone J.C.   115
Scanziani F.   202
Schelling F.W.J.   140, 174
Schickendantz C.   XI
Schillebeeckx E.   28
Schleiermacher F.D.E.   219
Schoonemberg P.   28
Schwager R.   173
Segalla G.   38
Semeraro MD.   115
Sennett R.   54
Sequeri P.   24, 55, 96, 204, 219
Sesboüe B.   9–10, 24, 27
Seung S.S.   119–120
Severino E.   25, 132
Shakespeare W.   137–138
Siegel D.J.   56
Siep L.   175
Simone Martini   91
Sinigaglia C.   45–55
Six J.-F.   115
Sobrino J.   76
Socrates   34, 96
Soloviov V.S.   25
Sonnet J.-P.   204
Spadaro A.   XI
Špidlík T.   178–218
Spielberg S.   191
Spinelli E.   47
Standaert B.   149
Steccanella A.   5
Stein E.   96
Studer B.   27

Taylor C.   54
Telfener U.   132
Teresa of Avila   96, 190
Testaferri F.   26
Theissen G.   38
Theobald Ch.   22, 25–26, 77, 96, 115
Thomas Aquinas   24, 204
Tillich P.   203
Tilliette X.   174
Tolkien J.R.R.   XVII
Tomasoni F.   25
Tomatis F.   174
Toniolo A.   175
Torcivia C.   115
Tremblay J.   219
Turoldo D.M.   203

Umiltà C.   43

Vaio S.   132
Vantini L.   71, 219
Vetö É.   176
Vidal J.M.   97
Vygotskij L.S.   218

Walter P.   203
Weiss D.B.   20
Williams R.   XIII

Yannarás Ch.   203, 218

Zeni S.   5, 157
Zizioulas I.   218
Zoja L.   203
Zollner H.   XI
Zourabichvili F.   220